Advance Praise for Daily

"Every person with that little voice in thei[r] ... write every day—must own this book. Ev[ery] ... [full of ho]pe and reality, just what we all need to keep us going."

—Steve Berry, *New York Times* and #1 internationally bestselling author of *The Patriot Threat*

"This must-have collection of inspirational nuggets will nudge you free of writer's block. Even if you're not blocked, a morning commune with some of writing's great minds will put you in the right creative space."

—Sara Gruen, bestselling author of *At the Water's Edge* and *Water for Elephants*

"I loved this book. Every page offered reasons to hope or reflect, to try harder or feel connected to writing's grand traditions. Seasoned pro or beginner—it doesn't matter. This book should be on every writer's desk."

—John Hart, *New York Times* bestselling author and back-to-back Edgar Award winner

"You don't have to be a writer to treasure *Daily Writing Resilience*, a unique and uplifting meditation book. It's chock-full of insights so profound you'll be tempted to gobble it up in one bite instead of savoring each daily portion as intended, slowly and appreciatively. For writers, it's a must-have!"

—Cassandra King, author of *The Sunday Wife* and *Moonrise*

"This book is something all writers need. Bryan Robinson's *Daily Writing Resilience* is not only wise but also marvelously practical. The daily mantras he offers, taken from the experiences of those who've kept to the path, will provide much needed encouragement along the way. Take this book to heart, and then take it with you wherever you go."

—William Kent Krueger, *New York Times* bestselling author of the multi-award-winning *Ordinary Grace* and the Cork O'Connor series

"This book is the Fountain of 'Youcandoit' that will sustain you as a writer day after day (recyclable for new insight year after year)—for as long as you reward yourself each day with one premeasured cupful of wisdom."

—Chris Roerden, author of Agatha Award–winning *Don't Murder Your Mystery*

"I urge both fledgling and experienced writers to get their hands on *Daily Writing Resilience* and keep it nearby for handy reference. Bryan Robinson knows his way around the head and heart of the working writer, and this book is a wonderful companion and a balm to the writer's soul."
—John Lescroart, *New York Times* bestselling author

"Bryan Robinson's daily compendium is like a gift you can open again and again. Full of wisdom, insight, and advice, this book will allow writers to soldier on in the face of the inevitable setbacks, delays, and frustrations of this writing life by bolstering mood and turning rejections into success."
—Jenny Milchman, Mary Higgins Clark and Silver Falchion Award–winning author of *Cover of Snow*, *Ruin Falls*, and *As Night Falls*

"For every type of writer—new, old, fresh, tired, impassioned, cynical, hopeful—this gem is flat out inspiring!"
—M. J. Rose, *New York Times* bestselling author of *The Secret Language of Stones*

"In this thoughtful and inspirational treasure, Bryan Robinson connects writers of all levels and provides exactly what every author needs: intellectual fuel and emotional sustenance. Don't start your writing day without it!"
—Hank Phillippi Ryan, Agatha, Anthony, and Mary Higgins Clark award-winning author

"The author's voice makes this book of meditations a true stand-out. Robinson offers a wellspring of wisdom shared with refreshing candor through daily doses of inspiration. A must-read for any author, whether at the start of the writing journey or well along the path of publication."
—Wendy Tyson, author of the Greenhouse Mystery Series and the Allison Campbell Mystery Series

"At last! A real tool for real writers, a reference book that should be on every writer's desk next to their thesaurus and Strunk & White *Elements of Style*. A practical guide that can be used as a daily devotional or motivational tool to hold your hand, to guide you, to encourage you, and to pull you back from the ledge. I can't wait to get my finished copy to put front and center on my desk."
—Karen White, *New York Times* bestselling author of *Flight Patterns*

DAILY WRITING RESILIENCE

About the Author

Bryan E. Robinson (Asheville, NC) is the author of 35 nonfiction books and two novels. His books have been translated into thirteen languages, and he's been featured on *20/20*, *Good Morning America*, ABC's *World News Tonight*, *NBC Nightly News*, NBC Universal, the CBS *Early Show*, and CNBC's *The Big Idea*. Robinson maintains a private psychotherapy practice and lives in the Blue Ridge Mountains with his spouse and four dogs. Visit him online at www.bryanrobinsonbooks.com.

To Write the Author

If you wish to contact the author or would like more information about this book, please write to the author in care of Llewellyn Worldwide, and we will forward your request. Both the author and the publisher appreciate hearing from you and learning of your enjoyment of this book and how it has helped you. Llewellyn Worldwide cannot guarantee that every letter written to the author can be answered, but all will be forwarded. Please write to:

Bryan E. Robinson
℅ Llewellyn Worldwide
2143 Wooddale Drive
Woodbury, MN 55125-2989

Please enclose a self-addressed stamped envelope for reply,
or $1.00 to cover costs. If outside the USA, enclose
an international postal reply coupon.

DAILY WRITING RESILIENCE

365 MEDITATIONS & INSPIRATIONS FOR WRITERS

Bryan E. Robinson, PhD

Llewellyn Worldwide
Woodbury, Minnesota

FIRST EDITION
First Printing, 2018

Book design by Bob Gaul
Cover design by Ellen Lawson
Editing by Aaron Lawrence

Llewellyn Publications is a registered trademark of Llewellyn Worldwide Ltd.

Library of Congress Cataloging-in-Publication Data (Pending)
ISBN: 978-0-7387-5343-0

Llewellyn Worldwide Ltd. does not participate in, endorse, or have any authority or responsibility concerning private business transactions between our authors and the public.

All mail addressed to the author is forwarded, but the publisher cannot, unless specifically instructed by the author, give out an address or phone number.

Any internet references contained in this work are current at publication time, but the publisher cannot guarantee that a specific location will continue to be maintained. Please refer to the publisher's website for links to authors' websites and other sources.

Llewellyn Publications
A Division of Llewellyn Worldwide Ltd.
2143 Wooddale Drive
Woodbury, MN 55125-2989
www.llewellyn.com

Printed in the United States of America

*Dedicated to aspiring scribes, debut authors,
and seasoned writers of all genres.*

ACKNOWLEDGMENTS

I don't claim to be an expert on writing, but if experience plays a role, I *am* an expert on the struggles and trials and tribulations of writers. Writing for forty years, I have paid my dues and earned the right to sing the blues. This book is a culmination of those turbulent yet exhilarating years of everything from writing hundreds of professional journal and popular magazine articles to several consulting editorships, thirty-five professional and self-help books, and three novels. Along the way, a stadium of people supported me.

I'd like to thank my spouse, Jamey McCullers, for his undying support over the trajectory of our years together. My deepest appreciation for my agent, Jill Marsal at Marsal-Lyon Literary Agency, for her steadfast belief in this project and me from the get-go and her pit-bull resilience and perseverance in finding this book a home. I owe a debt of gratitude to my publicist, Rowe Copeland, who saw this project through from beginning to end with her creative advice and support. And to Sara Wigal and everyone at JKS Communications and Literary Publicity for their enthusiastic promotion of this project.

Thanks to my dedicated readers and editors who did a magnificent job editing and providing feedback on the manuscript: Rowena Copeland,

Jennifer Fisher, Glenda Loftin, Edith Langley, and Debra Rosenblum. To all of my novelist colleagues and friends at International Thriller Writers who do the best job of any organization I know of supporting aspiring scribes, debut authors, and seasoned writers: Kimberley Howe, Jenny Milchman, Lee Child, Steve Berry, M. J. Rose, Wendy Tyson, Mark Leggatt, Barry Lancet, Elena Hartwell, Sheila Sobel, and Josh Frank.

I want to thank my technical advisor, Charlie Covington, for his masterful help with formatting the manuscript and guidance on internet and electronic issues of which I am totally ignorant. A huge shoutout to photo artists Carlo and Carol Pieroni for the generous time they spent taking the photograph for the book jacket. And I am so appreciative of all the wonderful professional folks at Llewellyn Worldwide, Vanessa Wright and Aaron Lawrence, and especially my editor, Angela Wix. You were all a joy to work with.

I extend my appreciation to all the talented writers of diverse genres who took their valuable time to read the manuscript and write a blurb when they could have been penning their own work: Steve Berry, Sara Gruen, John Hart, Cassandra King, William Kent Krueger, John Lescroart, Jenny Milchman, Chris Roerdon, M.J. Rose, Hank Phillippi Ryan, Wendy Tyson, and Karen White.

And last to all of you struggling writers of all genres whose love for writing fuels your grit and determination for inspiring me over the years to never give up no matter what.

No matter what.

CONTENTS

Writing is so difficult that I feel that writers,
having had their hell on earth,
will escape all punishment hereafter.
—Jessamyn West

INTRODUCTION

We have met the enemy and he is us.
—Walt Kelly

When you started writing on a regular basis, did you think it would answer all your prayers for fame and wealth, and you'd live happily ever after? Did you dream your book would be on bookstore shelves beside Lee Child, James Patterson, or J. K. Rowling? That it would hit number one on the *New York Times* bestseller list and garner the Edgar, the Barry, the Agatha, and Thriller Awards? That Steven Spielberg would beat down your door to sign you for the screenplay?

I did.

Were you perplexed to discover that nightmares come with the dreams? Did an agent's rejection, publisher expectations, blistering reviews, no-shows at bookstore signings, deadline pressures, zero awards, or agonizing writer's block besiege you? Did you have trouble locating your book on the shelves at Barnes and Noble? Did you make a little money but not enough to pay off the mortgage? Did you find that what few bucks you earned had to go toward paying a publicist? Are you still waiting for Hollywood to call?

I am.

After dashed dreams, do you still love to write?

I do.

Writers like me with ink in their blood have to write. Not writing isn't an option. When the going gets rough, we persevere through literary storms—albeit bruised, bereft, and beleaguered. I've seen them—writers frazzled from publishing's frenetic pace, spirits dead from unfulfilled and stressful career demands—empty shells comatose like zombies moving among the living.

The dead aren't supposed to walk among us, but they do. I know they do. I was one of them, too. In the still lonely hours before dawn, I plopped into the armchair, elbows digging into the knees of my ripped jeans. I dropped my head into my hands, grabbed a fistful of hair, and wept. That's right. This grown man cried. After finishing my best mystery yet, or so I thought, an editor I'd hired tore the plot to shreds. Rewrite after rewrite, dead end after dead end, confusion and frustration mired me. I wailed at the clock and shook my fist at the heavens, cursing, slamming things. At every turn, I met one roadblock after another. Distraught, I didn't know what else to do.

But cry.

I was my own biggest enemy, suffering from "dry-well syndrome," and didn't have a clue. Keep in mind this wasn't my first book. I had written thirty-five nonfiction and fiction books, tons of magazine and journal articles, blogs, and book chapters. I even won a few writing awards along the way. But I had never encountered that degree of writer's hell.

But hell is a state of mind. In the words of seventeenth-century author John Milton, "The mind is a universe and can make a heaven of hell, a hell of heaven." Truth be told, you and I make our own writer's heaven or hell. I can hear you gasp and see you roll your eyes, but listen up before you defriend me. Agents, editors, critical reviewers, or publishing houses don't hold the writing chains that bind us in place. We do, unwittingly perhaps, but we can rise up, overthrow our master, and unbind ourselves. And that's what this book is about: *Ask not how your writing life is treating you; ask how you are treating your writing life.*

By now you might wonder if it's possible to sustain joy, perseverance, and peace of mind in a hectic career filled with constant uncertainty and disillusionment. I'm here to tell you that it is. Like any profession, writing has its challenges, heartbreaks, frustrations, and exhilarations. Chances are, whether you're a seasoned author or an aspiring scribe, you've grappled with your share of meteoric challenges, repeated rejection, major setbacks, and devastating heartbreak. However, literary agents say the number one key to writing success—even more important than good writing—is perseverance, dogged determination in the face of disappointment.

For many years, in my lectures, books, and media appearances, I've taught people around the world techniques of resilience in the face of challenges and how to turn roadblocks into steppingstones. Just as grass grows through concrete, a resilient zone exists inside you. Once you find that place, you realize the power within you is greater than the challenges before you.

The 365 daily meditations in this book begin with January and go through December, but you can start at any time during any month. So if you pick up the book in May, you don't have to wait until January to start. The index provides key words that allow you the flexibility to select a particular writing issue that you might want to contemplate. You can select writing topics listed there that resonate on any particular day or explore certain topics of your choice in more depth.

The readings are designed to support authors of all genres. Perhaps you're one of them—juggling a full-time job, children, marriage, and household chores with a daily writing regimen and pressures from the business side of writing. As you navigate the ups-and-downs of the tumultuous writing world, this book will help you step back, take a breath, and contemplate a tried-and-true message geared to foster conscious living and free you from the clutches of your writing woes: an impossible deadline, a lousy review, bad writing habits, an agent's bludgeoning rejection, an editor's volcanic blast of disparagement, impassable writer's block, sounds of crickets at book signings, and the seismic rumble of your own spewing torrent of self-doubt.

Plenty of books teach the craft of writing, but this is the only guide on the craft of writing resiliency, necessary for you to become a successful author. You'll find tips and support through exercises such as meditation, breath work, yoga practices, the mind-body connection, stress management and relief practices, shifting habits for gratitude and positivity, decluttering to remove stuck energy, and self-care for health through sleep, exercise, and mindful eating. Daily contemplation provides reflection and mindfulness practices that will help you find your present moments and live more consciously through your writing pursuits. The simple messages in these daily readings have nourished and supported me, kept me resilient, and added meaning and joy to my own mindful writing journey.

Each daily meditation begins with a quotation from all types of writers—comics, novelists, poets, psychologists, cartoonists, spiritual leaders, journalists, songwriters, or philosophers—who serve up bite-size kernels of wisdom. Each quotation is followed by a passage of sage advice, warmhearted humor, concise heart speak, and touching inspiration. You can digest the morning meditation with a hot beverage then tuck it away to apply during your writing day or use it as a devotional to contemplate before falling asleep. Each reading concludes with a one-sentence takeaway that lodges within you, eventually becomes a part of you, living and breathing inside, and helping you navigate the ups-and-downs of daunting writing challenges.

At the conclusion of this book, I show you how I broke free from my inner chains, got unstuck, and finished that murder mystery. Meanwhile, I hope these daily meditations summon your inner resilience to escort you through the writing days ahead, support you in a deeply meaningful and mindful way, and help bring you the writing fulfillment you've been seeking.

JANUARY

JANUARY 1
Turn Endings into Beginnings

What we call the beginning is often the end
And to make an end is to make a beginning.
The end is where we start from.
—T. S. Eliot

One year's ending shepherds in the beginning of another year. We're ending and beginning our writing life all at the same time. Writing is a passion, an intensely personal calling, a long-time dream for most, and a solitary endeavor. It involves a lot of rejection and heartbreak at every stage. Many writers will review the past twelve months and set resolutions for the new year. We can begin again as we wipe the slate clean and contemplate beginning anew one day at a time.

Out of endings, fresh starts are born on our writing journeys. In the new year we can ask ourselves what we want to do differently to hone our craft. Develop better writing habits? Stop procrastinating? Create a healthier lifestyle? Cultivate a more positive outlook? Improve a faltering relationship? Learn to cope with rejection and self-doubt? Harness greater resilience and perseverance?

Everything we do outside our literary life contributes to writing success, whether it's tying up something left incomplete, changing habits, cultivating a more positive attitude, or thickening our skin.

Today's Takeaway

Start this new year with a clean slate and think about good writing habits, positive attitudes, or dedicated practices you can create to put your craft at the top of the charts.

JANUARY 2
Personalize Your Workstation

*I have a sofa on which I never nap, big windows with
an ocean view that I rarely see, because I keep the
pleated shades down at all times while working.*
—Dean Koontz

Dean Koontz says he knows he's a potential slacker, so he doesn't tempt himself with beach views. Each of us has to determine which surroundings work and then personalize them to suit our needs. A safe writing environment appeals to our senses in a different way from the settings we associate with daily life. It's a personalized space that contains everything we need to feel comfortable, creative, and productive. Under writing deadlines, a pleasant workstation eases stress, creates a sense of calm, and improves output.

There's no one-size-fits-all solution. Some writers prefer a little "comfort clutter" and disorganization so their surroundings don't feel like a museum. Some might be neat freaks, more at ease with tidy, streamlined areas. Other authors like Harlan Coben and John Hart prefer to write away from home to avoid distractions. Debut author Brian Panowich wrote in a closet at the fire station where he worked as a firefighter. What defines safety and comfort for you? Scented candles? Appealing paint colors? Vacation memorabilia with photos of loved ones, pets, and friends? Or anywhere, anytime?

Today's Takeaway

Lift your writing spirits by creating a safe, comfortable environment that attracts your five senses in a different way from the settings you associate with daily pressures.

JANUARY 3
Persevere Through Writing Storms

*Perseverance has so many guises, including standing up
in the face of rejection and getting back up when things
don't go smoothly, and yes, writing more books.*
—Jenny Milchman

Seasoned pros and aspiring scribes alike know the writing world is brutal—full of meteoric challenges, constant negativity, and devastating letdowns. Most agents, editors, and publicists say the number one key to writing success—even more important than good writing—is perseverance, dogged determination in the face of opposition.

A-list writers have worked long and hard. Author John Lescroart said, "I'm not an overnight success. My early publishing history, through my first five books, was unfortunate in many respects." Novelist Steve Berry said it took him twelve years and eighty-five rejections before he reached the bestseller list.

Rejection isn't personal; it's part of the package deal. And while perseverance is the cornerstone of success in anything we try, only the diligent survive the writing business. So let's be diligent and resilient. Every time we get up and brush ourselves off, we boost the chances of our work topping the charts.

Today's Takeaway

Persist when you get knocked down, don't take it personally, get up just one more time than you fall, and remember that acceptance and rejection are a package deal.

JANUARY 4
Monitor Your Writing Razzmatazz

There's always such a lot of razzmatazz
surrounding the first novel, and the doldrums
can appear after it has all died down.
—Christina Koning

A debut mystery or thriller writer once told me, "The moment I saw my first book cover was the moment it all started to feel real. I'm not sure when it will sink in, maybe when I hold an actual copy of my book. I'm so excited, I can hardly stand it!"

Any of us who published a first book can relate to this author's exhilaration. It's important for us to savor all the unrestrained joy and excitement we can muster but also to keep a healthy reality check on our "writer's high." The publishing world is rife with ups and downs that can rip us apart emotionally.

One minute we get a good review on Amazon, then the next one is lousy. Several agents reject our manuscript, and finally one wants to sign us. Our publisher sets a pub date for the fall then delays it to the spring. We promote our bookstore appearance like crazy and one person shows up. We lose a writing award then win another. It's important to celebrate your writing achievements to the fullest and ride the high. But be mindful that you need a fence around the drop-off so you can continue to move up and not down.

Today's Takeaway

Savor your writing razzmatazz, keep it in check, and prepare for a curveball of letdown that is sure to follow on your writing trajectory.

JANUARY 5
Outwit Your Negativity Bias

Your brain is like Velcro for negative experiences and
Teflon for positive ones—even though most of your
experiences are probably neutral or positive.
—Rick Hanson

Why do disappointments hurled at us from our writing challenges stick inside our skull? Scientists say it keeps us out of harm's way. Mother Nature hardwired us with a negativity bias that causes us to *overestimate threats and underestimate our ability* to conquer them. Most of us remember where we were on 9/11 but not the week after because downbeat news impacts us more. Forget the blooming azaleas along the roadside. If we don't see the car zooming at 90 miles per hour, we're roadkill.

What does this have to do with writing sustainability? The same bad-news bias that keeps us safe permeates every sphere of our lives. It's difficult to remain hopeful and persevere when our writing is bombarded by the same downbeat news that keeps us safe.

If we're searching for a solution to a plot, the mind automatically zeroes in on the problem, clouding out the range of possibilities. If we're anticipating the outcome of an editorial submission, a reviewer's comment, or an award nomination, our negativity bias creates unnecessary stress. We're more likely to feel fear instead of excitement. Our work as writers is to go beyond survival bias and prevent bad-news outcomes (known or unknown) from clobbering our writing potential.

Today's Takeaway

Outwit your negativity bias by offsetting it with a positivity bias: *underestimate your writing threats and overestimate your writing possibilities.*

JANUARY 6
Stack Your Positivity Deck

Don't be sad that roses have thorns;
be glad that thorns have roses.

—Lee Child

One of the cruel barriers to writing resilience is that negativity has a longer shelf life than positivity. For years I searched for my novel on bookstore shelves. Whether the book was on the shelves or not, my brain surmised the worst: the book wasn't selling. The solution to such no-win thoughts?

Experts say it takes three positive thoughts to offset one negative thought. Stacking our positivity deck has the cumulative benefit of allowing us to unlock a range of options and stir the creative juices. When we reshuffle our negativity deck while writing a draft or making revisions, our creative juices start to automatically dwarf stress juices.

A few tips can help you stack the deck in your favor, bounce back from bad news, and weather difficult writing days: avoid blowing things out of proportion; look for the upside of downside situations; focus on the solution instead of the problem; pinpoint the opportunity in a challenge; be chancy in new situations instead of letting survival fears hold the cards; step back from roadblocks and brainstorm possible stepping-stones; and hang out with positive people.

Today's Takeaway

Deal yourself a positivity card on a regular basis to build your mind's creative mojo and offset stress juices that could bring you to a screeching halt when you encounter a writing threat.

JANUARY 7
Lasso Your Wandering Mind

Cats are dangerous companions for writers because cat-watching is a near-perfect method of writing avoidance.
—Dan Greenburg

It's human nature for our minds to wander from time to time. In fact, yours could be wandering right now. You could be thinking about what you ate for lunch and what you "should" have eaten. You could be worrying about unpaid bills, an unfinished writing project, or a promised deadline to your publisher.

Take a minute and give your mind full permission to wander. Notice where it goes without trying to change anything. This counterintuitive strategy is much like leaning into a curve when riding a motorcycle—even though your thoughts might try to get you to lean the opposite way. This practice can actually relax the mind because we're leaning in by noticing, not struggling to make something happen.

Like Grand Central Station, wandering minds have so many thoughts coming and going they prevent us from being fully present during our writing moments and from pausing and catching our breath. Studies show when we stray, we pay—we're more stressed-out and unhappy when our minds wander than when we stay in the here and now. We're happier no matter what we're doing—even working overtime, vacuuming, or struck in traffic—if we're focused on the activity instead of thinking about something else.

Today's Takeaway

Pay attention and fully engage in each moment to keep your mind relaxed and alert at the same time; your writing will take on a fresh glow, plus wellbeing and productivity will soar.

JANUARY 8
Unveil the Light during Dark Hours

*Sometimes a change of perspective
is all it takes to see the light.*

—Dan Brown

When things are up in the air, career-wise, it can be a scary time. The words won't come, and we bite the skin around our fingernails. We missed an important deadline. Our dependable editor leaves the company, replaced by a new one who doesn't give us the time of day.

What does the future hold for our writing careers? What do we do now? Where do we go? Feeling adrift in the writing world can be terrifying, but we have a life raft: never underestimate the opportunity to persevere in a good crisis. During the darker hours of our writing lives, we *always* have the power to choose, starting with how we treat ourselves on the inside. We can wrap our arms around that scared, insecure part of us and, with nurturance and reassurance, talk it off the ledge.

No matter the outside conditions of our lives, we can choose to see the light. There are still many gifts waiting for us; we just don't know what they are. It's important to remind ourselves often of why we're doing what we're doing and let our love and passion for writing carry us through the darkest days.

Today's Takeaway

When all hope seems gone, turn darkness into light through conscious choice of your actions; remind yourself that no one can steal your love for writing and many gifts await you.

JANUARY 9
Take a Breather from What Others Think

*Sometimes it's good to take a break from
hearing what other people think about you.*
—Alanis Morissette

The singer/songwriter and author Alanis Morissette has been in the public eye since she was a child. Her groundbreaking songwriting, music, and looks have come under constant scrutiny, but she has learned to take a breather from the critics.

Whether we have the celebrity of Morissette or not, at some point someone will criticize our literary work. It goes with the territory. It's only natural that we want readers to hold our work to their chests and swoon, but to become better writers, we need constructive criticism whether it's from critique classes, editors, reviewers, or fans. At times, though, feedback can saturate us, drown out our own voices. Taking a break lets us settle within ourselves, appreciate our writing talents, and refuel our resilience and creative mojo.

We are the sculptors of our lives. Imagine a huge lump of clay in front of us as we clutch the sculpting knife. If we trim ourselves to suit everybody else, we whittle ourselves away, and there's nothing left. As writers, our main objective is to listen to our inner voice and *please* ourselves first then *prove* ourselves. Instead of handing the sculpting knife to another person, we carve our lives to our own true form. Do something that pleases you, such as a hike in the woods, instead of something that proves you, such as competing in a writing contest.

Today's Takeaway

Get out from under the microscope once in a while and be your own person by doing something that *pleases* you instead of something that *proves* you.

JANUARY 10
Curb Your Perfectionism

What is really hard, and really amazing,
is giving up on being perfect and beginning
the work of becoming yourself.
—Anna Quindlen

In its clutches, perfectionism tightens us in a stranglehold, injects its rigidity into our bloodstream and chokes the flow of spontaneous and flexible ideas. Uncurbed perfectionism causes us to set unrealistic goals, try too hard, and over focus on our mistakes. It blinds us from seeing our strengths and from generating our best creative work.

The only standard of perfection we have to meet is to be our perfect writing selves. Whether we write fiction or nonfiction or whether we're a plotter (write with an outline) or a pantser (fly by the seat of our pants), successful writing is determined by our ability to relax into the storyline and loosen perfectionism's iron-fisted grip so the creative juices can flow. As thriller writer Lee Child advises, "Don't get it right—get it WRITTEN!"

Take a few minutes and ask yourself what you can do to loosen your perfectionism and begin the work of becoming yourself.

Today's Takeaway
Give up on being perfect, set realistic writing goals, and allow yourself to make mistakes so creative juices, fresh approaches, novel ideas, and crisp writing can flow freely.

JANUARY 11
Engage in the Sweetness of Doing Nothing

*Creativity thrives on doing nothing. In the moments that
might seem empty, what has been there all along in some
embryonic form is given space and comes to life.*
—David Kundtz

Do nothing? I can imagine you rolling your eyes, glancing at your to-do list, booing and hissing. But I haven't been sniffing the ink cartridge from my printer, I promise. All the writing skill in the world won't help us meet our full potential until we have mastered the art of doing nothing. The Italians have a name for it: "il dolce far niente"—the sweetness of doing nothing. It doesn't translate in the United States, where tasks and schedules define us. The closest translation we have is "Killing time." But "il dolce far niente" demands more: to intentionally let go and put *being* before *doing* as a priority.

Doing nothing has been compared to the pauses that are an integral part of a beautiful piece of music. Without the absences of sound, the music would be just noise. Not long ago, I watched a writer, arms outstretched from his side, balancing on an old sea wall. In that moment, with all the time in the world, no hurry to get anywhere, all he cared about was navigating his body against the warm ocean breeze. Unbeknownst to him, his "il dolce far niente" provided an incubation period for his embryonic writing ideas to hatch.

Today's Takeaway

Indulge in the sweetness of being alive with "sweet nothings"—doing nothing for the sheer pleasure of it—providing an incubation period for writing ideas to come alive.

JANUARY 12
Weed Your Writing Garden

The book forces itself into my mind when
I am lugging furniture or pulling weeds.
—Robertson Davies

When we push away from our writing desks for a spell and do something on the physical plane, such as moving furniture or pulling weeds, we create a mental vacuum that quickly fills itself with creative ideas. Pulling weeds, for example, is like meditating. On the physical plane, we make space for flowers to grow while on the mental plane we clear out cluttered thoughts, making room for creative ideas to fill the empty space.

Sometimes daily stresses and strains clog creative channels, strangling us like Kudzu, choking off our creative flow. Some days the weeds of the writing world grow knee high, faster than we can keep up with them. Or sometimes we get so busy tending other people's gardens that weeds fill up our own.

Our ideas need to grow and flow freely if we are to be successful writers. What can we pull from our writing gardens to clear the underbrush and help us grow? Is it a cluttered writing space? A mental fog in our heads? A spiritual deadness? Worry, anger, or frustration? When we take a daily inventory of our writing gardens, we can weed out the undergrowth and blossom into the beautiful, scented, colorful perennials that we're intended to be.

Today's Takeaway

Tend your mental garden and clear away weeds that crept in while you were racing against deadlines, promoting your work, weeding another's garden, or postponing your personal life.

JANUARY 13
Steer Clear of the Scrap Heap

The man who lets a leader prescribe his course
is a wreck being towed to the scrap heap.
—Ayn Rand

When the rejection letters arrive—and they will—we don't have to let them turn us into a wreck hauled off to the scrap heap. If your writing path is anything like most writers' journeys, you will have someone telling you no every step of the way. The writing trajectory is like taking a hike in the woods. There will be logs to avoid, briars to endure, and undergrowth to trip us. But we face those hurdles and enjoy the hike anyway, keeping in mind that all successful writers before us travelled this path. But after tripping, they kept going, eventually stumbling into their dreams.

We are creators of our writing, not victims of it. Instead of letting rejection letters prescribe our course, we can prescribe theirs. We could haul them to the scrap heap. Or we could be creative and make a scrapbook, wallpaper a room, put them on our websites, read them at book signings, have a contest in our writing groups, use them for wrapping paper. Or we could do what James Lee Burke did. He saved his rejection slips in hopes of one day auctioning them off. You get what I'm saying? Are you feeling empowered yet? Think of a time you felt discouraged from a writing rejection and how you reacted. Then ask yourself how you can stay empowered in the face of your next rejection.

Today's Takeaway

Don't let rejections turn you into a victim and haul you off to the garbage dump. Remind yourself that, like your successful predecessors, you're a force to be reckoned with; breathe your second wind until you stumble into your dreams.

JANUARY 14
Emancipate Yourself from Damseling

I don't damsel well. Distress,
I can do. Damseling? Not so much.

—James Patterson

Does your mind get so creative that it puts you in a "damsel in distress" mode—that classic scene in world literature—even when you're watching the sunset? Mine does. Like James Patterson, I don't damsel well, but I can distress in the worst possible way.

Unless we're engaged in writing a thriller, our minds are using us when we get stuck in these internal dramas. Through the practice of mindfulness, we can bring present-moment awareness to what's happening inside and attune to the way we're treating ourselves so that we're more in charge of our minds. By simply noticing our thoughts, we start to see how many of them are worries about the future or regrets about the past. As we recognize that our thoughts are just thoughts, not truths, we learn not to make too much of them.

In a comfortable place with your eyes open or shut, bring your full attention to the thoughts streaming through your mind without attempting to change anything. Simply observe the thoughts for five minutes with curiosity and without judgment. Then notice what you're aware of in your mind and body. Don't be surprised if you feel an inner calm or gain aha moments that can help you approach your craft and respond to hard-hitting writing stressors in more effective ways.

Today's Takeaway

Emancipate yourself from "damseling and distressing"; notice where your mind goes during writing stretches, then bring it back to the deep richness of the present moment.

JANUARY 15
Sidestep Procrastination

We are so scared of being judged that we
look for every excuse to procrastinate.
—Erica Jong

Procrastination hits home. We hem and haw, terrified our finished product won't be perfect enough. Postponing and knowingly feeding the monster, we dust our desk, grab a snack, or arrange the spice rack—anything to avoid facing the fear of imperfection. Deadlines loom. Our editor sends an e-mail asking where the hell the manuscript is.

In the heat of the moment, stalling seems to relieve stress. But over the long hall, dragging our feet adds another layer of pressure, catapulting us into a swirl of adrenaline and cortisol stew. Deadlines pass, commitments pile up, self-talk beats us to smithereens. Now a second layer of pressure becomes another problem to reckon with.

In the initial writing stages, we don't have to get bogged down with dotting each *i* and crossing each *t*. Once we let go of everything our third-grade teacher taught us about spelling, grammar, and handwriting, we move from "I can either do a perfect draft or none at all" to "It's okay if my rough draft contains misspelled words or bad grammar." Giving ourselves permission to write "the shitty first draft," break big writing projects into tiny steps, and complete one easy item on our list gives us an instant hit of success.

Today's Takeaway
Face your writing tasks head-on imperfectly and early, instead of waiting until the last minute, and start with easy steps you can accomplish quickly to get you going.

JANUARY 16
Get Comfortable with Maybe

Maybe is just one change or perspective,
but it's one that changes everything.

—Allison Carmen

We writers, like most people, count on certainty and predictability. In fact, our very survival depends on it. We want to know what, who, when, where, and how things will happen with our work. When certainty is upended, it can feel as if the ground beneath us has opened up, threatening to swallow us.

One fact of life is that the only thing we can count on is that a writing life will bring us plenty of uncertainty. Things won't always go as planned. Our writing will go awry and unexpected things will blindside us. The car will stall in traffic. Flu will put us out of commission for a time. We won't always get the contract.

We don't get to tailor the writing life to our schedules. We have the choice to stew in the uncertainty of it or change our perspective to "maybe" and become more comfortable with uncertainty. Stepping into the arena of "maybe" loosens us up to the fact that for every possibility there are numerous ways a situation can resolve. We can live in serenity without having things our way and always knowing a definite outcome.

Take a few moments right now to meditate on an uncertainty in your writing life and on the possibility of accepting "maybe" with serenity.

Today's Takeaway

With uncertainty baked into the writing life, try to live with "maybe." Once you realize there are many possible outcomes, you're calmer and freer to focus on the writing at hand.

JANUARY 17
Be a True Writ Instead of a True Grit

*I try to be a regular sort of fellow—much like a dentist
drilling his teeth every morning—except Sunday.*
—John Updike

What makes us true writers? Is it when we land a contract from one of the Big 5 publishers? After we pen three novels? When we hit the bestseller list?

No. It's when we start to think of writing as our jobs like teachers, electricians, and doctors. We don't wait for idle times or until the mood strikes when there's nothing better to do. We don't *find* time to write. We *take* time to write whether we feel like it or not. It's our jobs.

When we compare writing to hard labor, it's easier to sit down and write. Writing can be as sweaty, dirty and grueling as digging ditches. Our job is to put words on a page, one beside the other, much like brick-layers arrange bricks. We use vocabulary and grammar instead of bricks and mortar. We are disciplined, and we make writing a priority and write on a regular basis.

Even if we're not published or if we have day jobs as engineers or lawyers, we are true writers when we're dedicated to the craft, make it a priority, and have such fierce determination that we can't *not* write. Contemplate on one action you can take to put writing higher up on your priority list.

Today's Takeaway

Think of yourself as a writer, call yourself a writer, dedicate yourself to the craft, and practice it on a regular basis one brick at a time, one word at a time.

JANUARY 18
Find Your Inner Sanctuary

Stillness is where creativity and
solutions to problems are found.
—Eckhart Tolle

When our creative writing juices have dried up and our thoughts are caught in futile repetitive mental loops, it's time to stop and let our minds meander.

The writing business is supercharged with tasks: bookstores, workshop panels, book clubs, interviews, writing deadlines, blogging, texting, social media postings, e-mails, voice mails, snail mail. Whew! The list is endless, and sometimes after hours we find ourselves exhausted, still on fast-forward.

The Rx for recharging our batteries is inner solitude. Within each of us there is a sanctuary to which we can retreat and gain insight and peace to help us navigate stressful moments. This inner stillness is a moment of reverie where neither thoughts of writing nor electronic devices are present.

We can create this inner place of calm, harmony, and peace anywhere, anytime: sitting at our desks for three minutes, meditating in a crowded airport, soaking in a warm bath. In this stillness, we rekindle our inner writing fires and hatch creative answers to unresolved writing questions.

Today's Takeaway

Take time out of the rat race to build breathers into your writing schedule where you get refreshed, relaxed, and recharged and discover creative solutions to writing roadblocks.

JANUARY 19
Say Goodbye to Worry

Don't worry about things...Just do your work and you'll survive. The important thing is to have a ball, to be joyful, to be loving and to be explosive...and you grow.

—Ray Bradbury

Asked how it feels to be a debut author, Dana Carpenter said, "Incredible and scary all at once. Some days I can't stop smiling and others I wake up in a sweat worried about reviews and sales and *the sequel* and all the things I can't control. But mostly it still feels like a dream."

I think Dana captured the ambiguity of the excitement and worry that most debut authors have. And if we're not careful, the worry can overshadow the excitement. First we worry about snaring an agent, then about getting published, then about reviews, sales, and all the other aspects we can't control.

At each stage of the publishing process, there are things to worry about, making it a constant companion and causing us to lose sight of why we wanted to write in the first place: our love for writing, desire to tell a story, or need to share a message. Will we ever be able to relax and enjoy the fruits of our labor? The final answer is up to each of us individually. Do you have writing worries you'd like to say goodbye to? Meditate for five minutes on your love for writing and see if that feeling can coexist with your worry.

Today's Takeaway

Savor the excitement of being a writer at every step of the writing process, and if the dream starts to slip through your fingers, say goodbye to worry and embrace the wonder.

JANUARY 20
Forego Biting into the Burnt Toast

*Objections will start to pop up like burnt
toast. These are your blurts.*

—Julia Cameron

In some ways the cells of the body are like the nosy neighbor from the TV sitcom *Bewitched*. They constantly eavesdrop on our thoughts—waiting in the wings to react to threats. When we're writing, negative self-talk can pop up like burnt toast with such lightning speed that we don't even notice.

Suppose we're asked to be on a panel at ThrillerFest—the conference for International Thriller Writers. Blurts pop into our heads: "You'll never be able to pull that off... You're kidding yourself... Who do you think you are?"

Burnt toast anyone?

Upon hearing these thoughts, the body's alarm system dumps a cocktail of cortisol and adrenaline into the bloodstream to deal with the threat. In a matter of seconds, we have a sinking feeling. We tremble at the mere notion of giving the talk. The mind takes us out of the present moment, and we imagine a bloodthirsty audience—hundreds of accomplished writers—staring us down. All the while the body is flooded with anxiety as if we're actually standing on the stage. Once we become aware of the "blurts" that exaggerate threats and underestimate our ability to deal with them, clarity heightens, stress drops, and serenity neutralizes the stress.

Today's Takeaway

Recognize when blurts pop up like burnt toast, remind yourself that situations can't trap you, then underestimate the threat and affirm your ability to deal with it.

JANUARY 21
Decide Your Writing Fate

Man does not simply exist but always
decides what his existence will be, what
he will become in the next moment.

—Viktor Frankl

If your writing path is anything like most authors' journeys, you will have someone telling you no every step of the way. The publishing pundits say the odds are against you making it as a writer. An agent says no thanks. Family, friends, and perhaps even your writing group tell you not to quit your day job. Worst of all is that voice that says you're wasting your time.

When bad news comes, something drops inside. No matter our sagging hearts, we always have the freedom to choose whether we *react* with despair or *act* with confidence. Author and psychologist Viktor Frankl wrote about his confinement at Auschwitz where he saw choices for himself, even as others dropped dead around him.

We can apply Frankl's powerful beliefs to the disappointment and frustration we feel with writing letdowns. Instead of allowing them to decide our reactions, we can always *act* by making conscious decisions about how we handle bad news. Regardless of negative consequences, no one can take away our writing will and our love for it. Reflect on a past reaction you had to a writing letdown then ask how next time you can *act* by holding positive beliefs in yourself instead of *react* with despair.

Today's Takeaway

Be conscious of the choices you make about writing letdowns. Hold your head high, look the world in the eye, and get back in the saddle; then write your best piece yet.

JANUARY 22
Put on Your Wide-Angle Lens

Occasionally... what you have to do is go back to the
beginning and see everything in a new way.
—Peter Straub

Just as we revise our manuscripts, sometimes we need to revise the way we're looking at our literary lives. When writing throws a curveball, we can ask if we're looking through a zoom lens or a wide-angle lens. One way to find out is to identify a career challenge. Perhaps our novel didn't earn the amount of royalties we expected. Maybe Kirkus didn't give us the starred review we thought we deserved—even gave us a negative one. Or perhaps we have to pull several all-nighters to meet a deadline for a writing class.

Whatever the writing challenge, typically the mind—operating like the zoom lens of a camera—zeros in on the problem, magnifies it, and eclipses the big picture. But we don't have to let the zoom lens create blind spots. Our wide-angle lens identifies the problem, pulls up the big picture, and observes the problem in the larger spectrum of our lives.

Once we broaden our outlook and put the complaint into a wider context, it loses some of its sting. When we can see a problem from more than one standpoint, it sharpens our clarity and brings peace of mind. Think of a writing complaint that you can view through your wide-angle lens then meditate on it and notice the calming sensation that emerges.

Today's Takeaway
Put on your wide-angle lens and look at the big picture of your writing career—especially the blind spots that your zoom lens clouds out—and your vision will morph into 20/20.

JANUARY 23
Don't Freak Out over Setbacks

Taking a step backward after taking a
step forward is not a disaster, it's a cha-cha.
—Robert Brault

Every author has had one kind of setback or another. If we plot the average writer's progress, it would make an upward zigzag, not follow an ascending straight line. As long as the zigzag keeps spiraling upward, we're "cha-chaing" our way to writing success.

It's impossible for us to move forward in anything without falling back once in a while. It's natural to grow disheartened when we feel defeated on the way to something new or unknown—something that we really want with our hearts and souls. A part of honing our craft of writing is to learn not to feel defeated after a setback. We don't get fooled into just looking at where we want to land and feeling disheartened that we haven't reached our goals. We learn to look back and affirm how far we've come instead of how far we have to go. This gives a truer picture of the map of the progress.

Just as brooks make rivers and rivers run into seas, the small steps slowly mount up over time. Next time we have a setback we can keep dancing forward until we cha-cha ourselves into our writing dreams.

Today's Takeaway

Tell yourself that setbacks are not disasters—they're cha-chas that form a zigzagged upward spiral—a natural part of a writer's progression, not an unbroken ascending line.

JANUARY 24
Stick Your Neck Out

Sometimes, if you aren't sure about something,
you just have to jump off the bridge and
grow your wings on the way down.
—Danielle Steel

Instead of constantly fleeing from the unknown, we strengthen our resilience as writers by stepping into the unfamiliar and unexpected. It's one of life's paradoxes. We build writing resilience by exerting a degree of control while stepping outside our comfort zone, risking our neck, and embracing novelty.

We cannot grow as writers unless we are willing to take risks. If we are too skittish or unwilling to stretch, we could unwittingly sabotage our talents. In fact, the risk of stepping into the uncertain and unpredictable—perhaps being criticized or contradicted—grows us as authors.

What edge can you go to in your writing today? What unpredictable bridge can you jump off to sprout your wings? What limb can you reach to get to the fruit of the tree and spice up your writing life? Anytime we take a risk, whether it be reading something we penned in front of a writing group or explore writing in a different genre, we gain confidence and stretch one step closer to the literary success we've been avoiding.

Today's Takeaway

Find that one place in your writing life where you've been hiding, then stick your neck out from your comfort zone and open pathways that can help you grow as a writer.

JANUARY 25
Put Down Your Gavel

Monsters are real, and ghosts are real, too.
They live inside us, and sometimes they win.

—Stephen King

All of us have an inner monster—that kick-butt voice inside that bludgeons us with criticism and tells us how worthless, selfish, dumb, or bad we are. It never rests and garners more airplay than the inner voice that tells us how great we really are.

But we don't have to let the monster's judgment sabotage our literary success. When a life event disturbs us, it is not the event itself but our judgment of it that causes our suffering. We can't help forming judgments; that's how we make sense of the world. In its own ironic way, the judge tries to help us weather literary storms with its kick-butt treatment. Much like the hard-ass drill sergeant who doesn't want to see a soldier's head blown off in combat, the judge pumps up the volume when we stumble, concerned that too much leeway will turn us into slackers and prevent us from finishing a writing project.

Coming down hard on ourselves after a mistake or failure reduces our creativity and chances of writing success. Substituting loving-kindness for self-judgment each step of the way is a powerful resilient tool, more likely to lead to literary success. So talk yourself off the ledge instead of allowing your judgment to encourage you to jump.

Today's Takeaway

Put away your gavel and amp up your kinder, more compassionate side when your inner judge overshadows you, and let it airlift you to untold heights of literary success.

JANUARY 26
Shun Turning Yourself into a Pretzel

I am afraid of people with too much charm. They devour
you. In the end you are made a sacrifice to the exercise
of their fascinating gift and their insincerity.

—Somerset Maugham

When we're afraid of disapproval of our writing, we avoid conflict by consenting to a request, even when we don't agree. Pleasing people puts us under pressure to keep up a façade. We seek approval by turning ourselves into a pretzel, smothering others with charm and manipulation that in the end is insincere—anything to save our skin.

Appeasing has a short shelf life before fellow writers find out the truth. In the writing world, no matter how hard we try, someone will disapprove of something—and it's only a matter of time before the crocodile will feast upon the appeaser.

The Rx? Get comfortable with disapproval—one of the few things we can count on in the writing business—and be honest and forthright in writing, because appeasement shows through. Also be willing to take a stand about your writing if you have strong opinions when others disagree with your creative ideas.

Today's Takeaway

Gauge your writing by your own set of standards: be true to yourself, be your own person, and throw your arms open to disapproval for it can only make your writing stronger.

Body Connection Practice: Practice Chair Yoga

*The most important pieces of equipment you need
for doing yoga are your body and your mind.*
—Rodney Yee

After sitting for long periods of time, our bodies need attention to keep up with our productive minds. Yoga is one of the best practices for attuning the mind and body. When practiced regularly, yoga brings down our cortisol levels and blood pressure, combats fatigue, and fosters sleep. And with certain types of yoga, our bodies get a 65 percent increase of dopamine squirts.

If you're in a writing zone and can't get to a yoga class, try practicing yoga in the very chair you're in. Make sure the chair has a back. Place your left hand over on your right knee. Place your right arm on the back of the chair. Stretch lightly with eyes open or closed. Notice the stretch and what happens inside. After sixty seconds, bring your body back to center. Then reverse the stretch. Place your right hand over your left knee. Put your left arm on the back of the chair. Stretch lightly again with eyes open or closed. Pay attention to the stretch, and notice what happens inside. After sixty seconds, bring your body back to center, and if you want to continue, you can repeat the cycle.

Today's Takeaway

Take three or four minutes to practice chair yoga; it gives you a deep sense of calm, mental clarity, and replenishes your mental and physical energy for longer writing spans.

JANUARY 28
Forgive Someone for Your Sake

I've known for years that resentments don't
hurt the one we resent, but they do hurt us.

—Anne Lamott

Are you eating rat poison, waiting for the rat to die? After a devastating writing experience, the hurt can morph into anger and cause us to become a storehouse of animosities. What purpose does this serve? Perhaps clutching resentment satisfies our hunger for revenge, our only means of retaliation—punishing the ones who hurt us.

But holding grudges creates self-harm, boomeranging and eating away at us like a disease—similar to a rat eating poison, then slowly waiting to die. Harboring resentments keeps the hurt at the center of our daily activities, depletes our energies, focuses us in a negative direction, and clogs creative channels.

Releasing antagonistic feelings creates a vacuum that unclogs our creative channels and clears open portals for our best writing to emerge. When we've been hurt by someone in the literary world and still want to pursue our writing goals, it's important to evacuate the grudges if we want to be successful. Once we have a vacuum, there's room for an open current of creative abundance and productivity to flow.

Today's Takeaway

Inventory your hurt feelings for old grudges, notice where they exist, then toss them into the dustbin of history, and move farther along the road to your writing success.

JANUARY 29
Transform Your Inner World

We do not need magic to transform our world. We carry
all of the power we need inside ourselves already.

—J. K. Rowling

Make sure your worst enemy doesn't live between your own two ears. Most of us writers think we are our thoughts and feelings. When that happens, the insecure thoughts, feelings, and judgments become our greatest enemy.

We're not our thinking or our feelings. When we can watch everything come and go in our minds, our true Selves with a capital "S" emerge. The transformed mind lets us see how we process what's coming at us. It allows us to step back, sit on the riverbank, and watch with a dispassionate eye the water we've been swimming in.

The power to detach from our thoughts and feelings exists in everyone, giving us a more honest and clear-minded view of what's truly happening inside and outside us. When we learn to stay in this objective place, we find that clarity, safety, and serenity surround us and we become more confident in our writing worlds.

Today's Takeaway

If your worst enemy is living between your two ears, try taking a bird's-eye view of your thoughts and feelings, watch them as they come and go then relish the magic of serenity.

JANUARY 30
Hook Up with Your Writing Tribe

*These people are your tribe. They get how hard
it is to get published and stay published, they
get the terror, and they have your back.*
—Jennifer Hillier

If you don't have one, a writing tribe is good medicine. Our tribes feel our pain. They know how difficult the writing and selling market is and how vulnerable it feels to strip down naked and expose our inner workings to the world through our writing.

Unfortunately, our loved ones often don't understand the challenges and triumphs of writing, and it can be a mistake to expect them to understand. But writing tribes—a friend, writing group, or critique class—carry us through the stress of our work being out in the world, the challenge to both write and promote at the same time, and the pressure of securing another writing gig. They provide a safe sanctuary where we can have face-to-face conversations about the upside and downside of writing and speak openly and honestly about our writing flaws, triumphs, and disappointments.

When a blistering review or writing rejection emotionally hijacks us, a supportive tribe can help us stay grounded, reminding us why we write in the first place, and give us the oomph to keep on going.

Today's Takeaway

Search for your own tribe of scribblers composed of people with whom you trust and feel safe, who nurture you, and provide encouragement and motivation to keep you going.

JANUARY 31
Summon Your Strength

Let the gentle bush dig its roots deep
and spread upward to split the boulder.
—Carl Sandburg

How many of us have allowed self-doubt to plummet us into despair? How often do we put our emotional wellbeing at the mercy of one unpleasant writing incident instead of mustering the strength to deal with it?

In the same way an acorn contains within it a mighty oak, we contain deep within us tremendous roots of strength. Are we in touch with those roots? Do we feel like an acorn or a giant oak? Do we recognize and nurture our strength so it can sprout into stamina to withstand the forces of the literary world? Not just physical strength but the determination and willpower necessary to withstand daily writing challenges—the kind author and newspaper journalist, Judith Viorst wrote about: "Strength is the capacity to break a Hershey bar into four pieces with your bare hands and then eat just one of the pieces."

As writing insecurities try to uproot you, remember that you have everything necessary to keep your feet planted on the ground, that your deep roots cannot be reached by a hard frost. As you harness all the strength within—like the sturdy bush that digs its roots deep—imagine spreading upward and splitting the literary weights that hold you down.

Today's Takeaway

Recognize and summon your inner strength to help you cope with writing uncertainties and resist crumbling under the stressors that accompany your writing journey.

FEBRUARY

FEBRUARY 1
Exercise an Attitude of Gratitude

*I am grateful that I experienced many things . . . and that
I have been able to write a dozen books, to receive
innumerable letters from friends, colleagues, and readers.*
—Oliver Sacks

The day-to-day annoyances we complain about are suddenly trivial when we face a major catastrophe. How many of us gripe and complain about minor inconveniences when our lives are already rich and full? After a writing project wraps, authors sometimes move on to the next one without taking time to savor the successful completion of the one they left behind. Taking time to underscore our completions and successes creates a deeper sense of fulfillment.

The gratitude exercise helps us see the flip side of the narrow scope that our minds build without our knowledge. Make a list of the many things you're grateful for—the people, places and things that make life worth living and bring you comfort and joy. After you've made your list, meditate on your appreciation for each item and visualize anything you've taken for granted—things that if you didn't have would leave your life empty. As you practice this exercise, notice that you are more aware of how full your life already is.

Today's Takeaway

Count your blessings for all that you have on this day, seize it and live it fully, and don't let pettiness distract you from the bigger, more important things in life.

FEBRUARY 2
Develop a Growth Mindset

The passion for stretching yourself and sticking
to it, even (or especially) when it's not going
well, is the hallmark of the growth mindset.
—Carol Dweck

Do you have a fixed mindset or a growth mindset? Your answer could determine whether you reach your dreams as a writer. Studies show we can fulfill our potential as writers by cultivating a growth mindset. Instead of viewing struggles, mistakes, and challenges as failure, we consider them part of a learning process that makes us smarter at our craft.

A growth mindset creates a passion for learning our craft, and instead of becoming discouraged by failure, it becomes part of that passion. The cherished quality of being a writer doesn't have to be inborn. It can be cultivated through ups-and-downs and challenges. That's why so many famous writers like Stephen King, Janet Evanovich, and James Lee Burke—who got tons of rejections—became successful. For writing "growthers," it doesn't make sense to stop trying. They learn from their struggles and refuse to give up. The poet Sylvia Plath said, "I love my rejection slips. They show me I try."

Today's Takeaway

Cultivate a growth mindset by considering failures, challenges, and struggles as a way to learn and allow you to thrive with resilience and become better at the craft of writing.

FEBRUARY 3
Scrub Writing Distractions

My house has too many distractions. There's the e-mail.
There's checking my Amazon ranking...There's the fax.
Too many distractions. I like to go out and write.

—Harlan Coben

Distractions in our writing environment can keep us in a state of low-grade stress and interfere with our writing capacity in subtle ways. Writers have different habits to avoid distractions. When writing, novelist Jeffrey Deaver has his own unique way of concentrating. He turns off the lights, pictures the scene in his head, and writes in the dark.

Studies show that under environmental pressures, our stress hormone levels escalate even when we're not aware of it. Rapid temperature changes of too hot or too cold can interfere with concentration. Fluorescent lights increase cortisol stress levels, and restricted sunlight can trigger depression and elevate stress. Well-lit spaces, using as much natural sunlight as possible, enhance our writing.

While blasting Lady Gaga's CD might help some writers concentrate, others are distracted by loud music or excess noise from barking dogs or children playing. In those cases, we can block out noise pollution with headphones, earplugs, or soft music or soundproof ourselves with good insulation, window treatments, or sound machines. Smoke-free, well-ventilated work areas with fresh air and low humidity also foster concentration.

Today's Takeaway

Inventory your workspace for writing distractions—lighting, temperature, noise and air pollution—to determine what steps you can take to bolster your concentration.

FEBRUARY 4
Eschew the "What-the-Hell" Effect

If you don't go after what you want, you'll never have it.
If you don't ask, the answer is always no. If you don't
step forward, you're always in the same place.
—Nora Roberts

Ever get so frustrated with the inability to finish a writing project that you bang your fist? After more futile attempts to find the right words, you might say to hell with it. Welcome to the club. When we have constant roadblocks, it's tempting to condemn ourselves and chuck the whole idea. This impulsive reaction—researchers call it the "what-the-hell" effect—is an attempt to bring quick relief to the misery of failing. We seek comfort in the very thing we're trying to conquer: writing failure. This action adds pain on top of heartache.

Studies show that after feeling a sense of failure, along with a bad mood, writers are more likely to give up their goals so they don't have to keep feeling disappointment. The bad mood eclipses perseverance, and the what-the-hell attitude gives us a way out—permission to give up.

We don't have to let writing frustrations catapult us into giving up. Accepting each and every disappointment without criticizing ourselves makes us more likely to succeed. If we consider that eschewing the what-the-hell attitude is a form of self-care instead of self-denial, it'll keep us from adding insult to injury.

Today's Takeaway
Face writing disappointments by taking the towel you want to throw in and use it to wipe the sweat off your face so you can continue on your literary journey.

FEBRUARY 5
Amp Up Self-Care

If I'd known I was going to live this long,
I'd have taken better care of myself.
—Eubie Blake

If you're like most writers who kick themselves for their shortcomings, you probably have a deep belief that this treatment can help you write better. Wrong. When writing pressures put us under the gun or we're stuck or frustrated in some way, it's important to be gentle and supportive with ourselves. It's more beneficial to catch ourselves when we fall just like we would a best friend. The more supportive we are of ourselves, the better writers we will become.

It's not selfish to love ourselves; it's selfish *not* to love ourselves, for our love for others and everything we do comes from self-love. Only as we cultivate the right attitude toward ourselves will we have the right attitude toward our writing.

We are taught that self-sacrifice is a virtue and that putting ourselves last is strength. But scientists say it's the other way around—that self-love stops frustration, worry, and other negative feelings in their tracks and leads us to treat others with more compassion and respect. How can you emotionally support yourself instead of turning on yourself in the middle of writing struggles?

Today's Takeaway

When you're going through a rough patch such as writing duress, love yourself with a nurturing voice and comforting words. Smiley face not required.

FEBRUARY 6
Outfox Your Pessimism

A pessimist sees the difficulty in every opportunity;
an optimist sees the opportunity in every difficulty.

—Bertram Carr

How many times has our hope and excitement been dashed with, "This project is just not right for me"? Then negativity clouds roll in and obscure our outlook, and we lose our enthusiasm and motivation. If you're sometimes pessimistic, you're in good company. Many successful writers tend to think in terms of worse case scenario. Most of us usually remember a negative situation (a) and how letdown we were (c). But we might not pay attention to how we thought about the situation (b). The first step is to outfox negative beliefs that unwittingly contribute to the letdown. Then write down a truer, more positive thought that can mitigate the negative feelings.

Here's an example: (a) "The agent I was hoping for turned me down" (activating situation); (b) "I'll never get my mystery published" (negative belief); (c) letdown goes through the roof (negative feelings). Now, go back to (b) and outfox the belief by looking at it from a different angle: "Publishing is a subjective business, and there are hundreds of agents. I'll keep searching until I find a good fit." Then notice a different emotion (c): Feelings of calm and hope prevail.

Today's Takeaway

If your writing career takes a nosedive, outfox pessimism and flip it around into a more positive outlook until you see less difficulty, more opportunity, and greater optimism.

FEBRUARY 7
Rein In Your Envy

Whatever you want, at any moment, someone else is
getting it. Whatever you have, someone else is longing for.

—Laura Lippman

Perhaps we've witnessed fellow authors envy other writers who have received more acclaim. Maybe some of us have been on the receiving end of envy or jealousy. Or perhaps we have envied prolific writers who pump out top-selling works faster than we can.

When we feel cheated at a colleague's good fortune, it reflects our own lack of writing confidence and success. Coveting the skills or accomplishments of others comes from the inability to see our own gifts or lack of belief in them. Envy can keep us from realizing that we are blessed with talents that the ones we envy don't have, and it can prevent us from penning our best work.

When we envy, we have an opportunity to look within and ask what we need to change about ourselves. A stroke of luck for a fellow writer doesn't have to be a slap in the face. When we genuinely experience the joy of another writer's good fortune, a curious thing happens. We suddenly have good fortune, too, because we share in their good feelings. Give it a shot and notice that as you participate in someone else's joy, you feel the joy, too!

Today's Takeaway

Rejoice in your talents and gifts instead of coveting other writers' abilities, celebrate the successes of every author you meet, and enjoy the boomerang of your own good fortune.

FEBRUARY 8
Immerse Yourself in Deep Play

There is a deeper form of play, akin to rapture and
ecstasy that humans relish, even require, to feel whole.
—Diane Ackerman

Deep play is a form of rapture created by an altered state that brings us joy, wellbeing, and inner calm. As we go deep into one pastime or activity that we are passionate about—instead of shallowly into three or four—it so engulfs us that time stands still. We feel blanketed in deep play's refuge and comforted from the stressors of life and the intensity of long writing hours.

Sometimes we can experience the comfort and satisfaction of deep play in our writing. I know I have. We call it going into the zone—that magical place where characters come alive, a fictitious setting becomes real, and we lose track of time. But when the demands of writing outweigh the reverie, we might need a different type of deep play in which we sidestep writing pressures, let go, and unwind.

Other forms of deep play are sailing, working with clay, gardening, painting, skiing, tennis, playing a musical instrument, or running—any activity where we can immerse ourselves. Excursions as simple as wandering aimlessly in antique galleries, milling around attic sales, or browsing bookstores also can engulf us and bring sheer enjoyment.

Today's Takeaway

Indulge deeply in a hobby, recreation, or creative outlet or hunker down with a good book to stimulate creativity, bring inner peace, and keep your life on even keel.

FEBRUARY 9
Read a Critique without Bawling

You know a heart can be broken,
but it keeps beating just the same.
—Fannie Flagg

It's inevitable. It will happen, and all of us writers must be prepared for how we deal with the hard news. A bad review can eviscerate our writing mojo, cut us off at the knees, throw us into tears, and make us not want to write again—ever.

Like most seasoned writers, I've been there and have the T-shirt. We haven't really been initiated as writers until the first rejection with perhaps additional ones to follow. Now that you know what to expect, what is the best way to prepare for a blistering review? For starters, it's okay to cry if you need to. When someone hurts you, it's not your fault that it's painful. And it's difficult to prepare for the heartbreak of high aspirations. So get out the tears—or other emotions—if they need release. You will find your broken heart keeps on beating to the finish line.

Once you empty the box of Kleenex, take a breath and try not to get defensive and angry. That will only work against you. As you examine the critique, let your dispassionate eye turn it inside out. Take in the good, ask what you can learn from it, and leave the rest on the page or screen. You have just turned a hurtful situation into a healing one that will move you further along your writing path.

Today's Takeaway

Read a writing critique with a dispassionate eye and heart; then use any beneficial feedback you find to improve your manuscript and leave the rest behind.

FEBRUARY 10
Affirm Your Tallcomings

Sometimes I want to write criticism a letter and tell
him to leave me alone. The problem is that when
I don't see him for a while, I start to miss him.
—J. Ruth Gendler

Do you blush when someone applauds your writing? Do you feel like you pulled one over on readers who praise your work? Do you feel discomfort if gushing fans glorify your talent?

There's a reason why the term *tallcomings* is not in Webster's and *shortcomings* is. There's no such word as *tallcomings*. I made it up because as writers we tend to ignore our positive attributes and clobber ourselves with negatives.

To be effective, it's important to have a critical eye, accept constructive feedback, and recognize our limitations and failures without dropping our heads in our hands. It's difficult to have an honest picture of ourselves if we cannot affirm the truth about who we are. And that includes acknowledging both our shortcomings *and* our tallcomings.

One tip is to replace fault-finding with favor-finding and give ourselves a fist bump when we reach a writing triumph. Another is to affirm our writing strengths on a regular basis so we Bookmarks see more literary possibilities, increase our reserves, and overcome future writing challenges. What writing tallcomings can you affirm about yourself right now?

Today's Takeaway

Throw modesty out the window and make a list of your tallcomings to build your writing resources so you can jump everyday hurdles that are sure to come your way.

FEBRUARY 11
Walk a Mile in Someone Else's Shoes

Hell is yourself and the only redemption is when a person puts himself aside to feel deeply for another person.
—Tennessee Williams

The ability to put ourselves in someone else's shoes and see their point of view is a powerful tool that takes us out of our own self-created hell.

Empathy connects us to what others are feeling and frees us from narrow, negative thoughts and snap judgments. It neutralizes our hard feelings and imbues us with a softer, kinder approach to disputes and difficult people. Empathy gives us control over situations that we cannot control, keeping us calm, cool, and collected. It keeps our integrity intact and helps us respond in a way that promotes fairness and good communication.

Think of just one person you can empathize with today—someone who has done something to upset you—and temporarily suspend your point of view (you don't have to give it up for good). Try to imagine walking around inside that person's body, looking at the upsetting event in their skin, through their eyes, with their heart. Then notice your hard feelings soften.

Today's Takeaway

Taking up residence in someone else's point of view gives you feelings of connection and power, brings you good feelings, and helps you cope in the uphill battle of your writing aspirations.

FEBRUARY 12
Spit Shine Your Electronic Habits

*I fear the day that technology will surpass our human
interaction. The world will have a generation of idiots.*

—Albert Einstein

Experts say Americans are more isolated because of their love affair
with the Internet, texting, e-mail, Twitter, and Facebook. The average
American has had a drastic drop in the number of people they call a
friend because of the attachment to their devices. Scientists report that
trading sleep, exercise, and relationships for electronics adds to stress
and poor physical and emotional health.

Writers who want to promote their work spend enormous amounts
of time on social media. While purportedly relieving stress, the very
electronic gadgets that save time and lives and improve the quality of life
can overwhelm us if not properly managed. Allowing constant wireless
intrusions automatically puts us in a foot race that can leave us frazzled.

Can we unplug long enough to enjoy life's other pleasures? Or are we
a click away from being leashed 24/7? As electronics invade private space,
we face the challenge of protecting our writing times, holding a reasonable pace, and staying connected to people in a human way. We can think
of electronic gadgets the way we would a romantic partner. It's great having them around, but it's nice to get a break once in a while, too.

Today's Takeaway

Turn off your devices during committed writing times, don't get duped
by the red alert chime that intrudes on your train of thought, and use
custom tones for family and friends.

FEBRUARY 13
Arm Yourself with an If-Then Plan

You can't hit a target you cannot see,
and you cannot see a target you do not have.

—Zig Ziglar

How many times have we resolved to improve writing habits and set writing goals? But a month down the road, we're still absent from our desks. Our vow is a distant memory. A magic potion, called the if-then plan, can help us stick to our writing promises.

The built-in strategy of the if-then plan inoculates us from a defeating "what-the-hell" effect. Having an action plan for what we intend to do before a situation occurs increases our chances of accomplishing a goal. Experts say being specific about when and where we will act on a goal automatically alerts the brain to be on the lookout for a specific situation (the "if") and the action that must follow (the "then").

Suppose I want to create more writing time. My if-then plan might look like this: "If it's Monday or Friday, then I'll work at my desk from 8:00 a.m. until noon." Now I have hardwired the situation (the day, place, and time) directly to the action (writing). My brain develops a heightened vigilance for the "if" situation. Once triggered, my brain is equipped with the automatic prepared response of writing (the "then" action).

Today's Takeaway
Set a target goal to improve your writing regimen and triple your chances of follow-through by creating your own if-then formula.

FEBRUARY 14
Get Cheeky with Those Who Have Your Back

*…Devote yourself to loving others, devote yourself to
your community around you, and devote yourself to
creating something that gives you purpose and meaning.*
—Mitch Albom

When we read the acknowledgments in books, we learn that wonderful family and friends stand behind published authors. They love and support their writers in a variety of ways. Today is a good day to make a list of all the people who've stood behind us in our writing careers. We can let them know how grateful we are that they are there for us, even though we're not always available to them.

We don't have to wait until we write our acknowledgment page. We can take time out from our writing day and let them know now so our relationships don't become stale and brittle from neglect.

There are many ways we can say I love you to the ones who have our back: a kind deed, a caring e-mail, a card, a hug and a kiss, a small gift, or special moments, such as taking time out for heart-to-heart talks and walks or dinner at a favorite restaurant. Contemplate all the people who support you, then show each one your love in a special way.

Today's Takeaway

Make a special effort to let the people around you know that you love them and appreciate how they take care of you while you get to do the thing you love most: write.

FEBRUARY 15
Get Plenty of Shut-Eye

The best bridge between despair
and hope is a good night's sleep.
—E. Joseph Cossman

In addition to healthy eating and regular exercise, scientists insist that a good night's slumber is the Holy Grail for a happy, productive life. After exercise and nutrition, it's the third cornerstone for joyful and productive writing. This trio of lifestyle habits gives us the stamina to withstand just about any challenge the writing world throws.

Many of us take sleep for granted, yet sleep's restorative nature makes it one of the best remedies to offset stress and maintain a sharp, creative mind. Sleep deprivation lowers our resistance to stress, harms the brain, and interferes with memory and learning. We're more forgetful, our attention is short-circuited, and we're grumpier.

Certain habits can promote sleep. Reducing the number of Chardonnays, Starbucks, or late night meals can offset insomnia. Forbidding electronic devices in the bedroom prevents tossing and turning. The glow from electronic devices within an hour before bedtime tells the brain it's daytime and interferes with falling and staying asleep. A midday snooze and exercise early in the day far outweigh the benefits of chugging several Red Bulls to get through long writing days. What habits can you add or eliminate so you can get to the Land of Nod?

Today's Takeaway

Try to get seven to eight hours of shut-eye a night for optimal writing resilience, and inventory your daily health habits if you find that you're regularly tossing and turning.

FEBRUARY 16
Wait without Clicking Your Nails

If you spend your whole life waiting for the
storm, you'll never enjoy the sunshine.
—Morris West

We are told that one of the best things we can do to build our writing careers is to write. Regularly. That's the easy part. It's the waiting for the outcome of our submissions that causes us to bite our fingernails to the quick. Haunted by a constant sense of urgency, many of us expect the writing life to match our hurried pace, dragging our iPads and cell phones everywhere, juggling two or three writing tasks at once. We dodge waiting lists, sidestep slow-moving lines, and shun waiting rooms as if Dracula were after our blood.

Although we white-knuckle our way through the wait, we don't have to. We can seize waiting moments and turn them into self-reflective writing moments—using them as valuable times to embrace lengthy pauses as fertilizer for our writing ideas. And we can turn waiting moments into present moments, enjoying the sunshine of now instead of waiting for future storms.

We can breathe deeply with the rise and fall of our breath, tell ourselves we're choosing to wait, and slow down our breakneck speed to a snail's pace. Above all, during waiting interims, we can continue to reflect on our writing.

Today's Takeaway

Next time you're waiting to hear about a writing project and catch your fingers drumming the desk, take a breath, let go, put yourself in harmony with the present moment, and find something else to pen.

FEBRUARY 17
Invite Mother Nature into Your Writing Space

Study nature, love nature, stay close
to nature. It will never fail you.
—Frank Lloyd Wright

Viewing nature from an office window or bringing the natural world inside reduces work stress and promotes calm and clarity. To bring the outside indoors, we can arrange writing stations to face scenes of wooded areas, water, wildlife, sunsets, or landscapes.

For those of us who don't have a view, scenic photographs or paintings are good substitutes. An opened window with a soft breeze and wildlife sounds adds a natural touch. Writers who live in urban areas can bring in potted green plants, fresh flowers, or a terrarium. And no matter the size of the writing space, there's always room for a tabletop trickling waterfall, a fish bowl, or a CD with nature sounds that create a calm and relaxing atmosphere. Stroking a pet—a bird, cat, or dog—and gazing at an aquarium lower blood pressure and promote relaxation.

Unless you're like thriller writer Dean Koontz, the presence of natural sunlight can help your writing potential soar. Keep blinds or shutters open, remove window treatments that block daylight, and wash the inside and outside of windows on a regular basis.

Today's Takeaway

Breathe natural life into your writing space to optimize your writing potential and capture the surprising twists and turns that bubble up from your creative depths.

FEBRUARY 18
Send Self-Doubt Packing

Your doubts are the private detectives employed by your
dislikes, to make a case against change or choice.
—W. R. Rodgers

Raise your hand if you've never had writing doubts. I thought so. There are days when self-doubt takes up residence in our heads and eats us alive. As long as doubt precedes our path, it keeps us from taking the necessary risks to grow as an author and a person. Plus it compromises our creativity.

What a relief to admit that we have self-doubt! All writers do, but we don't have to let it rent space in our heads. Doubt has the advantage of keeping us from blindly accepting every offer from the literary world. Once we give ourselves permission to doubt, it helps us move it out of the way and get to the truth. Doubt is a shadow over truth—a natural part of writing accomplishments. Unless we recognize it, doubt over-shadows the truth about who we are as writers. We want to offer more headspace to the self-truths.

Each time we step out of the doubt's shadow, we learn more self-truths. We can rewrite self-doubt's plot and accept the uncertainties with the certainties, the lows with the highs, the failures with the tri-umphs and use them as fodder on our forward writing path.

Today's Takeaway
Send self-doubt packing, move in self-confidence, and discover the real truth about yourself as a writer one writing project and one deadline at a time.

FEBRUARY 19
Stop "Shoulding" on Yourself

*If you have disconnected from your soul's desire
and are drowning in an ocean of "have to,"
then rise up and overthrow your master.*
—W. Timothy Gallwey

In a television interview, the news anchor, Diane Sawyer asked Oscar-winner Jennifer Lawrence if she would ever get married. Lawrence replied, "I don't feel a need to, but I might or might not." Sawyer responded, "When you don't need, you get to choose."

The words we use to weigh situations shape our attitudes. Oppositional self-talk like *need to, have to, ought, must,* or *should* reveal how we think and feel inside and drive our actions accordingly. When we sit to write, the words we use inside such as *should, need to,* or *have to* can limit creative ideas. We call these scolding, shame-based messages "should" thinking: "I should have gone to church" or "I should have written a better first draft."

Mere word substitution can make us feel more in charge of our writing agendas instead of at the mercy of them. When we substitute empowering words for oppositional self-talk (such as *could* for *should* or *want to* for *have to*), it changes the meaning and tone of the message and uplifts our emotions. *Shoulds* and *have to's* trigger oppositional feelings; *coulds* and *want to's* empower us with the freedom to choose.

Today's Takeaway

Notice whether you riddle yourself with inner talk that opposes your writing efforts or shower yourself with uplifting words that empower you, then make necessary changes that can help you write that barnburner.

FEBRUARY 20
Turn Negative Reviews Inside Out

A bad review is like baking a cake with all the best
ingredients and having someone sit on it.
—Danielle Steel

It's rare that authors don't want to hear positive reviews, but it's unrealistic to expect thumbs up every time. While many of us might not share the sales record of Danielle Steel, we probably feel the same pain when critics hurl lousy reviews at us. Let's face it: if we publish, critics will hurl, it will hurt, and we will howl.

It's okay to give ourselves permission to howl from the initial sting of a critical review. Once the hurt subsides, though, we can remind ourselves that painful isn't personal. Critics review our writing from a bird's-eye view through their own subjective lenses and rarely intend to eviscerate us. Think of it this way: If we turn a blistering literary review inside out, we can see the critic's desire of what they wished done differently, although it was stated in a critical way. We can extract each desire nested inside the criticism, assess it for value, and turn it inside out to see if there's anything that would improve our writing. If so, we apply the criticism to work in our favor then forget about the rest.

Today's Takeaway

Assess anything in a negative review that can bolster your work; then, as if removing a peanut from its shell, use what's helpful and throw the rest away before moving forward.

FEBRUARY 21
Debunk Murphy's Law

It's the circumstances that create fear. How
you respond is all you can control. Concentrate
on that, and you'll always succeed.
—Steve Berry

We can't control all that happens to us, but we can control our reactions. Murphy's Law is the age-old adage that anything that can go wrong will go wrong. The light bulbs burn out in the bathroom, bedroom, and at our writing desk—all at the same time. We get an e-mail rejecting our submission and our printer goes on the blink while we're racing to meet a deadline. "Murphy's Law!" We scream. We rant, "If something can go wrong in my life, it will." But is it really Murphy's Law?

Actually, science is at play. We drop a piece of buttered toast, and it always falls butter side down. Just your bad luck? Not according to scientists. The rate of spin for falling buttered toast is too slow to make a complete revolution and come face up before it hits the floor.

What about when we choose the slowest moving line? Murphy's Law? Not according to the law of averages. Two-thirds of the time either the line to the left or the right will move faster than ours. The light bulbs that burn out at once probably were installed at the same time with a similar life expectancy. The negative experiences we call Murphy's Law usually have little to do with bad luck. When we personalize these random events and conclude the world is against us, we create more obstacles to our writing success.

Today's Takeaway

Chalk up the things that go south in your writing days to life's roll of the dice so you feel less defeated in your literary efforts and more empowered to climb the ladder of success.

FEBRUARY 22
Harness Your Heartbreak

*Family dysfunction makes for rich literary soil... Betrayals
cut more deeply, pain lingers longer, and memory
becomes a timeless thing. For a writer, this is a gift.*

—John Hart

As writers we know that writing fiction is a creative blend of imagination, observation, and personal experience. In our writing, whether we are aware of it or not, we draw on our painful gifts from the past. We search for beauty and meaning amid the spiritual wreckage and harness it into prose, poetry, or lyrics.

In the same ways, we can consider our current frustrations and disappointments from the publishing industry as gifts. We can harness the pain of rejection and self-doubt into our art. But we need not go looking for it. It's already stored in our creative vaults, and the key phrase is "a certain amount."

A heavy dose of turmoil, confusion, and depression can be creatively debilitating. But a low dose of melancholy or anxiety can enhance creativity and provide rich literary soil for us to cultivate secrets and misdeeds and grow them into explosive stories.

Today's Takeaway

Harness the fertile soil of heartbreak and the unmapped mysteries stored in your creative vault and draw upon them for your plots, sense of place, and character development.

FEBRUARY 23
Bypass Blank Page Syndrome

People have writer's block not because they can't write,
but because they despair of writing eloquently.
—Anna Quindlen

How many of us ever thought that writer's block was time we block off to write? Unfortunately, that's not the case, but if you've had writing blocks, you're in good company. Authors F. Scott Fitzgerald and Joseph Mitchell, cartoonist Charles Schulz, and singer-songwriter Adele all struggled with the affliction.

Writer's block can occur from adverse conditions in an author's life, but it more commonly results from inner turmoil. When we push the river instead of letting it flow, desperation, criticism, or self-doubt can screech us to a halt. Or writing pressures can worm a path into our creative brain, usurp the lead, and blank us out.

Trepidation and creativity are opposites. They come from two competing areas of the brain: fear from our reptilian brain and creativity from our new brain. Fear and force throw the creative brain offline, hindering the creative flow.

Several tips help us bypass blank page syndrome and get back online: take breaks; try writing in another form of creative prose; brainstorm instead of judging your ideas; engage in free writing; and avoid the two competing tasks of revising while creating.

Today's Takeaway

Bypass blank page syndrome by turning off the critical brain, by writing as if you're playing, and by connecting with the joy that got you started writing in the first place.

FEBRUARY 24
Power Down and Clock Out

I'm pretty much a 9-to-5 kind of guy.
—Douglas Preston

Dolly Parton sang about 9-to-5—that it's enough to drive you crazy if you let it. And it will, if you let it. But you don't have to worry about 9-to-5 workdays anymore. Now we have the 24/7 workday that's enough to drive us crazy—if we let it. Easier said than done.

Are we stretching our days into the wee hours by overscheduling and juggling more tasks? Do we leash ourselves to electronic devices and make ourselves available 24/7, giving up much needed vacation time?

Living this way keeps our natural defenses on high alert, lowers our immune systems, and marinates us in stress juices (cortisol and adrenaline), clobbering us with mental and physical fatigue. Work stress (and yes, writing is a job) can turn us into disgruntled writers, making us less effective at what we do. Writers who spend longer hours at their desks are at greater risk for anxiety, depression, and burnout and have twice the number of health-related problems compared to those who reduce their work hours. We can recharge our batteries by telling ourselves there's a limit to what we can do. We put work out of the picture, take time out, and see this action as a strength, not a weakness.

Today's Takeaway

Power down and clock out from your writing desk at a certain time, master your electronic devices, and make more time for yourself and loved ones.

FEBRUARY 25
Accept Writing on Its Terms

*If a man has nothing to eat, fasting is
the most intelligent thing he can do.*

—Herman Hesse

Kayakers say the best way to escape when trapped in a hydraulic—a turbulent, funnel-shaped current—is to relax and it will spit you out. But our natural tendency to fight against the current can keep us stuck—even drown us.

In the same way, we must relax and accept writing on its terms. When up against a difficult publishing situation, we can welcome and watch the torrent of negative beliefs streaming through our minds. I can almost hear you hissing and booing, but this is another one of those writing paradoxes. Watching our negative reactions with curiosity, we let them come and go without personalizing them, resisting, or identifying with them and eventually they float away.

The more we *accept* painful writing conditions that we cannot change, focus on changing those we can, and learn to distinguish the difference, the less we suffer in our literary careers. Suppose our publisher finds a plot hole in our story that a 747 could fly through. It helps to completely accept the difficult situation. If salvageable, we can rewrite or revise. If not, we let it go and have a greater chance for serenity which gives us the clarity to take the next best step.

Today's Takeaway

Accept the writing life on its terms, give up the struggle to impose your will, and notice the fog of misery lift as peace and clarity of mind shine through the clouds.

FEBRUARY 26
Uncage Your Voice

*Each of you is an original. Each of you
has a distinctive voice. When you find it,
your story will be told. You will be heard.*

—John Grisham

Every writer needs a voice. Some of us know our voice. Others? Umm, not so much. Finding our voice is the key to getting dedicated followers and fans. If we're not ourselves, it shows through, and we eventually burn out like a fading star. If we're looking for attention, money, or fame, our voice will be mute. A lot of noise ricochets out there in the writing world. If we're going to be heard, we can't just raise our voices like a megaphone and shout words. We must set ourselves apart and let readers know we have something special to say and a unique way of saying it.

How do we get readers—other than our moms—to hear our voice? Passion and vulnerability. Many writers admit they write because their inner voice pushes to get out, so they have to uncage it. How many of us have a caged voice seeking release? When we give our caged voice freedom of flight, captivated readers raise their eyebrows and hold our books close to their hearts.

Today's Takeaway

Dedicate yourself to the passion of writing, not awards or approval, and you will free your own original voice, your story will be told, and you'll be heard.

FEBRUARY 27
Soothe Your Decision-Fatigued Brain

*Even when I am writing I usually take a break around
lunchtime and go for a little walk to clear out my head.*
—Patricia Cornwell

After writing for days on end, chances are the decisions we make about setting, storyline, character development, and backstory are different from the ones we make after the brain has a rest period. Why? Scientists have discovered a phenomenon known as "decision fatigue"—a condition that occurs when the brain is worn out, depleted of mental energy.

After hours of nonstop writing, the brain gets fatigued. The longer we sit at our desks and the more choices we make during our writing jags, the more difficult it is for a strained mind to make sound decisions. We start to take short cuts and ordinary decisions—such as what to wear, where to eat, or how to prioritize writing projects—become harder to make.

Our heads need restorative rest just like our bodies do. After a hard writing day, try these simple stretches to bring relief to your tired brain. Start by raising your arms over your head and lowering them back down. As you raise your arms, focus on increasing the height of your arms at varying angles: to the front, side, back, and face. Next, march in place until your muscles feel loose, then take longer strides, picking up your knees higher for about five minutes.

Today's Takeaway

Recover from decision fatigue with brisk exercise, relaxing in nature, power naps, deep breathing, a soaking bath, yoga, prayer, meditation, massage. You choose.

FEBRUARY 28
Rescue What You Might've Been

It's never too late to be what you might have been.
—George Elliot

For many aspiring authors, writing is what happens while we're making other plans. We postpone sitting down at the computer because the bedroom floor needs vacuuming, or we avoid our writing desks to arrange the kitchen spice rack.

We can ask what comes to mind as we realize tomorrow has no guarantees and ask ourselves some questions: If I had my life to live over, what would I do differently? Am I doing the things I want to do in my life? Am I telling myself I can't do them? Or am I putting them off?

The Latin phrase *carpe diem* cautions us to seize the day because we may not have this chance again. We can have more healthy days than sick days. Pay more attention to what goes right than what goes wrong. Create more peace than pandemonium. Live with more joy and fun. Try doing the things we told ourselves we couldn't do.

Once we are living our lives fully, as if each day is our last, we won't have to wonder or ask doubtful questions about what might've been. Now is the time to rescue an opportunity we've postponed or avoided because tomorrow brings no guarantees.

Today's Takeaway

Contemplate what actions you might take that would enrich your life—something that you may never get another chance at—then become what you might've been.

FEBRUARY 29
Steer Clear of Gobble, Gulp, and Go

Only men you can count on these days are Ben and Jerry.
—Janet Evanovich

The average American spends just minutes eating lunch at fast food restaurants or grabbing a bite at workplace cafeterias. Mindless eating—while standing, driving, on the run, watching TV or skipping meals altogether—makes eating an afterthought.

How many of us writers grab doughnuts and coffee then scurry to our desks, treating food as if it were a necessary evil? Or do we eat when we're not hungry to deal with writing stressors? When we're slammed and on the go, we're more likely to reach for comfort foods—convenient high-calorie, fattening carbs that are appealing and easy to grab. What would our writing lives be without Burger King or Ben and Jerry's?

A well-nourished body has a stronger stress-resistance shield and fosters greater writing stamina. What we put into our mouths influences what comes out of our creative brains: crap in, crap out. Wouldn't it be great if mindless eating increased our ability to turn out a viable writing project? Fat chance. When we treat eating as a singular activity to enjoy for its own sake, instead of a task to endure, then we will reach for the apple, not the Danish.

Today's Takeaway

Ask yourself how you treat food; avoid gobble, gulp, and go; then learn to slow down and give food—the fuel that provides stamina for your writing—the consideration it deserves.

MARCH

MARCH 1
Stop Throwing the Book at Yourself

Resilience is based on compassion
for ourselves as well as for others.
—Sharon Salzberg

As the spring rains nurture the land, we can imagine showering our bodies, minds, and souls with self-compassion. Sound hokey? Awkward? Irrelevant?

Not so fast. At first glance there appears to be no connection between self-compassion and writing resilience, but when we look closer, it's clear that they are inexorably linked. If we can't regard our writing selves with compassion, self-aversion takes charge with its whip and chain—nit picking and demanding, exhausting us of our creative mojo.

On the flipside, self-compassion is like a best friend, especially during tough times. It can talk us off the ledge and cheer us onward when we feel disheartened—fueling perseverance, and propelling us toward our writing goals. It credits us with what we've learned about the publishing world and the creative ways we've handled difficult writing situations.

How much self-compassion do you have? If your compassion tank is running low, brainstorm some things you can say to yourself or actions you can take to refuel it so that your writing resilience isn't running on fumes.

Today's Takeaway

Stop throwing the book at yourself and throw yourself at the book. Cultivate genuine self-compassion and notice how more resilient you feel and how much more perseverance you have.

MARCH 2
Meditation Practice: Sit with What Bothers You

*Mindfulness means paying attention in a
particular way: on purpose, in the present
moment, and nonjudgmentally.*
—Jon Kabat-Zinn

Many times we have the habit of ignoring unpleasant situations or problems stewing inside us. Perhaps we get busy doing something to escape: watch TV, shopping, clean house, or surf Facebook. Avoidance takes us out of our awareness to smudge the flames of unpleasantness and brings temporary relief, but it doesn't fix the unrest for the long term. Taking us away from the present moment, it eclipses clear-mindedness and self-understanding. But when we deliberately pay attention to the inner unpleasantness and sit with it in nonjudgmental awareness, it's a game changer.

As an experiment, think of a dissatisfaction that pops up regularly or one that has stuck with you lately. Go inward, welcome the feeling, then sit with the feeling in the present moment just as you might provide bedside company for a sick friend. Get to know this part of you with as much compassion as you can. Don't try to get rid of or fix it. Simply be present to the dissatisfaction with as much awareness as possible. Every time a thought or body sensation pulls you away gently bring your attention back to it again. After a while, don't be surprised if the bothersome feeling isn't as bad as before.

Today's Takeaway

Sit without judging or avoiding bothersome thoughts or feelings, letting loving-kindness cultivate clarity of mind, greater insight, and solid solutions to the problem.

MARCH 3
Exercise for the Health of It

Those who think they have not time for bodily exercise
will sooner or later have to find time for illness.
—Edward Stanley

You've heard it said a million times. By now you might be sick of hearing it. Physical exercise is a powerful remedy for stress relief, clear-mindedness, and productivity. So it doesn't take a rocket scientist to know how important it is for us writers after long stretches of sitting.

Raise your hand if the first thing you reach for after a long writing jag is a glass of wine, chocolate, or a cigarette. I thought so. Then you probably wiggle your body deeper into the sofa, thinking, "The last thing I want to do is exercise." Right?

But would you put on your sweats if I told you that scientists have found the fountain of youth—that exercise could add ten years to your life? Regular exercise, they say, changes the molecular and cellular building blocks and slows aging cells. One year of exercise gives a seventy-year-old writer the brain connectivity of a thirty-year-old scribe, improving memory and the ability to plan, deal with ambiguity, and multitask.

So which is it: Plopping into your La-Z-Boy or hopping on the treadmill? If you've been looking for the fountain of youth, you won't find it in a chill pill or cosmetic surgery. It's contained in your Stairmaster, swimsuit, or dancing shoes.

Today's Takeaway
Make exercise the first medicine you reach for before or after long writing hours, go to the gym, or take a walk for your happy hour.

MARCH 4
Buff Up Your Stress Hardiness

It is not the strongest of the species that
survives, nor the most intelligent. It is the
one that is most adaptable to change.
—Charles Darwin

When it comes to writing and publishing pressures, how do we hold up? We can think of ourselves as steel, plastic, or glass. If we're steel, stress bounces off. If we're plastic, stress leaves some dents, and if we're glass, stress shatters us.

We think avoiding stress is the best way to manage it. But is it really? It depends on our unique nature. Steel or stress hardy writers thrive on pressure. They view stressful events as opportunities to grow from pressures without avoiding or caving into them. They believe they have control over writing misfortunes and use them as motivation to fuel their successes. Glass or stress-sensitive writers are more vulnerable and believe external forces determine their writing success. In their eyes it doesn't pay to try hard because things rarely work in their favor. They think of themselves as downtrodden, focusing on hardships and problems that keep them stuck.

If you weren't born with stress hardiness, you can develop it with time and patience. As long as you're willing to cultivate more flexible, optimistic, and constructive reactions to writing stressors, you can become strong like steel and stress pings off you.

Today's Takeaway

Become the master of your writing fate, view obstacles as challenges instead of threats, and look for opportunities to overcome them instead of ways to deny or avoid them.

MARCH 5
Contemplate the Idea of Impermanence

*Nothing in the world is permanent, and we're foolish
when we ask anything to last, but surely we're still more
foolish not to take delight in it while we have it.*
—Somerset Maugham

When we stop to think about it, everything is impermanent. Every relationship ends in some way. Every material thing erodes, breaks, or decays. Each of us, too, will eventually die. Each of us has a limited number of mornings, breaths, and thoughts left, but we rarely consider how they will be spent. Life is temporary and tomorrow brings no guarantees. It helps us to consider more mindfully what's really important in our lives and to put writing frustrations, rejections, and even the highs of writing in perspective.

If we only had one more day to live, how do we want to spend it and with whom would we want to spend it? Impermanence awakens us to the finality of everything and the importance of living each precious moment to the fullest. It prioritizes the people and things that have gone unseen right before our eyes. It reminds us to take care of unfinished business, mend a relationship, or stop putting off something we've wanted to say to a loved one. When we're aware and awake with the gift of this day, we can make our moments of creativity extraordinary.

Today's Takeaway

Live this day fully, as though it were your last; put your writing practice in context of life's big picture, and focus on your priorities.

MARCH 6
Ask How You're Treating Writing Stressors

The best crime novels are not about how
a detective works on a case; they are
about how a case works on a detective.
—Michael Connelly

We might think there's little we can do about writing stress. Some stressors come from outside sources, others we unwittingly create ourselves. Just as Michael Connelly discerns the best crime novels, we can discern how much of our stress comes from outside of us and how much from within.

By asking how we're treating writing stressors, not how they're treating us, we start to see that we have more control than we thought. We realize we can turn a situation around, change a course of action, or reframe our outlook. It's a real eye-opener to ask with curiosity, not judgment, if we're adding to our writing stress without realizing it.

When we take a hard look at our own writing habits, excuses, and attitudes, we can identify the true sources of stress, much like the little old lady looking for her glasses when they're on her nose the whole time. This approach gives a clear picture of the origins of writing stress. We become empowered as we press outward against stress instead of victimized by the stressors that press inward upon us.

Today's Takeaway

Ask not how writing stressors are treating you but how you're treating writing stressors, and it will give you more writing clarity plus a clearer understanding of yourself.

MARCH 7
Keep an Unmade Mind

Your mind creates your reality. If you expect nothing,
you open up the universe to give you options.
If you expect the worst, you usually get it.

—James Patterson

Are you open-minded about an uncertain future or career outcome? Or have you crossed your arms, planted your feet, and made up your mind? I hope it's the former. Writers with unmade minds, void of expectations, garner more literary rewards and successes. But a clenched fist cannot receive a gift.

Superimposing expectations on a new situation masks opportunities and sabotages writing success. We might not realize that we enter unknown situations with made-up minds. Usually, when we expect a bad situation, it turns out that way because we unwittingly think and behave in ways to make it fit with what we expect. Known as the self-fulfilling prophecy, made-up minds close off possibilities, causing us to miss teachable moments and literary gifts.

We create positive outcomes by expecting nothing, staying open to new experiences, and behaving in ways that make them come true. Keeping an unmade mind in advance of the unknown bolsters creativity and literary success, taking us to untold artistic heights. The unmade mind found a cure for polio, painted the Sistine Chapel, put us on the moon, and created Harry Potter.

Today's Takeaway

Keep an open mind about writing expectations and approach your writing future with open arms ready to receive many gifts.

MARCH 8
Throw a Party Instead of a Fit

Some things in life are out of your control.
You can make it a party or a tragedy.
—Nora Roberts

Anger is a natural human emotion, as valid as joy or sorrow. When things don't go our way, it naturally hurts, disappoints, and frustrates us. We might rant and rave, stomp our feet, or throw things like kids who don't get their way.

Anger is only a part of us—much like a sprained wrist or sore ribcage is part of us. But once it grips our hearts, it can overshadow our true selves. When that happens, we can redirect it with the energy it deserves and release it so we don't direct it at others. We can have a catharsis instead of a fit by writing down feelings, pounding an old tennis racket on a mattress, or doing what Mary Higgins Clark suggests: "When someone is mean to me, I just make them a victim in my next book."

Once we realize anger is a separate part of us and let it go, we're ready to bring in our kinder side to speak *for* the anger instead of *from* it—either to the source of our anger or to a trusted friend, counselor, or tribe member. Speaking for anger means we talk it out using calm words to describe the feelings so that it recedes.

Today's Takeaway

Treat your anger as a separate part of you and speak *for* it as you would a sprained wrist, giving it the attention it deserves, and you'll be ready to throw a party instead of a fit.

MARCH 9
Make the Best of What Happens

If you can't change your fate, change your attitude.

—Amy Tan

On our writing journey, it's inevitable that big disappointments will hit us. Although we might not realize it at the time, a deeper lesson is concealed within the letdown. If we can't change our fate, our best option is to change our attitudes. That's where our power lies.

Writing disappointments won't stop coming simply because we get too miserable or too frustrated. As long as we continue to write, the downturns will join us. The solution comes in the attitude we take toward them. Losses contain gains, and clouds have silver linings. But we must look for them and ask ourselves what lesson is hidden in the letdown. This approach makes us an active learner instead of a passive recipient.

When bad news comes, we can remind ourselves that it isn't final and we won't have to stay in that place for long. We wait for it to pass, pinpoint the challenge contained in each negative situation, and ask, "What can I manage or overcome here?" or "How can I turn this matter around to my advantage?" Choose a recent writing disappointment. Then ask yourself what you can learn from the situation that will help you become a stronger writer.

Today's Takeaway

Make it a goal to use negative writing experiences—no matter how painful, frustrating, big or small—as lessons from which to grow.

MARCH 10
Think of the View from the Top

Winners take time to relish their work,
knowing that scaling the mountain is what
makes the view from the top exhilarating.
—Denis Waitley

We can get so bogged down with writing that it can seem like an impossible task to go on. It would be so much easier to just give up. But if it were easy, everybody would be writing and publishing.

The number one quality all successful writers need is persistence. One of the best tools to motivate us when writing seems like an uphill struggle is to think of the view from the top. We can visualize what it might be like to finish the paper, dissertation, or novel even though we feel like giving up. Imagining the feelings of accomplishment and the good body sensations that accompany the image gives us an extra dose of resilience. If we stick with scaling the mountain long enough, we start to see a progression. At first our goals seem impossible, then improbable, then as we persist onward, they become inevitable.

Persistence in the face of an uphill battle takes patience, commitment, and acceptance of failure along the way. Do we avoid the challenge or throw in the towel? Or do we think of the big picture and allow it to harden us into stubborn action and choose to persevere?

Today's Takeaway

Every time writing seems like an uphill struggle and you feel like giving up, just think of the view from the top, and that will motivate you to keep going.

MARCH 11
Muster Courage

Courage is being afraid and going ahead, anyway.
—Heather Graham

As a novice author, I never thought courage had anything to do with writing. As a veteran writer, I realize it has everything to do with it. The blank screen or note pad staring back at you can be one of the scariest events in the life of a writer. And many authors would rather have a root canal than face what can feel like an ominous vacuum.

When trepidation crops up on our writing path, courage is an essential quality to muster in order to soar through the winds of fear. Courage is the inner strength to accept and face *everything* that happens to us without avoidance or resistance. That might sound like a hard pill to swallow, and it is risky, but the payoffs are worth the efforts.

Building courage isn't about squashing our fears. It's about being afraid, feeling the fear, and letting life happen on its own terms. Then we stay the course, go forward anyway, and receive the fruits of our labors.

Today's Takeaway

With an open heart, embrace the courage deep within you to face writing challenges on their own terms, keep plodding on your writing path, and watch yourself blossom.

MARCH 12
Swear Off Acceleration Syndrome

*I find I am hurrying to get through my day's work. It is a
destructive suggestion. A book, as you know, is a very
delicate thing. If it is pressured, it will show that pressure.*

—John Steinbeck

When John Steinbeck's editor urged him to work faster, he refused. He realized pressure to produce would damage his writing. Is it possible that slow burn writers like Steinbeck, Donna Tart, Harper Lee, and Nelson DeMille have it right—that less is more?

Signs of *Fast Food*, *Quick Copying*, and *Speedy Service* line our highways, reflecting hurried and harried lifestyles. Has "acceleration syndrome" infiltrated current day writing, as if we've just chugged a couple of Red Bulls and are drumming our fingers to make words move faster?

Do we push ourselves thinking the only worthy writing projects are those we can finish quickly so publishers won't drop us? Let's ask ourselves if we compromise our writing standards due to outside pressures. Do we have a fast formula to slam out a piece to appease publishers? Do we pen in the clutches of fear, equating our writing worth with page numbers instead of quality work?

Today's Takeaway

Contemplate your writing craft, decide what form you want it to take, and follow your creative heart instead of conforming to destructive outside pressures.

MARCH 13
Consider Slow Writing

Slow writing is a meditative act: slowing down to understand our relationship to our writing, slowing down to determine our authentic subjects ...

—Louise DeSalvo

Author Louise DeSalvo adapted many of the ideas of the slow food movement to the speed of writing. The idea is that the slow writing process can enrich our work if we slow down enough to understand our relationship to it. In a world that values speed, if we make a commitment to take time to write, we commit to an important set of values.

Slowing down our writing pace isn't easy when everything around us moves at lightning speed. When we are consumed by a hurried lifestyle, we lose touch with our authentic writing selves. Slow writing doesn't just take time, but makes time. It's a way to humanize our writing in a world increasingly becoming more dehumanized. Slowing down can help us become more self-reflective writers: find our writing voice, fine tune our unique style, and see what works. We can eat slower, drive slower, and write slower. And we can imbibe the wisdom of the ancient Greek storyteller, Aesop, "Plodding wins the race."

Carve out time to slow write. Let the words slowly emerge and notice your relationship to them. After you finish, underscore how that felt compared to the way you usually write and note any self-reflections.

Today's Takeaway

Make a conscious effort to slow down the pulse and rhythm of your writing life so you can reflect on what you need to modify and your writing can blossom, bear fruit, and ripen.

MARCH 14
Discover Your "Tremor of Truth"

My courage is faith—faith in the eternal resilience of
me—that joy'll come back, and hope and spontaneity.
—F. Scott Fitzgerald

The phrase "tremor of truth" is used in physical fitness circles when we push ourselves to the max until our muscles tremble—a true sign that we're giving ourselves an optimal workout.

As writers we can ask ourselves the whereabouts of our "tremor of truth." We keep ploughing through that dull gray mist of uncertainty that comes down on all of us from time to time. When we tackle writing obstacles, there are times we want to give up. Then we find a hidden resource of resilience that we didn't know we had, and we push through.

We build our resilience and persevere by asking ourselves if we're pushing far enough through the gray mist to an optimal level. Or do we need to step up our efforts? And how far do we stretch ourselves before we reach the breaking point?

Sometimes it feels like we're pushing through solid rock, a vein of encased ore. We don't want to stop short, yet we don't want to overreach, either. Just before giving up, we tremble and shake with one extra push and feel our inner reserves kick in, moving us over the finish line.

Today's Takeaway

Develop eternal faith in your "tremor of truth" and find the hidden mental reserves you didn't know you had that enable you to push forward through writing obstacles.

MARCH 15
Dethrone Self-Doubt

I found my first novel difficult ... there are
so many opportunities for self-doubt that
you just kind of need to soldier on.
—Anthony Doerr

My first publication is out there in the literary world. Now, I don't have to do anything but sit back and wait for all those glowing reviews. Right? Wrong! During the lull, we work on our next projects *and* on our mindsets, preparing ourselves for all those opportunities for self-doubt.

We remind ourselves of the possibilities: negative reviews might thunder back to us, sales figures might slump lower than we hoped, and our publisher might not offer a second contract. But regardless of how disappointing the outcome, we soldier on, mindful of the conclusions we draw in our heads. We don't give self-doubt a free pass to steamroll over the facts.

We remember to separate facts from feelings. We refuse to let self-doubt tell us things like, "I felt that I could write, but obviously I can't" or "I feel like I've wasted all these months and years for nothing." We hold these emotional interpretations at arm's length and stick with the facts.

Today's Takeaway

Soldier on when negative feedback knocks, remind yourself that this is part of the literary package deal, and focus on the many opportunities *not* to give self-doubt a free pass.

MARCH 16
Mellow Out with Laughter Yoga

*Laughter is a form of internal jogging. It moves
your internal organs around. It enhances respiration.
It is an igniter of great expectations.*

—Norman Cousins

When was the last time you had a good belly laugh? Laughter yoga gives your body some of the same benefits as moderate physical exercise and is one of the best remedies against ills. After laughing, you probably notice you feel better within seconds. It reverses stress hormones and activates endorphins—the body's own painkiller.

Even fake laughing—laughter yoga built around forced laughing until it feels real— for one minute a day dampens stress, eases pain, stokes your immune system, and brightens your outlook. The science of laughter yoga is that even if you start with pretend laughing, your body can't tell the difference.

Here's how it works. In a standing position, look upward and hold your arms wide apart above your head. Start with forced laughing, engaging your shoulders, arms, face, and belly until the laughter starts to feel real. Continue for as long as you can, letting it rip: *Ahhh-hahaha-whoohoohoo-ha-heeheehee!* After hearty belly laughing, see if you agree that you get an instant lift.

Today's Takeaway

Practice "laughter-cise" often, especially when you can't get to the gym, and erase all your writing frustrations and clear your mind of stress.

MARCH 17
Celebrate Your Writing Triumphs

*People dress up for funerals. Why not dress
up to celebrate that you're alive?*
—Gay Talese

It's unlikely that we'll get a ticker-tape parade down Fifth Avenue when our novel is launched or after we win an award. Still, our accomplishments are important milestones worthy of recognition with great fanfare. After all of our hard work, we deserve to underscore the markers on our road to writing success whether it's an after party at a book launch, drinks with close friends, or a bash at our home. It could even be a silent fist pump we give ourselves.

Celebrations are the glue that binds us together with our families, friends, and our writing entourage. They provide memorable moments that mark our writing progress and successes. They create memories to look back on with joy and gratification—time-outs between the grueling deadlines and pressures for our souls to stretch, yawn, and spit before writing demands reoccur. Celebrations are our rewards for a job well done.

Today's Takeaway

Celebrate your writing triumphs with unrestrained joy in any way that allows you to give yourself the thumbs up and pats on the back that you deserve for all your hard work.

MARCH 18
Shy Away from Forecasting

The foolish reject what they see, not what they think;
the wise reject what they think not what they see.

—Huang Po

After a writer friend sold a book to a publisher, her sales went through the roof and she won several writing awards. But she told herself it was a fluke, that the next book would probably be a dud. I was floored. It's amazing how many writers unwittingly sabotage their careers with the self-defeating mental opposition called *forecasting*—the mind's tendency to predict negative outcomes despite positive circumstances.

If we're negative thinkers, our mind forecasts unpredictable writing experiences and collects evidence to support it. As with my author friend, positive indicators that contradict how we think of ourselves are discounted, minimized, or ignored. Despite everything coming up roses, we suffer the misery of our negative predictions.

Unless we're meteorologists, forecasting the worst without proof doesn't make it true. Taking the bird's-eye view of an outside observer, focus on the facts before a challenging situation, notice when you're caught in a stream of forecasting thoughts, intercept them, and turn them around to fit the facts. Usually you won't find evidence for the forecast; instead you'll find proof that *contradicts* it. Then use that proof to revise your cloudy forecast to sunny skies.

Today's Takeaway

Catch yourself when you forecast the outcome of a situation before it happens, identify your negative prediction, and ask yourself "Where's the evidence for this conclusion?"

MARCH 19
Recharge Your Batteries

If you neglect to recharge a battery, it dies.
And if you run full speed ahead without stopping for
water, you lose momentum to finish the race.
—Oprah Winfrey

How many of us write as if we're racing the wind? Whether we work at lightning speed or at a snail's pace, we need to take time out from writing once in a while, come up for air, and clear our heads.

We can indulge ourselves in simple pleasures: reading a good book to see what other authors are penning; immersing ourselves in meditation or prayer; watching nature; getting a massage; or enjoying a favorite craft. We can keep our exercise regimen going, get plenty of sleep, take short walks, and stretch for a few minutes each day.

If we want to go whole hog, we could consider turning the bathroom or hot tub into a spa for a day. Place scented candles around the tub, play soft music, and draw a warm bubble bath with essential oils or rose petals. Dim the lights, slide into the tub, sip a favorite beverage, and soak away the writing stresses of the day. Once finished, we can wrap ourselves in soft cotton oversized towels. Whether we need simple or complicated, let's keep our engines running with soothing moments that uplift and energize us.

Today's Takeaway

Keep your batteries recharged and fuel your momentum to finish that writing project so you'll have more to give your writing and your loved ones and friends.

MARCH 20
Watch for Moments of Gray

Basically I have two speeds...
Hostile or smart aleck. Your choice.

—James Patterson

How many of us talk to ourselves in black and white? "I can be either a prolific writer or a dedicated spouse, not both" or "Nobody supports my hard work." When we make these kinds of declarations, it's a sign that our minds are governed by the "all or nothing"—the affliction of trying to box life into neat categories.

Attempting to artificially categorize our lives into black-and-white traps us in one extreme or the other, blinding us between most writing solutions. It prevents us from seeing the truth about others and ourselves, limits endless possibilities, and leads to bad decision-making, hampering progress toward our writing goals.

Clear-mindedness doesn't come gift-wrapped in black-and-white; it's nested in the shades of gray—that dot somewhere between the extremes, also known as the middle way. If you keep your antenna up, you recognize when you're snared in an extreme point of view. Use of words like *always, all, everybody,* or *nobody, never, none* are cues that the "all or nothing" declarations are blinding you to limitless possibilities embedded in gray. "I have to be perfect at writing (all) or I won't do it at all" (none) becomes "I can be a good writer, take risks, and learn from mistakes."

Today's Takeaway

Watch for moments of gray and look for the middle way, and find greater clarity and more possibilities on how your writing life can work the way you want it to.

MARCH 21
Salute Your Inner Reptile

*The brain is a wonderful organ; it starts working
the moment you get up in the morning and
does not stop until you get into the office.*
—Robert Frost

Many of us might not know much about our own brain, yet our brain is who we are—the boss of our mind and body. It's important to know what this tool that enables us to write is up to. Besieged by a writing threat, our reptilian brain (survival brain) hijacks our prefrontal cortex (rational brain), throws it off line, and marinates us in stress juices. To keep us safe, our brain kicks into red alert, and we're so upset we can't think straight.

In the midst of writing threats, the good news is that the prefrontal cortex can help us take a breath, step back, and regain the perspective of an outsider. We can focus on the inner firestorm, listen to our feelings, and ask, "What am I feeling inside? What are these feelings telling me? If my heart wasn't slamming against my chest, what would I do?"

If we engage the brain's executive function under pressure, it's easier to separate from our inner reptile, stay cool, and make smart decisions. Once the reptile is activated, we must acknowledge our feelings, ask if we're angry or scared, and then have an inner dialogue: "I realize I'm upset, what can I do to calm myself?" This strategy throws the switch in the prefrontal cortex, separates us from our reptile, and enables us to act instead of react.

Today's Takeaway

When your writing is threatened, take a bird's-eye view in order to kick your executive functioning back on line, separate from your reptilian feelings, and act with reason.

MARCH 22
Refrain from Running with Scissors

*Although we walk all the time, our walking is
usually more like running. When we walk like that,
we print anxiety and sorrow on the earth.*
—Thich Nhat Hanh

Rushing, hurrying, and overloading subtract from our writing productivity. When we get overly stressed from endless writing jags, we can use the sensations of breath in the body to anchor our present-moment awareness and slow down. The acronym HALT stands for hungry, angry, lonely, or tired—a gentle reminder for writers to stop, slow down, and breathe when one or a combination of these four states overtakes.

When we feel HALT and use our intentional breathing from the diaphragm, it switches off the stress response. We take a deep abdominal breath through the nose, hold it as we count slowly to six, then purse our lips and exhale slowly through them.

When we repeat this breathing pattern several times, the body relaxes with each breath. Then we attend to whatever we need: eat a healthy snack or meal, let anger out in an appropriate way, contemplate our loneliness, or call a trusted friend and get restorative rest by napping or meditating. Afterward, we can slow down and take one challenge at a time, one step at a time. The irony is that HALT allows us to get more done, plus it renews our creative reserves.

Today's Takeaway

Tuck these reminders away in your memory so next time writing stress is too much you remember HALT, then slow down, breathe, and take care of yourself.

MARCH 23
Attest to the Gift in a Cosmic Slap

Cancer is a cosmic slap in the face. You either
get discouraged or ennobled by it.
—Richard Belzer

In a Barbara Walters interview, actress Elizabeth Taylor said she laughed when doctors told her she had a brain tumor. Walters gasped, but Taylor wisely replied, "What else are you going to do?" Taylor's attitude proves you can do a lot when adversity strikes.

Now, to be clear, losing a writing contract or getting turned down by an agent isn't cancer, but the principle is the same. Studies of trauma survivors show that adversity can have benefits called *post-traumatic growth*. Recovering alcoholics often say hitting bottom is their greatest blessing because it wakes them up to a brand-new way of living.

We have the power to choose how we respond to the seismic events in our writing lives. Instead of letting the situation dictate our state of mind, we can decide our perspective of the ups-and-downs and keep ourselves steady over the long haul.

When we look for the gift in adversity, we gain new meaning and broader appreciation for our losses. We can grow our spirituality and deepen our compassion, and we learn we're stronger than we thought. You, too, can practice these skills as you face the seismic surprises along your writing journey.

Today's Takeaway

When a letdown in your writing efforts causes you to feel distraught, turn it inside out and look for meaning in the seismic slap, then see if there's a gift nestled inside it.

MARCH 24
Accept the Bad with the Good

*You never know what worse luck your
bad luck has saved you from.*
—Cormac McCarthy

A Chinese farmer had an old horse for tilling his fields. One day the horse escaped into the hills. When all the farmer's neighbors sympathized with the old man over his bad luck, he replied, "Bad luck? Good luck? Who Knows?"

A week later the horse returned with a herd of wild horses from the hills. The neighbors congratulated the farmer on his good luck. His reply, again, was, "Good luck? Bad luck? Who knows?" The farmer's son attempted to tame one of the wild horses and fell off its back and broke his leg. Everyone thought this was very bad luck. Not the farmer, who replied, "Bad luck? Good luck? Who knows?"

Weeks later, the army marched into the village and conscripted every able-bodied man they could find to go to war. When they saw the farmer's son with his broken leg, they let him off. Was that good luck? Bad luck? Who knows?

The moral to this story is not to let the highs and lows emotionally hijack you and to remember that ups-and-downs come with the territory. This reminder can help you remain confident in your writing regimen and stay on the launch pad amid achievements *and* failures.

Today's Takeaway

Next time you encounter an uplift or letdown, remember to stay grounded, that no feeling is final, this one will pass, and a new change will come to turn things around.

MARCH 25
Take a Vacation Instead of a Guilt Trip

Guilt is the prosecutor who knows how to
make every victim feel like the criminal.
—Ruth Gendler

Guilt. Such a nasty word when it rolls off the tongue. How many of us carry guilt around in our minds where it nips at our heels on the way to our desks. As we pound the keypad, it lurks over our shoulders, pulls at our sleeves, distracts us from our best writing.

Guilty is a verdict we render on ourselves often unfairly or for minor offenses. No matter what we do, there's always something to feel guilty about. We write something that is honest and true, and someone takes offense at our opinion. We make a mistake, forget to reply, miss a deadline, say the wrong thing, lose notes, misquote.

Perhaps we say "I'm sorry" so many times we can start to feel like we *are* sorry. Let's ask if we prosecute ourselves unfairly for minor offenses. If so, can we acquit ourselves of the charge, render a not guilty verdict, and pardon ourselves? Can we forgive any unintentional harm done to others?

Ask yourself if you feel guilty about something. Have you treated yourself unjustly? What do you need to do to release guilt? Is it time to apologize or make amends to someone? Or is it time simply to let yourself off the hook?

Today's Takeaway

Stop guilt tripping yourself over minor offenses, follow your convictions, and take what you believe to be the right action.

MARCH 26
Think with Your Heart

Follow your heart. It rarely leads you astray.
It's thinking that gets us into trouble.

—Steve Berry

How often do we find ourselves overthinking our way through a storyline, hemming and hawing perhaps over a career decision? We need logic to a point, but in any creative endeavor—singing, writing, or painting—too much reasoning gets us into trouble. It can send our minds on a wild goose chase, lead to a whirlwind of confusion, and shut down our imaginations.

Effective writers need analytical reasoning skills, but they become ineffective when overused. Too much logic strips the heart of its rich literary beauty, making words sound dry, stale, and vacuous. Poetry and prose writer Tagore said, "A mind all logic is like a knife all blade. It makes the hand bleed that uses it."

It's important to know when to employ logic or cast it to the wind and think with our hearts—the other knowing, the poetry of the soul, that exists outside of thought and reason. When we're making writing decisions and the head and heart are in conflict, the heart rarely leads us astray. Once we consider the logic of a decision, we can add the test of closing our eyes, quieting the mind, and listening to what the heart says. Do that for yourself now.

Today's Takeaway

Listen more with your heart and less with your head when you're in the writing zone or making career decisions and notice the richness and clarity of the words that come to you.

MARCH 27
Don't Sentence Yourself to Confinement

Every writer must acknowledge and be able to handle
the unalterable fact that he has, in effect, given
himself a life sentence in solitary confinement.
—Peter Straub

Writing is a solitary job, but solitude doesn't have to be lonely. For me, it's as or more fulfilling than party hopping. My writing zone is populated with rich ideas and intriguing characters who engage in stimulating conversations and outlandish behaviors.

The solitude of writing is what we make of it. It can be a sanctuary, a retreat, where we get refreshed, relaxed, and recharged from the real world. Or we can feel cut off from life. For some writers, being alone is something to avoid at all costs for fear of what we find lurking inside of us. These writers experience solitude as a lonely torture while other scribes find it to be a deep spiritual and meaningful experience.

What about you? How do you feel about solitary writing? Do you dread it as an occupational hazard? Or do you welcome it as an enriching time of self-renewal?

Today's Takeaway

Try to think of your writing solitude as companionable—not as confining or lonely or restrictive—but as creative liberation that frees your spirit and lets it soar.

MARCH 28
Welcome Your Inner Voices

The voice is persistent, and it knows where you live.
It will find you in that long, dark teatime of your
soul and ask to come in for a cup or two.
—Susan Spann

Do you hear voices in your head? Of course you do, if you're a writer. Admit it. You might have a stadium of characters echoing in your mind. Perhaps you have one scolding you right now. What do you do when they're nipping at your brain? Chances are it depends on what they're saying. We have two classes of inner voices: closed books and open books. Open books—the voices of curiosity and creativity—are friendly voices flooding us with artistic direction, plot ideas, and a population of clever characters.

Closed books—the voices of judgment and criticism—eviscerate us with name-calling, discouragement, and putdowns. You recognize them, don't you? Their agenda is to douse our ambitions, talents, and dreams. But closed voices don't tell the truth. Only open voices do. We can't get rid of our inner voices, so ignoring, arguing, resisting, or steamrolling only make them stronger and louder.

Our best bet is to welcome all of the voices, distinguish between the closed and open ones, and then let the closed books jabber on in the background and take our direction from the wisdom contained in our open books.

Today's Takeaway

Welcome and observe your inner voices with open curiosity without personalizing them, resisting, or identifying with them, and eventually they will quiet down.

MARCH 29
Network with Lean-Time Writers

The people who count are the ones who are your
friends in lean times. You have all the friends
you want when things are going well.
—James Lee Burke

Misery loves company, and nowhere is company more essential than in the life of a writer. Many of us have a posse of like-minded folks who see our point of view and feel the ecstasy, pain, and heartache of writing. Our posse is there for us, not just when things are going gangbusters but during lean times, too.

What about you? Do you have a writing tribe with whom you feel a heartfelt connection who know you at your core? If not, it's important to search out members of a writing community to share deeper bonds. In writing groups or online forum support groups, we have an instant connection with one another on a deeper level without even sharing the details of our lives.

In some cases, these self-to-self connections can be psychological and spiritual—perhaps even sacred ties. This resonation, this deeper familiarity, provides us the safety to drop our day-to-day defenses. Without shame, we share our writing insecurities, negative beliefs about our capabilities, and bounce ideas off seasoned writers.

Today's Takeaway

Find the right tribe where you feel connected to writers who "get you," so you don't feel isolated in a career that "by its nature" is filled with hundreds of solitary hours.

MARCH 30
Write What You Long to Write

No teacher, preacher, parent, friend or wise
man can decide what's right for you—just
listen to the voice that speaks inside.
—Shel Silverstein

Most veteran scribes tell aspiring writers to "find your voice." Truth be told, we don't need to find our voice. It's already inside. We just need to listen and start to use it.

Our writing voice usually resides in our hearts, not just in our heads. It comes through as our hearts write what they long to say. When passion is our main pursuit, our heart goes off in search of itself, and that voice within us, nested in the depths of our soul, shows through. That's what we mean by "heart speak."

As writers, we can ask what our hearts long to say and what keeps them from saying it. If we can identify what stands in the way, perhaps we can move it over and side step it. We're often unaware of the small, petty things on our mental checklist that block us: agonizing over organizing a closet, unpaid bills, the carpet that needs vacuuming, or the unopened mail.

Ask what small stuff muddies your windshield. Once you identify what it is, wipe it from your mind and enjoy the clarity necessary to navigate around the blocks and speak from your heart.

Today's Takeaway

Consider all the small stuff you've been sweating that stands in the way of your heart speak, get it on the page, and let your voice speak what it longs to say.

MARCH 31
Erase the Omni from Your Presence

I've always believed human blood is red because
it really needs to draw attention to itself.
—Patricia Cornwell

Crime writers say that blood's lovely vermillion color is nature's alarm system signaling that something is very wrong and needs immediate attention. Like blood, all writers want a degree of attention. Perhaps that's one of the reasons we write: to be noticed. But how often does that need bleed over the line? Do we get carried away with our egos, hungering to be seen? Are we so bloodthirsty that we'll do anything to get noticed?

For sure, some writers have big egos and ride the highs of financial gain and notoriety. But in overdrive, EGO stands for "Ease Good Out." Promotion attempts by some writers, usually novices, can be cringe worthy and turn off fellow writers and fans. Yes, we're published, and that's a big deal, but it's important to maintain a degree of composure and self-respect. If we overwhelm our colleagues, family, and friends with requests for help in marketing or hints for recognition, it will turn them off.

Know the line between vulgar self-aggrandizement and smart self-promotion. It's considered good form to honor the fine line between good and bad promo. One of the best ways to build your brand is to mentor aspiring scribes in your blogs or Facebook.

Today's Takeaway

Ask yourself how much you recognize the works of other writers on the same path you're on, and if you have lent a helping hand just as one was lent to you.

APRIL

APRIL 1
Plug Into Your Patience

The two most powerful warriors are patience and time.
—Leo Tolstoy

How many of us get impatient with early drafts of a manuscript, wanting to quickly race through to the finish line? I thought so. Would we serve guests lasagna that is not fully baked? Doubtful. Then why would we submit a half-baked manuscript?

Many successful writers talk about twenty or thirty rewrites before submitting their work. When we push ourselves faster than the project can bake, we might unwittingly torch our success. Impatience and rushing diminish our creativity.

Great writers know that patience is our friend and it saves us from rejection and failure. Plus, they have learned not to allow today's fast and furious pace to outrun careful thought and reflection.

As we underscore the need for patience, we notice that we slow our decision-making and ease into waiting until projects simmer from rare to well done. Let's ask what aspects of our writing we need to simmer from a hard boil, so haste doesn't make waste. Without judgment, contemplate on what causes you to rush a piece of work. Then take a breath and a break before going back and reworking the piece. Chances are you will find more that needs to be done before submitting it to critical eyes.

Today's Takeaway

Practice patience in all your daily affairs; learn to wait until projects are ready for critical eyes to save yourself from the burn of rejection and failure.

APRIL 2
Meditation Practice: Stay Awake at the Wheel

*If you're having difficulty coming up with new
ideas, then slow down...Creativity exists in the
present moment. You can't find it anywhere else.*
—Natalie Goldberg

How often do we race through the day without considering who we are and what we want from writing? The trance of productivity robs us of the presence needed for happiness and creativity. Being active is still a waste of time if we busy ourselves just for the sake of being busy.

Take one minute right now and try this simple exercise. Turn your attention to your fingers and focus on them. Wiggle your fingers. Notice how this sensory experience feels. Focus on how the wiggling looks and sounds. Do you hear crackling in your joints or sounds of skin against skin? Do you appreciate how hard your fingers work for you when you put pen to paper or fingertips to keyboard? Do you judge yourself or the exercise? Is it difficult to stay focused? How does it feel to slow down?

If you were fully engaged during the exercise, you might've noticed that previous worries or stressful thoughts were absent. As we navigate through our daily writing regimen, let's not let treasured moments slip through our fingers like quicksilver. We can stay attuned to the present moment, remain productive, and have a happier more creative writing life.

Today's Takeaway

Move at a steady, calm pace, mindful of your moment-to-moment experiences, and feel life under the earth beneath you, letting it come through your writing.

APRIL 3
Write "As If"

You and I as writers must write as if we were highly paid,
even though we may not be. We must write as if we were
top-shelf professionals, even though we may not (yet) be.
—Steven Pressfield

Sometimes if we feel self-doubt nipping at our heels, there's value to acting as if it's a snap. What does it mean to act "as if?" When we're angry and unforgiving, we act like we forgive someone who offends us. When we're feeling cold and detached, we act as if we're interested in a fellow writer's good news. If we're having difficulty getting words down, instead of fighting tooth and nail, we convince ourselves it's easy, act as if it's easy, and we tackle it with ease.

When we really give ourselves to the performance of "as if," the mood we pretend becomes a reality. Acting as if we're the way we want to be changes our mindset to the way we want it and helps us get through the mental sludge. When we proceed with "as if," our mood follows suit. This tool can salvage a bad writing day or prevent a squabble with a member of a writing group. Next time you have a writing problem, tell yourself it's easy and approach it with ease.

Today's Takeaway

Convince yourself that a writing challenge is actually a piece of cake, act as if it's true, then notice the ease with which a problem becomes a cinch to work through.

APRIL 4
Murder Your Little Darlings

In writing you must kill all your darlings.

—William Faulkner

I have to confess. I've committed murder and recommend you do the same. I realize that's a tall order and, although many of you write about murder, you might not be ready to kill. Yet. Or perhaps you've already committed the act. If you've written for any period of time, you've likely been forced to kill your babies. Writers F. Scott Fitzgerald and Stephen King endorsed it.

How could Faulkner, Fitzgerald, and King coldly suggest we kill our precious ones? This kernel of wisdom imparted by the greats is often misunderstood. Killing your darlings doesn't refer to killing off characters. For the greater good of our literary work, the experts urge us to dispose of self-indulgent passages—the words to which we are attached and hold in high regard.

This effectively means removing our personal favorites that don't translate to readers in the same way. This could be an entire piece of a story that has survived many revisions and editing passes—a true beloved held dear in our hearts—but from an objective perspective is completely unnecessary and disposable. After we kill our little darlings, we breathe more richness and life into our narratives.

Today's Takeaway

Strike your precious words from the page when, from a bird's-eye view, your readers don't receive your precious darlings in the same light as when you wrote them.

APRIL 5
Get Shovel Ready to Declutter

*Don't own so much clutter that you
will be relieved to see your house catch fire.*
—Wendell Berry

Disorganization and clutter. Grrrr. They can be roadblocks to locating our writing tools, cutting into valuable time and adding another level of frustration, chaos, and stress when we could be writing that best seller. Sometimes when we hang on to junk, we harbor something else inside and don't realize it could be clogging our motivation or creative flow.

Mounting debt, cluttered desks, undeleted spam in our computers, disorganized writing spaces—all point to something deeper inside, often stuck energy seeking release. Decluttering our physical environments unclogs inner blocks, making room for inspiration, clarity, and creativity.

There is an old saying that nature abhors a vacuum. When we move out of our lives anything that no longer serves us, we automatically make room for what serves us best. So what about that yellowed manuscript stored in a drawer for the last five years? Start digging out by organizing unusable items into four action categories: keep, recycle, donate or trash, getting rid of as much clutter as you can.

Today's Takeaway
Declutter by deciding what is critical for your writer's journey and what is blocking it; then toss, donate, or recycle and watch your clogged energy lighten and lift away.

APRIL 6
Take Midday Catnaps

I catnap now and then, but I think
while I nap so it's not a waste of time.
—Martha Stewart

Not only is catnapping not a waste of time, it actually makes us more productive and creative writers. Some of the most accomplished authors take power naps—short midday snoozes of no more than thirty minutes in order to fuel their energies. It far outweighs chugging a Red Bull or five cups of coffee to keep alert through the afternoon. Brain activity, memory, and the mood of power nappers stay higher throughout the day compared to brain activity of non-nappers, which declines as the day drags on.

If you're interested in improving your mental clarity and writing creativity, give the power nap a try. It flips off your power switch and reboots your engine for the rest of the day. The best time to catch midday z's is around two or three o'clock in the afternoon. Set an alarm so you don't fall into a deep sleep and wake up groggy with a headache. Turn off your electronic devices and nap in a quiet place. Reboot gently when you wake up. I rub my arms and thighs to feel myself back in my body and splash cold water on my face. Then I'm ready to write another few hours.

Today's Takeaway

Take midday time out from your writing to go to the Land of Nod and wake up refreshed, energized, and clearheaded, ready to pick up where you left off in your writing.

APRIL 7
Show Genuine Happiness for Others' Success

*Part of becoming a wise man or a wise woman, is to get
to that point where you can have a friend for whom you
are genuinely happy when he or she has a success.*

—Norman Mailer

Some of the most famous and successful writers wouldn't win the congeniality award when it comes to their comments about fellow authors. Truman Capote flippantly dismissed Jack Kerouac's work: "That's not writing, that's typing." Flannery O'Conner was none the more favorable about the work of Ayn Rand: "The fiction of Ayn Rand is as low as you can get..."

As writers we can ask ourselves if it's really worth spending our energy downgrading our colleagues. When we spend our time that way, it puts the spotlight on us, raising such questions as what does that say about our internal landscape? Where does the need come from? Is it envy, jealousy, displaced anger? Or is it fear of our own failure?

Our own success has a greater trajectory when we express genuine happiness for the successes of fellow writers. We don't have to like or even appreciate their style. But somebody out there does, and that deserves recognition.

Today's Takeaway

Instead of using your energy to put down fellow authors, use it to uplift them, be genuinely happy for their success, and other writers will in turn look up to you.

APRIL 8
Write Even on a Bad Day

It's unimaginable to me that I wouldn't write, but it's very imaginable that I won't write for a little while.
—Anne Rivers Siddons

When our writing plans seem to unravel around us, we question if it's all worth it. Most writers have days when we consider chucking it and finding another craft. Next time we have a "when it rains, it pours" day, we can consider the wisdom Norman Mailer imparted: "Being a real writer means being able to do the work on a bad day."

If we were bus drivers or teachers, bricklayers or computer programmers, we wouldn't give up and walk away on a bad day. We would fix the problems and continue on. And we'd know that bad days come and go just like the good days do.

And as far as *not* writing, what are the options? If we let our disappointments and frustrations get the best of us and give up on a bad day, would we feel better? Not if we're true writers. Keep writing especially on the bad days, even when it feels like the earth is crumbling under your feet and everything is unraveling around you because it isn't.

Today's Takeaway

Don't stop writing no matter how hard the climb, then after the bad mood lifts, you'll feel better even on the worst days than if you hadn't written at all.

APRIL 9
Fly in Formation with Someone

I live with the people I create and it has always made my essential loneliness less keen.
—Carson McCullers

Geese fly in a V formation because it assists with the communication and coordination in the group. The V formation greatly boosts the efficacy and range of their flight, especially over long migratory routes. When a goose gets sick or wounded or shot down, two geese drop out of the formation and follow her to help and protect her. They stay with her until she is either able to fly again or dies. They are connected to one another in and out of flight. And it's those connections that help them soar.

As writers, we too want to fly in formation, to have someone to keep us airborne or catch us when we fall. Whether it's the characters we create, our pets, a writing group, we want to know that someone else is there.

You know, that feeling when you can just be with someone and not have to say anything—no words at all? You know, that warm cozy connection that runs deep within us that all is right with the world? Too few of us have those kinds of connections. Is there someone in your life with whom you would like to fly in formation as your soaring partner?

Today's Takeaway

Fly in formation with someone who is there to spread their writing wings with you or pick you up when you fall—be it your characters, fellow authors, pets, family or friends.

APRIL 10
Dodge the Second Book Syndrome

*Such is the noise that accompanies a
triumphant first novel that writers are finding
it increasingly difficult to write a second.*

—Jasper Rees

Chances are that most of us have heard of the variously known writer's jitters called "second book syndrome," "secondbookitis," or the "sophomore slump." Perhaps others, like me, have experienced it. Ugh! The second book is well known to make us bite our nails and break out in hives because of pressures to produce a work of equal value to or far exceed the first.

Sometimes we forget why we wanted to write a book in the first place and let performance anxiety trump our love for writing. Did book one take all of my stored-up artistry and despair of a lifetime? Will book two be as good as book one? Can I get back in the right voice? Do I have another book in me or am I a one-hit wonder?

Performance anxiety blocks our entrance into the writing zone—that magical, effortless place where words flow and characters write their own story. Our love for writing keeps that zone open. If we're lucky enough to have the second book syndrome, we can remember that however hard it is for authors to follow up on a debut success, it's far harder for the majority who are not.

Today's Takeaway

Cut your second literary work some slack, sidestep panic and frantic, and let your love of writing snatch victory from the jaws of self-doubt.

APRIL 11
Never Give Up

Failure is the condiment that gives success its flavor.
—Truman Capote

From time immemorial, all the great writers in every field of endeavor have doled out the same wisdom one way or another: "Never give up." From the ancient Chinese philosopher Confucius, who said, "It does not matter how slowly you go as long as you do not stop" to Twentieth Century American inventor Thomas Edison, who said, "Our greatest weakness lies in giving up. The most certain way to succeed is always to try just one more time," the message has been the same.

As writers we will have many days when hopelessness sets in. After a failure to achieve a goal, we tell ourselves we can't go on and want to give up. We don't really want to give up. It just feels like that's the only option. But it isn't. We haven't actually even failed; that's just what we call it when expectations aren't met. We're simply traversing a valley most writers go through until they reach the mountain of success.

Baseball great Babe Ruth, arguably one of the best ballplayers of all time, said, "Every strike brings me closer to the next home run." We can use Ruth's wisdom in our writing pursuits and tell ourselves that rejection and failure bring us closer to our publication dreams.

Today's Takeaway
Instead of giving up, do what every successful writer before you did: keep swinging until you hit your dreams out of the park.

APRIL 12
Hang On to Your Dreams

*Nothing is as real as a dream. The world can change
around you, but your dream will not. Because the
dream is within you, no one can take it away.*

—Tom Clancy

Few things insult me more than when someone says, "Someday I'm gonna write a book." It's like a thirty-year chain smoker, taking a puff off a cigarette and saying, "Someday I'm gonna quit." It's obvious from the lack of grit in their pronouncement that someday will never come. Empty words and dreams are different. Some wannabe writers want to get published but never take time to put pen to paper because their empty words are not real dreams.

But writing dreams are real, and it's important to think of them as real because it makes them more tangible and achievable. Things on the physical plane change around us every second: We miss a deadline or rejections come back in our e-mail inbox faster than we submit proposals. But our dreams remain intact.

No one in the outside world can take the dreams that reside inside us. If you dream of being a writer, you don't talk about it the way someone would wish about winning the lottery—a gamble, a game of chance, of luck. Writing dreams are real—the stuff success is made of.

Today's Takeaway

Hang on to your writing dreams as real possibilities, not some pie in the sky wish, and your dreams are more likely to come true.

APRIL 13
Take It One Word at a Time

When you're climbing Mount Everest, nothing is easy.
You just take one step at a time, never look back and
always keep your eyes glued to the top.
—Jacqueline Susann

How does a chihuahua eat an elephant? One bite at a time. How does a mountain climber scale great heights? One step at a time. How does a writer complete a three hundred page-writing piece? One word at a time, one paragraph at a time, and one page at a time.

When we're partway through a writing piece and the rest of it stretches out ahead of us like a hike up Mount Everest, the temptation to do something else can often win out. When we gaze at an insurmountable writing task, we wonder how we'll achieve our goal. Focusing on the end result divides our attention from the blank page and plops us into the future, causing us to feel anxious and hopeless.

Progress is guaranteed if your writing is centered on the present page, not on scribbling the mountain of pages before you. As you focus on the small steps—one word or one page at a time—you feel calmer and more patient, and the words and pages weave together into a full manuscript.

Today's Takeaway

Break huge writing tasks down into small steps and write one word at a time, one page at a time, and it will add up to the full manuscript before you know it.

APRIL 14
Trumpet Your Defiance

With the pride of the artist, you must
blow against the walls of every power that
exists the small trumpet of your defiance.
—Norman Mailer

Defiance is not a dirty word. Many writers like Norman Mailer claim that their best work is written in a state of defiance. Have you blown your horn of defiance against those who slam the door in your face? If not, how long will you wait before sounding your trumpet?

When publishing powerhouses tower over us, it can feel like a Samson and Goliath battle. Defiance, not submission, is the slingshot against any overbearing authority. It's a snort of contempt in the face of the powers that stiff-arm with, "Don't call us; we'll call you." When we tap into the strength and courage of defiance, that power puts us on equal footing with the powers-that-be.

Defiance of writing obstacles exalts and glorifies the artist in us. Be willing to blow your trumpet of defiance. Blow it in the face of anyone who tells you no. Blow it when you're told by the publishing honchos, "We just didn't love it enough." Blow it when someone says, "You can't." Blow it when the oppositional voice within says, "You might as well give up." In the end, it's our defiance of those who stonewall us that redeems us.

Today's Takeaway

Blast your trumpet of defiance when you feel downtrodden and hopeless and let your singlehanded strength help you persevere in your writing goals.

APRIL 15
Grow Thick Skin

*Character consists of what you do
on the third and fourth tries.*
—James A. Michener

When things go south in your writing life (as they inevitably will from time to time), do you find yourself crumbling under the hard knocks? Do you struggle to take action for fear of making the wrong decision? Or are you able to accept bad news, quickly recover, and move on with your writing?

Resilience is the emotional ruggedness necessary to persevere after ninety-nine rejections so we can succeed on the one-hundredth try. Making our marks in the writing world is tough and requires cultivating a zone of resilience. Some people are lucky to be born with it. Many of us who are not can develop it painstakingly over time by staying the course and never giving up, especially during the hardest of times.

Developing thick skin is just as important as developing the craft of writing. Without both we don't have the total package necessary to be successful authors. Real resilience is when we believe we won't make it but we start anyway, trust in ourselves and the outcome, and let our thick skin see it through to the end.

Today's Takeaway

Grow thick skin in the face of opposition on the third or fourth tries, with many different avenues to writing challenges, until a path is cleared for you or you clear a path for yourself.

APRIL 16
Stand Tall and Wear Away the Stone

The fall of dropping water wears away the stone.
—Lucretius

Do you think of yourself as "i" or "I"? That might sound silly, but it isn't. You're not lower case, but if you think of yourself as small instead of tall, regardless of your stature, it will show through in your writing and interactions with people in the writing world.

The size of our frame, our gender, or our stamina to pump iron—none of that really matters when it comes to writing success. What matters is that we think of ourselves and treat ourselves first-rate inside our skin. "Nobody can make you feel inferior without your consent," wrote Eleanor Roosevelt. When you're up against the publishing giants—agents, editors, publicists, booksellers—who've been doing their jobs for a long time, don't consent. Stand tall instead of crouching in your negotiations, your demeanor, or your self-talk.

It's not only the words we pen, but also how we present ourselves that sells our writing projects. Holding ourselves in high esteem and being our own cheerleaders, with "atta-boys" or "atta-girls," is important for writing success. We must think of ourselves as powerful, never sell ourselves short, and never be afraid to be who we are.

Today's Takeaway
Instead of selling yourself short, stand tall and think of yourself as capital I when it comes to your writing, and you'll feel forsaken no more.

APRIL 17
Outlast Defeat

In fact, it may be necessary to encounter the defeats, so you can know who you are, what you can rise from, how you can still come out of it.

—Maya Angelou

If we fall short of our goals—no matter how unreasonable they might be—how many of us torture ourselves with self-defeat? How often do we put ourselves down for innocent mistakes or for the risk of putting ourselves out there and failing? Instead of scolding ourselves, we outlast defeat by giving ourselves credit for our grand efforts.

Success and defeat are a package deal. And nowhere are feelings of defeat more pervasive than in the writing and publishing world. Writing defeats give us a chance to know ourselves better and hone our resilience. We learn not to participate in someone else's underestimation of ourselves. We adamantly refuse to reject ourselves when we get a rejection. Tough times never last; tough people always do.

Contemplate some specific ways you could outlast your next writing defeat. Then write them down and put them in an easily accessible place. Perhaps you could avoid turning on yourself with negative self-talk. Or you might make a special effort to affirm your positive writing qualities. When you encounter no's, you are never really defeated, as long as you use "defeat" to remember to rise above self-loathing and remember who you are.

Today's Takeaway

As you encounter writing defeats, reign victorious by being true to yourself, learn what you can rise from, and never participate in someone else's underestimation of your ability.

APRIL 18
Abstain from Jumping to Conclusions

The mind, which is most capable of receiving impressions,
is very often the least capable of drawing conclusions.
—Virginia Woolf

Can we read minds? Great writers, like Virginia Woolf, know that mind-reading doesn't go hand in hand with great writing, although sometimes we might think it does. Over lunch suppose we pitch a book idea to a publisher. After two weeks, we haven't heard a word. Our conclusion? "Obviously she didn't like the concept." We might even rationalize, "I didn't like her anyway." A month later we get a phone call accepting our proposal. But after hours of agonizing, our mind and body underwent unnecessary suffering because we concluded the worst-case scenario.

The culprit that got us into this worry torment is called *mind reading*—jumping to conclusions based on thoughts that pop into our head instead of hard evidence. We believe what we think is what someone else thinks. When we accept our negative thoughts as truth and our pessimistic feelings as fact, we sell ourselves a bill of goods.

We can save ourselves a lot of unnecessary suffering by questioning automatic thoughts and waiting to see if the hard evidence supports them. The more we practice this approach, the more we learn that impressions are not conclusions and that it's better to wait to connect the dots *after* instead of *before* the hard evidence is in.

Today's Takeaway
Instead of automatically doing someone else's thinking for them and thinking the worst, wait for the hard evidence to save yourself from a lot of unnecessary torment.

APRIL 19
Develop a Keen Sense of the Marketplace

To create something you want to sell, you first
study and research the market, then you develop
the product to the best of your abilities.
—Clive Cussler

You've launched off into the wild blue yonder with your writing. That's great, but there's another side—the business side—that needs attention. There's a certain amount of hard research that goes into writing success: the business market for which you're writing.

To become successfully published authors, we must develop a keen sense of the marketplace through research. We go to bookstores and look around to learn what people read and what sells. Most booksellers have restricted shelf space, given to books that fly off the shelves. We look at titles spotlighted on the end aisles to see what's selling big.

We read books on how to get published and how to find an agent. We sign up for webinars that show everything from how to navigate the rapidly changing social media landscape to negotiating contracts to building a fan base. We attend writing conferences and take classes to learn how to prepare for a pitch or how to build our writing platforms, and we go online and subscribe to e-magazines.

Today's Takeaway

Do your homework about the writing marketplace in order to break into the writing business and to sustain a long and satisfying career as an author if that's your goal.

APRIL 20
Dare Writing as an Adventure

*Life is a song, sing it; life is a struggle, accept it; life
is a tragedy, confront it; life is an adventure, dare it.*

—Mother Teresa

Writing woes are a consequence of the situation combined with our perspective. There's a fine line between excitement and terror. Does your heart race when you write that heart-pounding scene the same as it does when you read a scathing review? Chances are you label the writing as fun and the bad review as stressful.

When we consider a situation as a problem, we experience stress, but if we dare to consider it as an adventure, we feel excitement. Faced with a writing challenge, we can move the needle from fear to daring adventure. Adventure triggers the rest-and-digest response and *opens us up* to creative possibilities. But if those same challenges become problems to solve, it activates our stress response and *closes us off* to creative solutions.

Our writing life won't always go our way, but when we can't control difficult situations, changing our perspective changes our attitude. We consider our next writing challenge as an adventure and worry less about the problem side of the equation. This U-turn makes insurmountable events feel like a breeze.

Today's Takeaway

In the above quote, substitute the word "writing" in place of "life" and read it silently to yourself often: "Writing is a song, sing it; writing is a struggle, accept it, writing is a tragedy, confront it; writing is an adventure, dare it."

APRIL 21
Expect a Miracle

Miracles do happen. You must believe this.
No matter what else you believe about
life. You must believe in miracles.

—Augusten Burroughs

Authors speak of writing miracles that happen all the time—story after story of unknown writers plucked from obscurity and catapulted into the spotlight: J. K. Rowling with her Harry Potter series or novice writers who self-publish their own books that fly off the shelves. The psychologist Wayne Dyer packed his car full of self-printed books and drove cross-country from bookstore to bookstore until he hit the bestseller list.

So expect a miracle in your writing. I can see you rolling your eyes after I've stressed how next to impossible it is to get a major publisher interested in your work. Still miracles—not all of the J. K. Rowling variety—do happen, some huge, some small. While many of us get stuck worried about how to surmount problems, life often takes us around them in ways we could never imagine.

Miracles cannot be quantified or dissected under a microscope; they happen unplanned and when we least expect them. That's why we call them miracles. Our disbeliefs are the major hindrances to their manifestation. The two common denominators among writers who've been blessed by writing miracles are faith and persistence.

Today's Takeaway

Have faith in the possibility of miracles without getting bogged down wondering about the science of how and when they'll happen, and keep your beliefs loose enough to accept them.

APRIL 22
Don't Just Do Something—Sit There

I think we all get too caught up in
doing instead of just being sometimes.
—Anne Rivers Siddons

How many of us hit the ground running as soon as our feet touch the floor, checking our electronic leashes, slurping coffee, bolting to our desks with a million ideas exploding in our heads, worried if the publisher will like the finished product? Perhaps we believe frantic and panic are the best ways to accomplish our writing goals.

But we don't have to be frazzled to become good writers. Calmness is a more effective state to hone our craft. When we are in a peaceful center, heart and respiratory rates slow down. The mind is open and clear, and actions and decisions are reflective and balanced. As worry and fear recede, a blissful serenity makes everything seem right with the world.

The more we still the anxieties of our hurried mind and center on the quiet places within us, the more the calm state will be available to us even in times of upheaval. We can be more productive when we maintain a peaceful awareness in the stream of our writing and moving at a reasonable pace while staying attuned to our inner world and our surroundings.

Today's Takeaway
Bathe yourself in the slow-moving waters of calmness in the stream of your writing instead of giving external stressful demands authority over you.

APRIL 23
Outsmart Your Limitations

The only limits to the possibilities in your
life tomorrow are the buts you use today.

—Les Brown

It's amazing how many of us get trapped by the way we use our minds without even being aware of it. When things don't work out the way we want, it looks and feels as if life is treating us badly, but that's usually not the case. Although our capabilities are limitless, our minds often put bars on that potential. The need for security causes us to become attached to our negativity and perceive limitations as real.

After a certain number of rejections, it's easy to think of ourselves as downtrodden. Self-victimization, negativity, and self-pity become habitual ways of thinking. These limitations manifest themselves in our chronic patterns of living without a writing project, alone, bored, miserable. The bars are the old judgments, fears, and worries put there by previous experience, recycled through the present.

Once we understand it's our limiting thoughts—not the reality of the world—that get in the way, our writing lives change for the better. The awareness that it's not the situation that imprisons us but the way we think about the situation can free us from our mind traps and our suffering.

Today's Takeaway

Replace your "buts" with "ands," outsmart your negative thinking, and remove the bars that you thought were holding you back from reaching your writing goals.

APRIL 24
Accept Uncertainty

*If uncertainty is unacceptable to you, it turns
into fear. If it is perfectly acceptable, it turns into
increased aliveness, alertness, and creativity.*
—Eckhart Tolle

"Accept uncertainty?" you might ask with a grimace. At first glance that sounds like a tall order. But when you think about it, it's worth the payoff. Truth be told, uncertainty is certain; it's one of the few things we can count on. The ability to accept it beforehand brings us peace of mind, contributes to our creative writing, and helps us persevere in the topsy-turvy literary world.

The writing life is full of unexpected curveballs. Resisting uncertainty drains our writing energy and dooms us to fear. Expectations about a situation can cause us to become overly attached to the outcome, setting ourselves up for disappointment and resentment. We spend a lot of energy getting upset over things we cannot control instead of welcoming uncertainty.

As writers, it's important to develop the ability to fit into any unexpected situation. We can ask ourselves if we've forced or resisted an uncertain, uncontrollable situation and notice the accompanying tension in our bodies. On the heels of surrendering to the uncontrollable situation, we notice the aliveness and calmness that enshrouds us. Take a minute now to go within and imagine accepting uncertainty with open arms then notice what happens.

Today's Takeaway

Contemplate the uncertainty you encounter, welcome it, and see if you can befriend and fully accept it in order to create an open heart, clear presence, and peaceful mind.

APRIL 25
Replenish the Soul in Your Writing

Writing, for me, is a search for God.
—Carson McCullers

Veteran authors often describe writing as a spiritual experience, a journey deep within themselves, or a state of altered consciousness. A zone lifts us to another sphere where hours go by that seem like minutes. Novelist Amy Tan described it best: "The muse appears at the point in my writing when I sense a subtle shift, a nudge to move over, and everything cracks open, the writing is freed ... ideas pour forth ... "

From the time I could wrap my fingers around a pencil, I, too, experienced that zone, spending hours alone in my room writing mystery stories with characters, hands over mine, willing to do whatever I wanted, granting me control over an unwieldy life that threatened to engulf me. Even today, constructing words into sentences expresses the depths of my soul with great satisfaction and joy.

As we deal with the business side of writing, it's important to keep the soul in our craft and not yield to requests of "write faster, write more." As creators of our own worlds, the deeper connections within us are not only psychological; they're spiritual—some would even say sacred moments. Never forfeit your muse for money.

Today's Takeaway

Keep the soul in your writing instead of letting schedules, deadlines, and rejections in the business side rob the very spirit that inspired you to write in the first place.

APRIL 26
Psst, Reframe Your Writing Hell

... Ultimately we'll never encounter
anything more terrifying than the monster
among us. Hell is where we make it.

—Dean Koontz

Imagine two passengers on an airplane preparing for takeoff. Neither have flown before. Ann is excited; Molly feels trapped, stressed to the max. Ann listens to her iPod and relaxes. Molly white-knuckles it and grips the armrest during takeoff, worried that the plane might crash. Both women have the same external experience but a different internal experience. Ann sees the flight as an adventure. Molly sees it as dangerous.

When we perceive a threat (real or imagined), the mind constricts and targets the problem with worry or fear. The body responds with fight-or-flight as though the threat is real even when it isn't. You probably know writers who think of their careers as heaven and others who call them a living hell.

We have the power to turn writing practices into a heaven or hell simply by the perspectives and actions we take. We have the power to shift from negative to positive self-talk during a challenge to create heavenly moods, feelings, and actions.

Today's Takeaway

Reframe your negative attitude toward writing pressures into a positive outlook so you can harness the tactical muscle memory to turn a hell into a heaven.

APRIL 27
Ditch Your What-Ifs

*Do not lose power over the what-ifs of
your life. They are unlimited and endless.
Keep your power in the now, in present time.*

—Gary Zukav

One of the most common ways we overestimate threats is waiting for the ax to fall. *What ifs* are those cruel ghosts that haunt us day and night. "What if my writing class doesn't like my piece? What if my novel doesn't sell? What if I can't think of a plot for my next story? What if my publisher turns me down?"

What ifs are endless exaggerated thoughts streaming through our minds that we latch onto as fact—worries that interrupt our enjoyment of writing. Truth be told, most things we worry about never happen or at least not in the way we imagine.

What ifs are out-of-the-moment episodes that disconnect us from our present selves. Before jumping to conclusions with such thoughts, we can keep our power in the present moment. Imagine you're a private detective in a murder mystery and ask, "Where's the evidence for my prediction?" When we wait to connect the dots *after* instead of *before* the hard evidence is in, we discover that *what is* usually contradicts *what ifs*. And we save ourselves a lot of hand ringing and wasted time that we could put into writing that heart-pounding scene.

Today's Takeaway

Next time you catch yourself mired in writing worries, turn your foresight into 20/20 and use your hindsight as a reminder that *what ifs* are unreliable sources of information.

APRIL 28
Don't Let the Past Steal Your Present

We inhabit ourselves without valuing ourselves, unable
to see that here, now, this very moment is sacred;
but once it's gone, its value is incontestable.
—Joyce Carol Oates

Many of us go through life, inattentive to the moment, trying to get to the Nirvana of pleasure, missing out on what's happening now. If we start to watch, we might be amazed at how the mind skips the present. We push through the traffic jam instead of *being* in the traffic jam. We hop in and out of the shower to our writing desks instead of *being* in the shower. We rush through dinner to watch TV instead of *being* present with dinner preparation.

The present moment is a gift. Don't let the past steal it and let life slip through your fingers, for the past is already gone and the future never arrives. There's a way to practice present-moment awareness. We can start during a morning shower by focusing on the thousand beads of splashing water popping against our skin, the rushing sounds they make hitting the tub. We're aware of the smell and feel of the slippery soap gliding over our faces, the soap bubbles swelling on our necks, arms, and chests. We notice the fluffy towel against our bodies. We continue with awareness while brushing teeth, eating breakfast, and going through morning routines. Anytime your mind wanders—even now as you read these words—bring it back to the present. As you mindfully inhabit yourself, you'll have a renewed appreciation for the richness and calmness of these sacred moments.

Today's Takeaway

Be mindful with your writing self throughout the day, let it anchor you in the place where true life occurs moment to moment, and you'll view the world in a totally different way.

APRIL 29
Toss Your Resentments in the Dustbin

*There is no point in burying a hatchet if
you're going to put a marker on the site.*
—Sidney Harris

On your writing journey, someone will hurt you, probably unintention-
ally. Perhaps they already did. Do you harbor anger because it gives
you emotional satisfaction? If so, there's an old saying that those who
anger us, conquer us. Each of us can decide whether we'll be *conquered*
or *strengthened* by someone's wrongdoing. When we forgive others for
wrongful acts, we conquer them. Forgiveness is an act of self-compassion that frees us from a negative prison on the inside. Letting go of
negative thoughts and feelings brings inner peace, softer hearts, and a
loss of resentments.

Would you like to forgive someone on your writing journey? Are
you ready to forgive *entirely* and *completely*, even for things the person
has yet to do or will continue to do? If so, write down the name and the
behavior that arouses strong feelings. Visualize whatever bothers you.
See yourself forgiving the person *completely*. After you feel true forgiveness in your heart, open your eyes, tear the paper into tiny pieces, and
throw it into the trash bin. The next time you have negative thoughts
about this person, remind yourself you've already consigned those feelings to the dustbin of history.

Today's Takeaway
Forgive someone for your own sake and substitute loving-kindness for
long-held resentments, then forgive yourself for carrying the burdens
for so long.

APRIL 30
Stretch Your Chest and Arms

You are only as young as your spine is flexible.
—Joseph Pilates

You might have noticed that your chest muscles and the muscles in front of your underarm are often tight from repeatedly reaching your arms out in front of your body. Typing on the computer, holding a book, or working at your desk are activities that shorten these muscles after a long time. Here is a simple stretch for these muscles:

- Stand in a doorframe at the end of a wall with the front of your right shoulder pressing against the end of the wall. Reach your right hand directly out from your shoulder down the wall. Your hand and arm should be touching the wall parallel to the floor.

- Begin to turn your body away from your right arm and feel the stretch.

- Repeat the same pattern with your left arm on the other side of the doorjamb, taking the turn a little further to gradually increase the stretch. You might feel your shoulder blade move closer to your spine when doing this stretch.

Stretching for ten minutes releases the stress that builds up in your body while you're writing. Not only does it feel good, but stretching your body is one of the easiest ways to discharge tension and relax your body.

Today's Takeaway

As you move into stretching, remember that stretches should never hurt or cause you pain, so make sure you practice them slowly, gently, and often—at least three times a week.

MAY

MAY 1
Rewind the Movies in Your Head

*Everybody, everybody everywhere, has his own movie
going and everybody is acting his movie out like mad, only
most people don't know that is what they're trapped by...*
—Tom Wolfe

The brain runs constant mini-movies—brief clips of past or future events that at one time wired us for survival. Through repeated neural firing patterns, the brain strengthened our learning of life-sustaining behaviors. Because of our genetic heritage, the human brain continues to produce short films that have nothing to do with actual survival or with what's happening in the present. Even if we know that, it's easy to become swooped up in the movie's storyline and stress.

When faced with writing challenges, the clips pull us out of present time. The movie might take us thousands of miles away, where we fret about how our writing will be received, agonize over writer's block, or rehearse with trepidation for a reading appearance.

Take a few moments and pay attention to the theater playing in your head right now. Notice how it can become bars on an invisible cage that traps us in a life that's smaller than the one we can actually have—much like a tiger released into a large zoo that continues to crouch as if it's still confined to its old pen. Then bring your awareness back to the present and notice the expansiveness.

Today's Takeaway

You can create a horror movie or a musical/comedy in your head when you notice the clips playing and bring yourself back to connect with the current moment.

MAY 2
Meditate Instead of Medicate

*Stop. Take three deep breaths and smile everywhere in
your body, observing what's happening in your body.
Proceed now with kindness and understanding.*
—Deepak Chopra

Meditation is good medicine to comfort the writer's mind because in some cases we overuse our minds. When we devote ourselves to meditation, our mental burdens and unnecessary worries drop off one by one. A good way to meditate is to close our eyes, breathe in and out, focusing on each in-breath and each out-breath. We follow our breath through to a full cycle from the beginning of an inhalation where the lungs are full back down to where they're empty. Then we start over again.

As we stay with this cycle for five minutes, thoughts usually arise. We wonder if we're doing the exercise right, worry about an unfinished writing project, or question if it's worth our time. We accept anything that arises with openheartedness. Each time the mind wanders off and gets caught in a chain of thought, we gently step out of the thought stream and come back to the sensations of our breath. After five minutes, we slowly open our eyelids and take in the colors and textures. We stretch and breathe into our vivid awareness and notice how much more connected we feel to the moment.

Today's Takeaway

Devote yourself on a regular basis to being with your breathing—where true life occurs moment-to-moment—so worries drop away and your writing runs more smoothly.

MAY 3
Bend It Like Beckham

Blessed are the flexible for they will not allow
themselves to become bent out of shape!
—Robert Ludlum

Bend It Like Beckham is a good soccer strategy, and bending in the writing game can help authors score big, too. The ability to bend is an essential quality to fuel creativity and persevere against the inflexibility of literary storms.

What insecurities do we hide behind when we order and over plan our lives like a blueprint for a skyscraper? How many wonderful opportunities and people do we exclude with our inflexibility? Flexibility keeps us from getting bent out of shape when things don't go our way. It assists us in our work if there's a hole in a plot or inconsistency in a character so that we can make creative revisions. It enables us to work cooperatively with colleagues at writing conferences, collaborate on projects, or on panels at bookstores. Flexibility helps us bend our defensive walls in reaction to constructive criticism.

Ask yourself if you need to scrub ruts and routines that straightjacket you. Do you welcome opposing views that can improve your craft? Are you able to accept feedback from mentors about the direction to take that might sustain you as a writer?

Today's Takeaway

Loosen and bend in just one area of your writing life, no matter how small, then stand back and watch your creative juices flow and your writing ideas bloom.

MAY 4
Honor Your Scars

The world breaks everyone and afterward
many are strong in broken places.

—Ernest Hemingway

What doesn't kill us as writers makes us stronger. I know, don't throw rotten tomatoes at me. I didn't say it. They did, since the beginning of time; first with philosopher Friedrich Nietzsche, then Ernest Hemingway, and then singer-songwriter Kelly Clarkson popularized the phrase in her pop song. So there must be some truth in this old adage somewhere.

The last thing writers want to hear when we're struggling uphill is that the journey will make us stronger. It's easier to embrace this message once the letdown has settled. Truth be told, we couldn't write about broken, fallible characters if we didn't know what rejection, failing, and hurt felt like.

When we strain against our writing limitations and burst through them, it enables us to grow and strengthen. All of us writers have a bullet lodged somewhere in our hearts and souls—bullets that give us fodder for creativity and resilience. We can harness the strength that resides in those places where we feel broken, letting it drive us forward to writing success.

Today's Takeaway

When it seems as if you've failed, remember that you haven't failed at all, that you're strong in those broken places, building firepower to succeed in your love for writing.

MAY 5
Find Your Bookends

You can't have an up without a down, a right without a
left, a back without a front—or a happy without a sad.

—Harlan Coben

Writing has bookends. Whatever you're seeking is also seeking you. But in order to wrap your arms around it, you must first accept its opposite. I realize that sounds crazy, but you can't have success without failure, light without dark, or ecstasy without agony. Are you driving yourself up a wall trying to get accepted as a writer? If so, you must first accept that gain and loss work in concert.

You want your manuscript to be accepted, but can you accept its rejection? You desire readers to be your fans, but can you tolerate no-shows at book signings? If you want to succeed at writing, are you willing to accept failure at a writing task? You want critics to praise your writing, but are you willing to accept a scathing review?

Everything has opposites. To attain what we want, we must be willing to accept what we don't want. Choosing acceptance fertilizes our motivation to get up and dust off one more time than we fall. That's where firepower comes from.

Today's Takeaway

Open your writing arms to good and bad and you'll find it easier to face disappointment and rejection, plus the taste of writing success will be sweeter once it arrives.

MAY 6
Grieve Dashed Dreams

When there is chance of gain, there is also chance of loss.
Whenever one courts great happiness, one risks malaise.

—Walker Percy

When we chase a life's dream of writing, we risk great loss, but it's a gamble most writers are willing to take. After a series of disillusionments and discouraging feedback, however, many writers become sad, even depressed. Devastation and heartbreak bring tears, and it feels as if the writing journey has come to an end—even if it hasn't.

It's important to take time out of the rat race to touch the pain of long-held grief. Not that the dream is over, just that it usually doesn't happen when and how we imagined. That, too, is a loss that calls for mourning.

Instead of freezing our emotions when we feel a sense of loss, it's important to fully mourn them, no matter how big or small. Feeling the inner hurt and pain soothes and heals and helps the sting thaw.

As members of a writing family, we're never alone in our grief when dreams are dashed. Grief is universal, and all writers know it inside out. Sharing with another author who understands the pain strikes a deep cord within us and cuts our hurt in half.

Today's Takeaway

Grieve your writing losses alone with tears, in meditative silence, or talking with a trusted confidant; whatever you do, give yourself permission to feel the losses in your own way.

MAY 7
Stiff-Arm Harm

Self-compassion is actually a courageous mental attitude that stands up to harm—the harm that we inflict on ourselves everyday by overworking, overeating, overanalyzing…
—Kristin Neff

Self-compassion gives us the emotional strength to stand up to the harm of constant disappointment. It allows us to recover more quickly from bruised egos to acknowledge our shortcomings, forgive ourselves, and respond with care and respect. Self-compassion enhances emotional well-being. It boosts happiness, reduces anxiety and depression, and gives us courage to stick to our writing regimens amidst ongoing disillusionment.

Staying the course one defeat after another takes courage. If you're like most people, you hear a voice that says you might as well give up: "You've been at this for a long time. You haven't had one single bite. You're wasting your time and your life." The defeating self-talk overtakes us, eventually taking us down, but only if we believe it.

Critical self-talk is the defeating force, not the writing challenges that we undergo. We don't have to listen to the voice. Just because it's there doesn't mean it's telling the truth. Instead, we can hold the negative voice at arm's length, let it chatter on, keep separate from it, and connect with inner courage and belief in ourselves.

Today's Takeaway

Stand up to harm with the courage to stick to your writing path, no matter what is thrown your way, no matter how downtrodden you become, no matter how discouraged you feel.

MAY 8
Treat Your Writing as Your BFF

Writing is the only thing that, when I do it,
I don't feel I should be doing something else.
—Gloria Steinem

When Gloria Steinem called me one day, her first words were, "Bryan, I feel like I know you." Although we had never met, she had read a book of mine called *Chained to the Desk*. We had both written books about our childhoods and although the circumstances were different, the psychological underpinnings were similar. To cope with early hardships, Gloria and I found writing as a healing salve to our childhood wounds.

Writing is a silent friend for many of us. Novelist Ann Patchett thinks of her writing as an imaginary friend that she drinks tea with in the afternoon. For many of us, it's the source of comfort, entertainment, and enlightenment available anytime of the day and in the wee morning hours when no one is around. It lets us escape from an unjust world to find safety and consolation in a place where our justice rules.

We can use journal writing as a friend, helping us come to terms with our thoughts and feelings, providing insight into difficult problems. Creative writing can be an outlet to release writing stresses or vent about injustices inflicted upon us when we were too young to do anything about them.

Today's Takeaway

No matter why you write, treat it as your BFF, using it lovingly for the common good of others and yourself to provide insight, inspiration, and healing heart speak.

MAY 9
Befriend Writing Stressors

Whether it's anger or craving or jealousy or fear or depression—whatever it might be—the notion is not to get rid of it, but to make friends with it.
—Pema Chödrön

Yes, you read right. It sounds counterintuitive, but forging a friendly relationship with writing stressors actually helps reduce stress levels. If you're scratching your head, think of it this way: fighting, conquering, battling—and all the other words we use to deal with stress—create an adversarial relationship that leads to greater frustration and anxiety. So instead of going to war against stress, an accepting attitude can help lower the stress needle.

The elegant design of our nervous system prewires us for stress so we can survive. But as we begin to think of stress as a protector, we can consider all the ways it takes care of us. It watches out when we're driving in heavy traffic, searching for our car in a dark parking garage, or trying to meet writing deadlines. In many ways it's our friend, constantly on the lookout.

I can hear you gasp, but give it a shot. Once you start to contemplate all the times stress had your back when you thought it was against you, notice how your appreciation starts to calm you down, and you learn that combating stress does more harm than good.

Today's Takeaway
Instead of going to war with writing stressors, befriend them, then watch your stress needle drop, your combative frame of mind subside, and your writing waters calm.

MAY 10
Prepare for Orphan Grief

*The truth is you can be orphaned again and again and
again. The truth is you will be. And the secret is this will
hurt less and less each time until you can't feel a thing.*
—Chuck Palahniuk

In the publishing industry, the likelihood of orphan grief rises each
year. When we get published and our publisher shuts down, we face
huge repercussions. Chances are you will experience it, too, whether
your parent company gets sold, goes out of business, or drops you from
its stable of authors. As small independent publishing houses close their
doors or get swallowed up by larger companies, authors find themselves
without a home.

Some writers become orphans when publishers decide not to publish their sequels, leaving authors with orphaned works that are difficult,
if not impossible, to get another publisher to adopt. Being an orphaned
writer isn't unlike having a parent abandon us. It's disorienting at first
and then we traverse several stages of grief: shock, denial, bargaining,
anger, and ultimately acceptance.

Once we finish moaning and crying, it's important to start writing
again, as mystery writer Debra Goldstein did: "My best hope for moving forward from being an orphan is to continue writing short stories
and novels." Just as life goes on, our writing life continues as the best
way to overcome orphan grief.

Today's Takeaway

Your best hope if orphaned by a publisher is to give yourself time to
grieve then take a deep breath, connect with your love for writing, and
get back to it again.

MAY 11
Be Gutsy with Self-Promotion

Don't think of your website as a self-promotion machine, think of it as a self-invention machine.

—Austin Kleon

Your perseverance has finally paid off and you're a published author. You might have editors like I did who suggested that I learn the art of shameless promotion. Your chest tightens. You flush. *I'm a writer*, you think, *not a marketer*. Besides, it belittles my craft to commercialize it. Is it appropriate to reach out to local bookstores, libraries, or businesses? Or is that too weird? And where's the line between tooting our own horn and blasting people?

Self-promotion isn't second nature for most writers, but our comfort with it is essential for success. Not only is it okay to reach out to let people know about our publications, it's necessary. Otherwise, how can the public know what we've done? Usually bookstores and libraries appreciate knowing about our literary works.

One way to think about self-promotion is that we're inventing our Writing Self—our persona as a writer. Once we get our feet wet, we discover how welcoming most people are and how much they want to support us. So instead of shying away from self-promotion, let's get comfortable sharing and promoting our hard-earned work and tooting our horn, just not blasting too loudly.

Today's Takeaway

Be gutsy and toot your own horn when you get published. Make sure you blow it softly, and think of it as the invention, debut, and celebration of your Writing Self.

MAY 12
Give Middle-Aged Creep the Brush-Off

*Whenever we feel stressed out, that's a signal that our
brain is pumping out stress hormones ... those hormones
can ruin our health and make us a nervous wreck. "*
—Daniel Goleman

Middle-aged creep isn't the jerk in a trench coat leaning over your shoulder with his camera phone. It's the added spare tire, usually caused by stress that refuses to budge no matter how much we diet or exercise. A Yale University study found that under threat, even insects like grasshoppers—which normally feed on protein such as grasses—switch to munching on sugary goldenrod plants. The sugary foods provide fuel to quickly feed their amped-up bodies in case they need to flee.

Wonder why we crave pizza? When we're frazzled with writing, we are more likely to seek out sugars, fats, and carbs for a quick energy boost. The brain acts as an internal slingshot, pumping a cocktail of stress hormones into our bloodstream. We stew in its cortisol and adrenaline juices, and glucose levels spike to give us energy, readying us for action. The fats and sugars we eat go straight to our bellies, depositing fat, making us more vulnerable to stress.

To break this cycle, we can find stress reducing activities such as exercise, meditation, or yoga. Couple the activity with healthy eating and a good night's sleep. These habits give us healthier ways of managing writing stressors.

Today's Takeaway

Writing and stress (good and bad stress) go hand-in-hand, so the key is to develop a healthier lifestyle and find productive ways of managing stress.

MAY 13
Admonish Self-Sabotage

---

*Sit down once a day to the novel and start working
without internal criticism ... without the need to look at
your words as if they were already printed and bound.*
—Walter Mosley

Sometimes it seems like too much. The enormous changes we need to make can be overwhelming. The literary road is too long, too steep, too rocky. Urgency outruns patience. We find ourselves rushing the words instead of letting them speak. In the end the manuscript doesn't work.

We sabotage our writing with unrealistic expectations and impatience. Great things take time. The Grand Canyon didn't form in a day. The key is to slow down and take our writing one word, one sentence, one paragraph at a time. Day by day each word adds up and BOOM! We eventually have pages. We must give time for our writing to blossom and bear fruit then ripen.

Let's ask if we're rushing ahead of the words and creative juices, leaving them in the dust. We don't push our writing; like the river, it flows by itself. The philosopher Augustus said, "Make haste slowly." Today we can tackle only what demands resolution in this moment, this hour. Tomorrow we will deal with tomorrow, and next week we will make it through each writing day word by word.

Today's Takeaway

When discouraged, give yourself credit for the tiny gains you pen each day and remember each word adds up to sentences, paragraphs then pages, one word at a time.

MAY 14
Trust Your Inner Muse

In the depths of winter, I finally learned that
within me there lay an invincible summer.
—Albert Camus

Many writers, poets, and musicians say their creative inspiration comes from an inner muse. Among them novelist Amy Tan, painter Pablo Picasso, and songwriters John Lennon of the *Beatles* and Jim Morrison of *The Doors* called on their muses to inspire their creative works.

Sometimes we writers forget what lies inside. We spend days and weeks away from our writing, wondering if we're still up to the task. During our absence, the process of writing can feel foreign—like a far away land almost forgotten. We fear losing our ability if we get too far away from it. Perhaps some of us are afraid to take time off, that our muse will die or take a permanent leave of absence.

The muses within us never go away. During the dead of winter when we're dealing with the distraction of life events, they hibernate until we return. Learning to trust the invincible muse's devotion and giving it time to penetrate our mind cultivates a clearer, calmer, more creative mind. We are indebted to our inspirational muses who love and guide our creative endeavors. Without them literature would be an impoverished world.

Today's Takeaway

Learn to trust that the muse dwelling within you—like a dedicated, invincible companion—is patiently waiting to assist and always looking forward to your return.

MAY 15
Unearth Your Quirky, Creative Side

Many people hear voices when no one is there.
Some of them are called "mad" and are shut
up in rooms where they stare at the walls
all day long. Others are called "writers."

—Ray Bradbury

Inside us writers is an entire universe waiting for exploration. Some of us might have discomfort with "the other side." While clinging to the familiar puts us in a more comfortable and secure zone, it can put us at odds with the creative process. Do the three R's run our lives: ruts, rules, and routines? If so, it's time to stretch and let our wild and imperfect selves out of the cage of judgment and mistrust.

If we live by the book, it's time to try something that requires spontaneity and flexibility. If we're perfectionists, we can intentionally do something "imperfectly." If we're logical and systematic, let's lighten up the creative and intuitive sides of our brain with art, dancing, or poetry. If we fly by the seat of our pants, we can organize our writing life. If we're shy at parties, we can get in touch with our outgoing side by introducing ourselves to strangers. If we're on the go 24/7, we can try gardening, yoga, or quiet contemplation. If we're sedentary, we can fast walk or try aerobics. Stretching where we've never been unearths buried parts of us that can maximize writing possibilities.

Today's Takeaway

Unearth your quirky, creative side by doing just one thing differently, and discover more of you using the stretch to infuse more creativity into your writing craft.

MAY 16
Place Imposter Syndrome on Life Support

Like most other creatives, I struggle
with self-sabotage, self-doubt, and feeling
like an imposter more often than not.
—Jeff Jarvis

Journalist Jeff Jarvis is not alone in feeling like an imposter. It's a common feeling among high-achieving creative people. When actress Jane Fonda won her second Oscar, she told a talk show host she felt like a phony and feared the Academy would find out how talentless she was and take the award back. Even American author and poet Maya Angelou said, "I have written eleven books, but each time I think, 'Uh oh, they're going to find out now. I've run a game on everybody, and they're going to find me out.'"

If we think of ourselves as unworthy writers or believe that something is deeply flawed in us, we'll take those beliefs and treat them as facts in our everyday lives. Even when situations contradict the beliefs, we superimpose our beliefs on the situations. We call this the "impostor syndrome"—writing successes marked by the inability to internalize the accomplishments and a persistent fear of being exposed as a "fraud."

Despite huge writing successes with our craft, many of us writers discount or downplay our achievements as flukes, tell ourselves we didn't earn them, and fear they won't happen again.

Today's Takeaway

Send your imposter syndrome packing, radically accepting the external evidence that spells out your success, letting it rule over your internal feelings.

MAY 17
Fizzle, Drizzle, Then Laugh Instead of Sizzle

Laughter and tears are both responses to frustration
and exhaustion. I myself prefer to laugh, since
there is less cleaning up to do afterward.

—Kurt Vonnegut

After an expectation or bright writing idea disintegrates, frustration and exhaustion hit. When writing fizzles, tears drizzle. If we tried to collect all the tears shed by writers, they would fill an ocean. And oh, how we hate the pain of grief. Who doesn't?

When we're down and out and a tear rolls down our cheeks, we can think of it as another drop of salt water in the writer's ocean of tears. We will feel less alone and more connected to scribes who came before us and who come after us. But we don't have to remain sad and lonely.

Sometimes we get so used to moping and crying about our writing frustrations that we forget there's a flipside. As we let the sadness run through us, it allows us to move forward. Forcing ourselves to laugh at the frustration, even when we don't get the results we want, can help us release the hurt.

Look back on a frustrating or exhausting time in your writing. Is it possible to muster a chuckle or even a smile when you look in the rearview mirror?

Today's Takeaway

Balance your day with humor and laughter, and try not to take yourself too seriously; it will brighten your writing path, and you'll have less cleaning up to do.

MAY 18
Write Disappointments as Your "Mentor"

*Anything that doesn't take years off your life and
drive you to suicide hardly seems worth doing.*
—Cormac McCarthy

In the midst of disillusionment, short of slitting our wrists, the easy solution is to give up and surrender our writing pens. But if we want to be resilient writers, we shelter in place and stay on the path. A teacher doesn't get tenure. An attorney doesn't make associate. A construction worker doesn't get promoted. But they keep working until they meet their goals. As writers, we too stay the course until we secure an agent, sell our first piece, or hit the big time with our third or fourth novel.

We can think of writing disappointments as our "tor-mentors" and ask what we can learn from each one. We look the "tor-mentor" in the eye. We try to see the upside of a downside situation, pinpoint the challenge or opportunity in the disappointment, and discern what we can manage or overcome with each seemingly discouraging situation.

Contemplate the viewpoint that writing disappointments are lessons from which to learn, not failures that must be endured. Then focus on the opportunities they contain to make you more resilient. Share those insights with a fellow writing companion.

Today's Takeaway

Think of each writing disappointment—no matter how discouraging—as your mentor that gives you an opportunity to cultivate inner strength and become more stress resilient.

MAY 19
Muzzle the Domino Effect

*When it seems impossible, like nothing is
going to work, you are usually just a few
millimeters away from making it happen.*
—Tony Robbins

"No matter how hard I try, I can't find a publisher. I thought I could write, but obviously I can't. I've wasted all this time for nothing." Sound like you? The domino effect occurs when our emotions jump overboard and exaggerate a factual event. The only fact is "I haven't found a publisher." What remains are feelings that magnify the facts. But when the domino effect hits like a tsunami, the emotions feel true, causing us to make the biggest mistake of our lives: hang up our writing pens and put our manuscripts in a drawer.

No one except ourselves can keep us from success. When we get discouraged, our lizard brain floods us with negative emotions, throwing the rational brain off line. Caught in a riptide of negativity, we have a way out. First, take a breath and ask if the messages are facts or feelings. Most of the time, we're reacting to feelings. Second, let the domino effect run its course. Once the dust settles and your rational brain is back online, you can pinpoint the truth and change the negative feelings into the facts. Then you're back in the saddle again.

Today's Takeaway

Don't be too quick to throw in the towel when you have one writing roadblock after another because you could be just a step away from acceptance and success.

MAY 20
Spring-Load Post-Traumatic Growth

*I think persistence in the face of adversity is
an essential part of a writer's job description.*

—Lawrence Block

Dramatic, positive changes can occur as a direct result of facing an extreme challenge to our writing efforts. Although these challenges are not life or death, sometimes they might seem traumatic to us. If you're not a natural-born optimist, you can muster the necessary coping skills to face the seismic events that could otherwise devastate you in the writing and publishing world.

Instead of post-traumatic stress, we can face extreme writing challenges with post-traumatic growth. As strange as it might sound, writing adversity has benefits. Overcoming such adversity can help us see that we're stronger than we thought, bring new meaning to our writing lives, take us deeper into our spirituality, and deepen the sense of closeness with others and ourselves.

What benefits can we derive when expectations don't turn out the way we want? We cannot change the result, but we can alter how we cope with the outcome. Therein lies our power for positive growth. When we learn to think of our visions as ironclad and our actions as steadfast, we surmount and benefit from all the earthshattering situations.

Today's Takeaway

Face your next extreme writing challenge with post-traumatic growth instead of post-traumatic stress, and it will make you a more resilient writer.

MAY 21
Outpace Turmoil with a Calm Heart

Peace does not mean to be in a place where there is no
trouble, noise, or hard work. It means to be in the midst
of those things and still be calm in your heart.
—Unknown

Staying calm in your heart and mind when everything around you seems to be falling apart isn't easy, but it's not impossible to do. We are more alive when we're at peace with ourselves, when we have a mind that's resting. A resting mind is a mind without imperative—one in which we don't need anything to be different.

With practice, we can relax and enjoy things around us without the urge to change them, get rid of them, or stay busy to avoid them. We can respond with thoughtfulness instead of thoughtlessness. A kind word diffuses a sour attitude. Calm in the face of hysteria has a soothing effect. Compliments reverse aspersions.

Resting minds and calm hearts allow us to act instead of react in stressful situations. With repeated success, heart speak can heal the body from the wear and tear of everyday writing stressors.

Today's Takeaway
Stay calm in the face of turmoil, accept what's happening around you, and make the best of every moment that you have.

MAY 22
Stalk Inspiration with a Club

You can't wait for inspiration.
You have to go after it with a club.

—Jack London

To become good writers, we need intentional inspiration—the tender listening to our inner wisdom. If we're impatiently rushing to the finish line, we can't hear our inner wisdom because it comes slowly and in its own time. And it appears when we least expect it, usually when we're doing something other than writing or thinking about writing.

Some world-famous writers go after inspiration with a club by putting themselves under intentional, unforced conditions that nurture it. Virginia Woolf, Alice Munro, and Ian McEwan are just a few of the legion of writers who found inspiration by simply walking. It made them feel alive and helped their inspirational juices flow.

D. H. Lawrence found inspiration writing outside in nature—facing the sea, distant mountains, in the snow or the English countryside under a shade tree—which made him feel safe and soothed his restless spirit. What about you? What calms you down or excites your soul to soar? What makes your blood boil? What makes your heart leap?

Today's Takeaway

Go after inspiration with a vengeance by placing yourself under circumstances that allow you to wait for it and welcome and seduce it to the surface.

MAY 23
Body Connection Practice: Try Micro Self-Care

It's the paradigm shift to targeted micro
self-care, the cultivation of small replenishing
moments... that continues to make a crucial
difference in my ongoing stress level.

—Ashley Davis Bush

Sometimes even when we're writer-fried and undernourished we must keep plugging away to meet writing demands or deadlines. Under writing pressure, we might not have time for substantial commitments for macro self-care, such as exercising at the gym, twenty minutes of meditation, or even walking around the block.

But there's always time for thirty seconds of micro self-care to reduce stress and refresh our minds without getting up from our writing stations. One micro self-care exercise lets us strengthen our backs for support and soften our chests for compassion while continuing to write: Pull in your belly button toward your spine and straighten your back as you imagine a string pulling you up from the top of your head. Take a deep belly breath, relaxing your stomach outward and mentally softening your entire body.

The deep breathing stimulates your rest and digest response, offsetting your stress response, and you feel immediate relaxation. This simple micro self-care exercise clears your mind so you can continue writing with less physical stress.

Today's Takeaway
Find quick and simple strategies for self-care to keep you replenished and clear-minded when you're under writing duress and don't have time for macro activities.

MAY 24
Shed Self-Defeating Attitudes

We don't see things as they are, we see them as we are.

—Anaïs Nin

We enter most situations with a mindset based on our attitude toward ourselves. When we set our sights in a certain direction, we'll eventually see whatever we expect to see. If we look for misery, we'll find it. If we look for success, we'll find success. This seems like a very simple idea, but let's not permit the simplicity to obscure the firepower and far-reaching possibilities it injects in our writing.

We create our writing experiences in the things we find and hold on to. Whatever we look for is waiting for us. When we expect a bad writing outcome, it can turn out that way simply because we think and behave in ways that fit with that outlook.

Just as water takes the form of the vessel that holds it, our behaviors take the form of the thoughts that mold them. It's not *what* our writing practices deal us that determine our happiness; it's our *attitudes* about what our writing practices deal us that makes the difference in our writing success. What are you looking for in your writing craft? Have you found it? Why or why not?

Today's Takeaway

Identify a self-defeating outlook that blocks your writing success, replace it with a positive attitude, and take necessary steps to make the positive thought a reality.

MAY 25
Plan to Sweat

Sweat, sweat, sweat! Work and sweat,
cry and sweat, pray and sweat!
—Zora Neale Hurston

Writing is hard work. It's tough on mind and body and requires blood, sweat, and sometimes even tears. If you love writing, you learn how hard it is. There will be days when it feels as if you've sweated in ninety-degree heat. There will be others when it feels like you're floating on a cloud. But because you love it, the benefits outweigh the drudgery.

We might have to go through long stretches when our writing isn't where we want it to be. Getting to where we produce consistently satisfying work takes patience, time, and practice. But with stick-to-itiveness we learn how and under what conditions to write and what works and what doesn't as we develop the best writing regimen for ourselves.

We immerse ourselves in literature and discover how people in other fields create. We talk with our contemporaries about their processes, and we connect with other writers and learn where they find their inspiration. We ask authors whom we trust and respect to critique our writing. We take writing classes, join writing support groups, and read about how great writers learned their craft. It's all work, but in the end it's worth it.

Today's Takeaway

Be willing to work and sweat and practice daily as you learn to write, and be willing to persist and sweat the extra mile when your writing isn't as good as it needs to be.

MAY 26
Own Your Power

The most common way people give up
their power is by thinking they don't have any.
—Alice Walker

As beginning writers, we often give our power away when making choices about publishers and contract details. We need patience and fortitude as we wait months in between submissions to hear from agents or publishers. Once we get a bite, it's difficult not to be impulsive and jump at the first chance to get our work in print.

There are several secrets to holding on to our power as published authors. If we learn these skills, we equip ourselves with all the power we need to stand our ground: develop a tough skin, learn to persist, and practice resilience in body, mind, and spirit. Acquire a keen sense of the marketplace by visiting bookstores and learning what's selling and what people are reading. Cultivate a professional attitude toward writing, and hone the skill of meeting deadlines. Study the publishing industry and understand the ins and outs of how it works. Learn the art of self-promotion and social media skills.

We grasp our power by connecting with it on the inside and by taking practical steps to gain knowledge that propels us forward on our writing journeys.

Today's Takeaway

Take the time to acquire the essential knowledge to be a successfully published author so you have the mojo to hold on to your power and not give it away.

MAY 27
Restore Wind in Your Sails

Right where you are is where you need to be.
Don't fight it! Don't run away from it! Stand firm!
Take a deep breath. And another. And another.

—Iyanla Vanzant

Your publisher is suffocating you with impossible demands. An editor's critique is taking the wind out of your sails. Your spouse is breathing down your neck for more attention. You're under a writing deadline that causes you to hold your breath. And you're on the verge of a meltdown. Your breath becomes short, shallow, and rapid. Perhaps you use your shoulders instead of your diaphragm to move air in and out of your lungs. You might stop breathing or hold your breath and not even realize it.

Notice your breathing right now. Do your breaths come from high in your chest or deep in your abdomen? Are they fast or slow? If stress tries to steal your breath, causing shallow breathing higher up in your chest, you can calm yourself by practicing abdominal breathing.

When you breathe from your abdomen, you can't get as worked up with the extra oxygen you get in your bloodstream. Your diaphragm flattens downward, pushing the muscles in the abdominal cavity upward, creating more space in the chest so your lungs can fill up.

Today's Takeaway

Under stress, practice natural abdominal breathing—going deeper and slower from your abdomen until you feel calm and relaxed and can get back to your writing.

MAY 28
Let Your Wild Thing Run Free

---

*If you cage a wild thing, you can be
sure it will die, but if you let it run free, nine
times out of ten it will run back home.*

—Fannie Flagg

If we cage our creative juices for too long, they can dry up. If we let our wild, creative thoughts run free and focus on another activity, they will be there when we return.

We can schedule a hole in our calendars for unplanned moments, when there's nowhere to go, nothing to do, nobody to see. This allows us to create reflective moments where our minds can drift, our bodies can melt, and we can watch the grass grow.

We can lose ourselves in a calming view of nature, kick a ball along the seashore, sip tea by a warm fire while stroking a pet, plan heart-to-heart talks with someone close to us. These soothing moments recharge our batteries, let our minds run free, and become the building blocks to wellbeing, being well, and well-filled creative juices.

Today's Takeaway

Let your mind go between writing projects and refrain from forcing, resisting, or clinging to creative ideas, allowing them to hatch on their own.

MAY 29
Table Going for the Jugular

If I worried too much about publisher
expectations, I'd probably paralyze myself
and not be able to write anything.
—David Baldacci

Sometimes stress dogs us with self-doubt, telling us we can't write or we'll never learn the craft. Or if we do learn the craft, we won't be able to get published. Or if we get published once, we can't pull it off a second time. If publisher expectations can paralyze David Baldacci, it can happen to any of us.

What do we say to our best friends or children if they thought they couldn't do something? We wouldn't say, "Of course you can't, my darling, you're not very good, so you might as well not even try." Instead, we believe in them and encourage them with compassionate pep talks. It's important for writers to give ourselves that same type of internal support.

Instead of going for the jugular when self-doubt nips at our heels, we can ease our minds with positive affirmations. These present-tense statements are not tricks to convince us that a situation is better than it actually is. They are prescriptions of encouragement within our reach that we might not totally believe but we want to believe. Think about the kind of support you need in your current writing regimen. Then give it to yourself.

Today's Takeaway

Before you start writing, imagine the best of outcomes and whisper silently to yourself, "I can do what I set my mind to do, and I can do it well."

MAY 30
Don't Let Your Mind Stunt Your Writing

*The aim of the life of a rosebush is to
be all that is inherent as potentiality in the
rosebush: that its leaves are well developed
and that its flower is the most perfect rose...*

—Erich Fromm

Like the rosebush, the aim of most writers is to pen the very best words that we can. In order for roses to blossom into their full beauty potential, the rosebush needs a specific kind of soil, moisture, temperature, and sun or shade. For us writers to reach our full potential, we, too, need certain conditions and optimum care.

Without proper conditions and care, the rosebush will do the best it can on its own. It might grow crooked in the direction of the sun to get more nourishment. Many writers inevitably allow our minds to get in the way of our own growth. Our negative and discouraging thoughts deprive us of the moisture, sunlight, and fertilizer we need to become our best.

The attainment of self-love, self-encouragement, and self-compassion create optimal conditions to enrich the soil of our writing so that we can grow into the best writers possible.

Today's Takeaway

Flourish as a writer by providing for yourself uplifting, compassionate, and positive thoughts that nourish you on a daily basis, then watch your writing bloom.

MAY 31
Schedule Time to Quiet Your Mind

*Boredom, anger, sadness, or fear are not "yours," not
personal. They are conditions of the human mind. They
come and go. Nothing that comes and goes is you.*
—Eckhart Tolle

As a child growing up in the South, I remember church camp meetings where believers fanned away sweltering heat as they worshipped under huge tents. I often peeked through slits in the tents to watch them raise their arms to the heavens, clap their hands, speak in tongues, run up and down aisles, and sometimes cut cartwheels in ecstasy as they became "slain in the spirit." Little did I understand that they were engaging in practices that contributed to stress resilience.

We don't have to get stirred into a frenzy to calm down the comings-and-goings of the mind and get the benefits of spiritual euphoria. One of the best ways to quiet the mind is to set aside time for solitude and reflection, allowing the creative self to take the helm.

Contemplation of nature, meditation, or prayer reduces stress and puts the body at ease. This state occurs with the rush of a beautiful sunset, heightened bliss from deep meditation, or natural highs from spiritual connection through prayer.

Today's Takeaway

Quiet your mind so when you return to your writing, the comings-and-goings in your head no longer eclipse your creative self, and the quiet fills up with rich, creative ideas.

JUNE

JUNE 1
Glue Your Butt to the Chair

Writing is the art of applying the ass to the seat.
—Dorothy Parker

When beautiful weather beckons, it can be difficult to stay at our writing stations. Even in bad weather it can be difficult to plant ourselves in the chair if we lack inspiration. Most successful authors would agree that true writers don't let a beautiful day or waiting for inspiration to strike dwarf their craft. Still, how many of us wait for rainy days or until we're in the mood? Nobody's waiting for us, and we're accountable to no one. Except ourselves.

A real writer goes to work on gorgeous days when we're depressed or downtrodden and on days we'd rather sleep in. Everyone in all walks of life has bad days—plumbers, secretaries, surgeons, electricians—but they still go to work rain or shine. Don't let the weather or your mood dictate when you write. If you want to be a writer, plant yourself at your writing station and work, even if it's just for fifteen minutes.

Today's Takeaway

If inspiration isn't there, go after it by writing what you can instead of waiting for it to come to you; you will find that it will meet you halfway.

JUNE 2
Get Your Writing Business Done

It is often said that before you die your life passes before your eyes. It is in fact true. It's called living.

—Terry Pratchett

Do you ever get the feeling your writing life is zipping by and you're not taking advantage of it? *Carpe diem*—Latin for "seize the day"—reminds us to live our lives fully, get our business done, and not worry about the past or future. On our deathbed, we don't remember the time we spent working in the office or mowing the lawn. We regret we didn't get important business done.

If we had our lives to live over, what would we do differently? Talk less and write more? Invite our writing group over even though the carpet is stained and the sofa faded? Burn the midnight oil to get that story finished? Say more of "I can do this" and less of "There's no way"? Pay more attention to what goes right instead of what goes wrong?

Once we live as if each day were the last, we won't have to give a second thought to the haunting question: Is my life flying by and I'm not getting my writing business done? So what are you waiting for? It's time to get writing business done.

Today's Takeaway

Write that novel, craft that short story, join the critique group; don't wait any longer to get your business done because tomorrow offers no guarantees.

JUNE 3
Know When to Hold and When to Fold

*Some people with awful cards can be successful
because of how they deal with the tragedies they're
handed, and that seems courageous to me.*
—Judith Guest

The cards that our writing life deals us don't determine our happiness or unhappiness. It's how we think and respond to the hand we're dealt that determines our happiness. We are the masters of our writing fate, and we have the power to create the nature of that experience—to either hold or fold.

If we think of ourselves as victims at the mercy of the hard blows of the writing and publishing world, then we will be truly miserable. If we view ourselves as survivors of our writing disadvantages and use them to learn and improve our work, then we create a positive experience out of a negative one.

How we think about what happens to us on our literary journeys creates our success or misery, not the acceptances or rejections. Staying focused on hardships and problems keeps us stuck, and we trick ourselves into believing that we are made miserable by writing circumstances. We become attached to being downtrodden. Failure, despair, and pessimism become chronic feelings in our writing days. And they start to show. Our challenge is to remain focused in our positive outlook, courage, and self-confidence.

Today's Takeaway
Be the master of your writing fate, bear responsibility for outcomes without self-judgment or blame, and use disadvantages to strengthen your perseverance and resilience.

JUNE 4
Meditation Practice: Sidestep Mind Fogs

*Much of the time we're going through life, inattentive
to what's happening, trying to get to the Shangri-La of
pleasure, missing out on what's happening, here and now.*
—Ronald Siegel

Chances are that you judge yourself and your writing much of the time. Think about the last time you took a shower or brushed your teeth (I hope it wasn't too long ago). Caught up in thought streams, you probably thought about other things, about your writing maybe, besides what you were doing at that moment.

For writing resilience, we want to be in charge of our minds instead of letting them take charge of us. That makes us stronger, more clear-minded scribes. Try an experiment in the next day or so to notice your thoughts while preparing a mindful meal.

Pay close attention as you assemble the ingredients. Notice the unique character of each vegetable, fruit, or piece of meat—the myriad of colors, diverse smells, and varied textures of foods. Even the different sounds as you chop, slice, cut, grind, and pound. You might pop an ingredient into your mouth, noting its taste and texture against your tongue. As you combine the different ingredients, notice the visual transformation and aromas as the separate become one. Then take in the smells and colors before you dig in.

Today's Takeaway

Stay alert to mind fogs by taking charge of where your mind goes. Does it go where you want or where it wants? Take necessary steps to develop more mindfulness, hence better writing.

JUNE 5
Dwarf Appeasing with Self-Pleasing

I cannot give you the formula for success, but I can give the formula for failure—which is: Try to please everybody.
—Herbert Bayard Swope

A writer feared his second novel wouldn't be a success. He was in a writer's critique group that didn't "get" the plot, and it sent him into a tailspin—months of writer's block and anguished writing. He changed the plot, forfeiting his own truth in order to please group members.

For those writers among us who are still trying to be a good boy or good girl so everyone will like us and we'll never be rejected, listen up. People pleasing is a direct result of our writing insecurities and is a poison for authors.

It's possible to be open and flexible to feedback without compromising the integrity of our work, but the quality of our writing doesn't depend upon the acceptance or approval of others. If we forfeit our own writing voice to appease the opinions of others, we shortchange ourselves, our writing suffers, and we lose our true identity as an author.

Reflect on a time when you gave your writing self away to someone else's opinions instead of sticking to your own. How did you feel later? If you were to develop a game plan for future writing challenges around people pleasing versus self-pleasing, what would it be?

Today's Takeaway
When push comes to shove, the key to writing success is to get comfortable with your own writing and please yourself first with your own voice as the final stamp of approval.

JUNE 6
Banish Your Procrastinator

I never put off till tomorrow what
I can possibly do the day after.
—Oscar Wilde

Procrastination is often based on fear of failure. Putting off a writing task that we're not sure about gives temporary relief. We don't have to deal with the immediate unpleasant fear of not getting words just right or blanking altogether.

However, stalling only makes matters worse. It adds a second layer of pressure, throwing us into a stress cycle and possibly into writer's block. Dragging out writing tasks raises our tension levels. Long lists and piles of daily chores weigh us down, overwhelming us even more.

Let's not become a bunch of knuckle draggers. Simply choosing one item from our to-do list that we can accomplish quickly then completing it gives us a jumpstart and lifts the burden of procrastination. We can face writing commitments head-on and early instead of waiting until the last minute. When we have several items on our list, we can distinguish between essentials and nonessentials and work through the tasks that need immediate completion one at a time. Reflect on some aspect of your writing that you've put off. Then face it head-on by biting off just a small piece to get you started. Then notice the tremendous unburdening.

Today's Takeaway

Take an inventory of the overlooked details of your writing life then tie up loose ends and savor the relief and serenity of the mental unburdening.

JUNE 7
Be Careful What You Ask For and From Whom

Be careful what you wish for... Wishes are brutal,
unforgiving things. They burn your tongue the moment
they're spoken and you can never take them back.
—Alice Hoffman

Chances are that most of us welcome feedback on our works-in-progress. And any publicist, agent, or editor will say their evaluations are subjective. When we ask for feedback, it's important to consider our sources, not let the pool get too big, and take advice with a giant grain of salt.

Soliciting feedback from too many people can backfire. We might get as many contradictory answers as the number of people we question. A barrage of conflicting ideas can catapult us into confusion and mire us in writer's block.

Limit the number of people from whom you solicit opinions of your craft; make sure they possess knowledge of the writing craft and of the ins-and-outs of the publishing industry; and trust that you can rely on their subjective judgment.

Today's Takeaway

After you ask for an honest writing critique, prepare yourself for subjective and occasional negative feedback; consider the source, then consult with yourself before deciding what to change and what to leave on the table.

JUNE 8
Learn to Say No

You know I say just what I think and nothing more nor
less; I cannot say one thing and mean another.
—Henry Wadsworth Longfellow

Some of us say yes when we'd like to say no. Fear of saying no comes from fear of rejection. We put our likes and preferences behind the desires of others in order to be liked and, as a result, we have a pile of unmet needs that often lead to resentment.

Saying no means we are taking care of ourselves by asserting our honest opinions and choices. When we are honest with others and ourselves, we feel better, our needs are more likely to be met, and the resentment melts away.

If we're always saying yes, we're not living freely until we say no at least once in a while. When we assert our honest views, we discover that we like others and ourselves much better. To whom do we need to say no? A fellow writer who asks for the e-mail address and phone number of the agent that it took a year to land? A family member who asks us to critique a short story when we're under deadline and don't have the time? The friend who calls, asking to read passages when we're in the middle of dinner? Who then?

Today's Takeaway

Say no at least once in a while so you're true to yourself, not whittling yourself away by saying yes all the time.

JUNE 9
Stave Off Writing Despair

I too have felt despair many times in my life,
but I do not keep a chair for it. I will not
entertain it. It is not allowed to eat from my plate.
—Clarissa Pinkola Estés

After a while, beginners and seasoned pros alike can start to feel despair with their writing. Despair can knock on our door at any literary stage. And it has many messages. Aspiring scribes can lose steam from trying and getting nowhere. Some debut writers, plagued with fear, despair that the second book won't measure up to the first. The continued humdrum success of seasoned authors can become so old hat that despair dwarfs the enthusiasm we once had.

The key is to find a way to push through writer despair instead of letting it stop us in our tracks. We don't have to entertain despair. We don't have to invite it in for tea at our table. Instead of losing heart, we can remind ourselves that we were made for these times, that this is part of what writers are trained to do. When despair comes calling, we go inside, find our resilience, and allow it to eat from our plate.

When the excitement and wonder are gone, we can challenge ourselves with a different genre, new characters, or a different form of writing. Inspiration is unending. We can search in different places to renew our writing spirits. What are some ways that work for you to break through when you are mired in despair?

Today's Takeaway

Dig deeper into your creative soul. Take your resilience by the hand and go seek the ordinary and the usual with fresh eyes and gaze beneath the surface to see what writing treasures lie buried there.

JUNE 10
Nail Down Your Writing Style

Writing is like driving at night in the fog.
You can only see as far as your headlights,
but you can make the whole trip that way.
—E. L. Doctorow

Some authors, known as "plotters," lead their writing process by starting with an outline. They know where they're going every step of the way and how the book will end. Other authors, known as "pantsers" fly by the seat of their pants, let the writing process lead, have little or no idea where the storyline is going and no clue how the story will end.

Author Charlaine Harris said, "I've often wished when I started a book I knew what was going to happen." Novelist Ann Patchett said, "Sometimes not having any idea where we're going works out better than we could possibly have imagined."

I'm a plotter with nonfiction and a pantser when I pen a novel. Some authors combine styles. It's okay not to know where we're going with our writing or to know exactly where we're going. There's no right approach. Don't let anyone tell you there's only one way. Each of us must nail down what works best. What's important is that you find your own unique way of writing that fits. Are you a pantser or plotter or combination?

Today's Takeaway
Nail down your writing style so you know what best fits you, and don't let anyone try to redirect you down a road that doesn't resonate within your writing heart and soul.

JUNE 11
Ramp Up the "Umph" in Triumph

A pat on the back is only a few vertebrae removed
from a kick in the pants, but it is miles ahead in results.
—Ella Wheeler Wilcox

After months of sending out queries, I landed an agent for the book you're reading, and I screamed and yelled and jumped up and down. My spouse and friends looked at me with blank faces and stepped backward. When my agent snagged a publisher, I ran around in circles in my kitchen. My spouse grabbed the phone and started to call 911 to have me evaluated. Not really.

But truth be told, many of us go through literary ups-and-downs alone. Most writers have times when we feel underappreciated, that no one understands how hard we work. Maybe it's unrealistic to expect non-writers to get as excited as us. Still, it's important to recognize our contributions from within ourselves.

We can give ourselves two thumbs up, a fist pump, or atta-boys when we score big in the writing arena. Recognize yourself in a demonstrative way. Underscore and validate your writing success so you're motivated to continue onward. Give yourself an affirmation, a special treat, or a simple two thumbs up. I promise no one in a white jacket will come for you.

Today's Takeaway

Hit the pause button now and then, and put the umph back in triumph for all the writing challenges you overcame, the literary triumphs you attained, and all those achievements that lie ahead.

JUNE 12
Be a Good Will Hunter

It is literally true that you can succeed best
and quickest by helping others to succeed.
—Napoleon Hill

You've heard the old adage that it's better to give than receive. It might sound odd, but helping other writers has a boomerang effect. Commonly known as the helper's high, dispensing good will boosts our mood, calms us down, and relieves us of stress-related illnesses. According to scientists, brain scans of benevolent and generous people show stronger immune systems, calmer dispositions, and better emotional health.

We're in the writing game together. We don't compete against one another. The more we spread good will and help other writers, the more it helps us. Reaching out and supporting fellow authors gives us a break from our own stressors. It makes our lives feel worthwhile and gives us a sense of purpose, and meaning.

There are many online mentoring sites such as International Thriller Writer's Debut Author Forum, where writers share advice, exchange information, and guide debut authors in their first steps as published authors. Performing kind acts for other writers—no matter how small or brief—connects us to them in a deeply meaningful and humane way. By taking good care of fellow writers, we're taking good care of ourselves.

Today's Takeaway

To forget your writing woes for a while, get a good feeling in return and acquire a new lease on your writing life, lend a helping hand to another writer; you'll be glad you did.

JUNE 13
Be Willing to Split Open

Write what disturbs you, what you fear,
what you have not been willing to speak
about. Be willing to be split open.
—Natalie Goldberg

All writers have fear. We're damned if we write and damned if we don't. Even literary agents are scared. They usually start off their rejection letters with, "I'm afraid I have to pass." If you're a writer, you're in a boat with a bunch of scaredy-cats. We're afraid what we pen won't be good enough. We'll be judged. We'll reveal our inadequacies. We'll be rejected. We'll fail.

Fear can squeeze the life out of us and diminish the joy. It can restrain us from taking on new challenges, forming new relationships, and deepening intimacy with old ones.

You might as well face and feel the fear and write anyway—willing to reveal what disturbs you, to split open and write about what you're afraid of, what you haven't been able to speak about. When you do, your writing will take on a deep richness. And readers and fellow writers will feel right at home because chances are they feel what you feel inside, too.

Today's Takeaway

Be willing to split open and your fear will dissipate because you won't chance anything or expose anything that every writer before you hasn't already experienced and revealed.

JUNE 14
Build Confidence with the Bricks Thrown at You

*A successful man is one who can lay a firm foundation
with the bricks others have thrown at him.*
—David Brinkley

Debut author John Hickman wrote, "It is one thing to get that proverbial dreaded note from a publisher: 'Thank you for your interesting submission. However ...' But it is entirely another thing to have a close friend or spouse hear or read your work and just not get it."

This is sage advice for an aspiring scribe. Chances are if we write for any length of time most of us will experience what Hickman describes. The key is what we do with the bricks that are thrown at us and to make sure we use them to build a strong foundation. If you're like I was, you might want to show your really good stuff to everyone you know. The problem is friends and family might not understand the craft and give conflicting or misleading feedback that could shut you down or make you angry.

It's important to be selective about with whom we share our writing drafts. When negative feedback befalls us, we must have the confidence to make an objective call in response to it and build from there. We might create something different based on the feedback or strengthen our confidence to keep it as we originally intended. Meditate on the bricks that have been thrown at you and ask how you can use them to build your writing confidence.

Today's Takeaway
Build a firm writing foundation with the bricks thrown at you by avoiding defensiveness, being objective, and having the courage to move forward with confidence.

JUNE 15
Balance Your Writing and Personal Life

Live a balanced life—learn some and
think some and draw and paint and sing and
dance and play and work every day some.
—Robert Fulghum

Today average Americans are challenged with finding work-life balance. With more things to do life moves faster. Many of us notice our personal time is shrinking. We leash ourselves to wireless electronics and watch our work-life balance go down the toilet. If you're like debut author Ann Farnsworth, you're stretching long hours juggling a daily writing regimen and pressures from the business side of the tumultuous publishing world with family commitments: "As a mother, the biggest obstacle I face is trying to balance the very real needs of my family and the push I feel to write. How does a mother ever find a quiet place to write? I write in the early morning hours, and the creative high gets me through the day."

Whatever your story, take a breath, step back, and view your life from a bird's-eye slant. Are you truly living the way you want to? Is your life balanced or lopsided? If so, pinpoint where the imbalance is and ask yourself what you can do to bring back some equilibrium. Consider playing enjoyable music, practicing relaxation exercises, watching nature, meditating, exercising, or spending time with your family.

Today's Takeaway

Examine your life to determine how to insert more personal time and, in addition to writing, do other things that bring you joy, peace of mind, and fulfillment.

JUNE 16
Brace for Your Rite of Passage

If one is not careful, one is soon writing to please reviewers and not their audience or themselves.

—Louis L'Amour

You're excited about the release of your first publication. Your publisher is pleased, the ARCs look terrific, and you have great feedback from relatives, friends, and your writing group. All is going well. You're waiting for your first glowing review. Then from out of nowhere a critic kicks in your teeth. You lose faith in your writing ability and your writing journey ends—at least it feels that way. Sound familiar?

It's a rite of passage to get a negative review. If you haven't received one yet, you will. All writers get their fair share. Writing is a subjective business, and reviews are based on personal tastes. One reviewer will trash a literary piece while another will extol the exact same work.

When you get a bad review at the starting line, you just got it out of the way, like eating your vegetables. When you get bad reviews after years of publishing, learn to take the bad with the good. Discern what insights you can glean about your work and adjust accordingly. Leave the rest on the table. Dessert is coming.

Today's Takeaway

Stay the course in your writing ability, especially in the rough swells of the publishing seas; after a bad review, think of it as a rite of passage all writers sail through.

JUNE 17
Design Visual Rest in Your Workspace

Clutter is what silts up exactly like silt in a
flowing stream when the current, the free flow
of the mind, is held up by an obstruction.
—May Sarton

Disorganized and cluttered writing spaces can make our work chaotic and stressful. Productivity wanes as we bounce from one task to another. Clutter creates roadblocks to finding things we need, cutting into valuable writing time, and adding another level of frustration when the writing business is already stressful enough.

An organized system for electronics, keys, mail, and other writing tools eliminates the pressure of searching for something when we're already behind schedule. After our writing space is uncluttered, visually appealing, and functioning smoothly, we are more productive and our writing is more creative.

Order conveys a feeling of calm and stability—a feeling that things are under control and all is right with the world. Visual rest un-obstructs the creative flow of our minds and frees us to pay attention to what really matters: our writing. Reflect on one or two actions you can take to bring visual rest into your workspace.

Today's Takeaway

Create visual rest in your workspace so you don't waste valuable writing time searching for your work tools; your creative juices will flow more freely.

JUNE 18
Capture Plenty of Snooze Time

*It is a common experience that a problem
difficult at night is resolved in the morning after
the committee of sleep has worked on it.*
—John Steinbeck

Many of us take sleep for granted, yet the restorative nature of sleep makes it one of the best remedies for cultivating great writing. Lack of sleep can cause foggy thinking and block creative thinking. The writer Arianna Huffington called sleep nature's Ambien.

We know that sleep deprivation interferes with memory and learning. The brain moves slower. We're more forgetful, our attention is short-circuited, and we're grumpier. We are prone to greater risk for heart attack, stroke, and depression.

When we're struggling with plot, character development, or waiting jitters around a writing submission, a good night's sleep gives us a whole new lease on life the next day. Experts say the average person needs seven to eight hours of sleep a night for optimal health. Those who doze eight or more hours are less stressed, have fewer colds and viruses, and live longer. Remembering these facts contributes to us being better writers all around.

Today's Takeaway
Catch plenty of Zs to keep your health optimal, your mind unruffled, and your writing fresh and crisp.

JUNE 19
Reassess Failures as Success Builders

Some of the biggest failures I ever had were successes.
—Pearl S. Buck

The Rx for failure as a writer? There's no such thing—failing as a writer that is—unless we choose to put that frame around the picture when something doesn't go our way. Yes, of course, an agent, editor, or writing mentor might reject our work. And it might feel crappy, but is that really failure?

Let's take a scenario that actually happened. Suppose I get a publisher's rejection on a Friday and torture myself. I tell myself I've failed and beat myself up. I feel like crap. Then out of the blue another publisher accepts the same piece of work on Monday. What happens then? How can I be a failure on Friday and a success on Monday with the same literary work?

It's all in how we choose to look at it. Failure is in the eye of the beholder. If we insist on the label "failure" when bad news comes knocking, we can face the failure then get back to writing. But the best policy is not to label our writing as a failure to begin with. Instead, try to see it as an integral part of the writing submission process. Look back over some past writing "failures" and see if in hindsight you can see them as successes.

Today's Takeaway
Avoid labeling yourself as a failure, and don't let someone else's critique of your writing determine how you view your accomplishments as an author.

JUNE 20
Drench Yourself in Courage

Fear lives in the head. And courage lives in the heart. The job is to get from one to the other.

—Louise Penny

Playwright and novelist Elena Hartwell said, "When I do the first draft, I'm partially consumed with terror that it will be awful and unfinishable and well … not work at all." As writers, most of us can get into a state of terror or panic that we won't be successful. But we have more power over that fear than we think. More courage dwells inside us than we're aware of. The key is to get from our heads into our hearts and trust the journey.

Courage and resilience come from being mindful of the attitude we take as we write and the knowledge that we can choose that attitude. When terror slugs us—as it surely will from time to time—we can face it head-on by going around it, over it, under it, or changing our outlook.

But we must never run away from it, for that would mean running away from ourselves. Fear dwells inside us, not in the outside world, where we can throw a net over it. It takes courage to stand up and say that we won't allow fear to intimidate our writing abilities or cast self-doubt over us anymore. Think of a time you were intimidated by a writing challenge. Then contemplate mustering as much courage as you can and drench yourself in it.

Today's Takeaway

Outsmart your consuming writing fears with courage, and face them head-on so that your journey from head to heart is effortless and flawless.

JUNE 21
Relinquish the Five-Napkin Burger Appetite

If it came from a plant, eat it;
if it was made in a plant, don't.
—Michael Pollan

When we're burning the candle at both ends or rushing against deadlines, many writers become stress eaters. To calm our stress, we eat what's convenient and appealing even if we're not hungry. We're more likely to reward ourselves with fattening, high-calorie meals such as fast foods, frozen dinners, and comfort items because they're quick and appealing. It can become such a habit we don't even realize we're doing it.

A well-nourished body has a stronger stress-resistance shield that protects us as we write and yields greater writer sustainability. We can dine on complex carbs and slowly digested high-fiber foods like whole grain breads, cereals, and pastas to stabilize blood sugar levels. Snacking on raw fruits, nuts, and vegetables gives us more energy over the long haul than cheese puffs and potato chips. Substituting high-fat meats with omega-3 fatty acids found in fish such as salmon and tuna prevent surges in stress hormones.

The key is to feed our writing soul instead of our physical body with nutritious eating habits and healthy munchies so it will become second nature to reach for the apple (which came from a plant) instead of the Danish (which was made in a plant).

Today's Takeaway

Fuel your creative appetite instead of your stress hunger, eat healthy food, and fuel the quality of your writing with high-test.

JUNE 22
Challenge Your Mind Traps

*Within each experience of pain or negativity
is the opportunity to challenge the perception
that lies behind it, the fear that lies behind it,
and choose to learn with wisdom.*

—Gary Zukav

All of us writers need a healthy dose of reality. But what happens when the cold hard facts of disappointment and failure continually overshadow the moments of happiness and victory? We get stuck in a mind trap of discounting the positives. We draw illogical conclusions and over-personalize negative writing situations. We downplay our accomplishments and positive qualities and dwell on the negatives: "Oh sure, I got a positive review from one critic, but the other reviewer raked me over the coals." This mind trap can keep us stuck in depression and anxiety and create an outlook of hopelessness.

The good news is that we can make our own silver linings. There's usually a "but" in a mind trap that can help us catch ourselves when we insist that positive aspects don't count as much as the negative ones. Once we are aware of our outlook, we can take the viewpoint of an outside observer, challenge the mind trap, and put the situation into better perspective. Think of a mind trap you've had about your writing ability then challenge it with an affirmation about the truth about your ability.

Today's Takeaway

Challenge your mind traps when disappointment seems to outweigh victory, then give victory equal weight to disappointment, and notice what happens inside.

JUNE 23
Conjure Conditions of Sustainable Creativity

Creating the culture of burnout is opposite to
creating a culture of sustainable creativity.
—Arianna Huffington

Burnout is creativity's poison, more serious than stress or fatigue. Once burnout takes hold we're out of gas. All hope of surmounting disappointment is gone. There's a deep sense of disillusionment and hopelessness that our writing efforts have been in vain. Writing loses its meaning, and small tasks feel like a hike up Mount Everest. Our interests and motivation to write dry up, and we fail to meet deadlines and obligations.

Fortunately, we can create writing sustainability so that our writing trajectories are longer and more productive over time. Once we acknowledge the problem, we can start to say no and practice self-care.

Successful writing and self-care work in tandem as twins, not enemies. As we develop confidence to persevere in reaching our writing goals, lead a healthy and balanced life, and hone our craft, we are on the road to writer sustainability. What actions can you take to create writer sustainability to prevent burnout in your life?

Today's Takeaway

Instead of drinking the poison of burnout, create a culture of sustainable creativity and think of drawing a line that protects you from burnout as a sign of strength, not weakness.

JUNE 24
Remain Sincere to Your Craft

*What are the qualities that cause a book to sell like
soap or breakfast food or Ford cars? It is a question
the answer to which we should all like to know.*

—Aldous Huxley

Some agents and editors want us to write popular knock-offs of what's selling, and they want it quickly. Where do we draw the line between commercializing our craft like a box of laundry detergent and remaining sincere to it?

Novelist Aldous Huxley winced at the idea of commercializing writing because he believed it shrinks the creative endeavor. He wrote, "All literature, all art, best seller or worst, must be sincere if it is to be successful." So the question for us writers becomes: What kind of writing appeals most to us? Fiction? Nonfiction? Commercial? Academic? Journalism?

Regardless of the path we take, most writers consider sincerity to be the cornerstone of success. A sincere writer cannot successfully be anything but true to herself or himself. We write what we know, what we're passionate about. We eschew copycat writing or deliberate forgery based on what's popular; however, if our sincere writing brings those material rewards, that's all the more satisfying. Contemplate on your sincerity to the craft of writing then note if there's anything that needs changing.

Today's Takeaway

Remain sincere to your craft and don't let commercial success compromise your integrity or your creative endeavors; consider it an added bonus.

JUNE 25
Quiet the Chorus in Your Head

What I've learned to do when I sit down to work on a
shitty first draft is to quiet the voices in my head.

—Anne Lamott

Many of us writers speak of kick-butt voices that put us under the micro-scope with a running commentary about how inept we are or how bad things will be. Much like the hard-ass drill sergeant trying to save his soldiers' lives, the critical voices—or *parts*, as we call them in psychol-ogy—point out our failures and judge our flaws to help us survive.

Writers have given these voices a bum rap. It can feel like the voices are working against us when, in fact, they're working hard to protect us from the threat of having our heads blown off in writing combat, to get us what they think we need for a good life.

I don't know about you, but I have a stadium of *parts* trying to pro-tect me from the slings and arrows of life. *Worry* warns me of a threat out there somewhere. *Judgment* tries to give me courage not to be ner-vous about an upcoming challenge. *Frustration* and *Anger* give me a good kick in the pants so I'll take a risk that I resisted. To quiet our minds, we learn to appreciate and accept the earnest intent of our inner voices and to refrain from fighting or resisting them. What are the loud-est voices in your head pertaining to writing? And what actions can you take to quiet them when they blare at you?

Today's Takeaway

Close your eyes and acknowledge and accept the chorus of voices in your head without fighting or resisting them; as you carefully listen, they will quiet down.

JUNE 26
Separate Your True Self from the Inner Chorus

*One day, to our astonishment, we will find that the True
Self for which we are searching is also searching for us.*

—Stephen Cope

Many writers refer to themselves in ways that reflect the messages people bestowed on them growing up. As we internalize the messages, they become *parts* of us, and we learn to define ourselves by the parts. We might call ourselves a worrywart, sad sack, or penny pincher.

Even if those traits describe us, they're only *parts* or aspects of us, not all of us. If I think of myself as a control freak, that identity eclipses the rest of me and limits all that I can become. If I think of myself as an angry person, my identity with the anger makes it's difficult for me to know the rest of who I am. "If we are not the voices in our heads, then who are we?" you might ask. We're the ones watching and listening to the voices in our heads: the True Self or Watcher.

Try this exercise. With the curiosity of a private detective, look inside and watch and listen to your inner voices as separate aspects of yourself. As you pay attention to who's listening and watching, you can feel a deeper connection to your True Self.

Today's Takeaway

Start to think of your *parts* as aspects of you, then as you separate from them, make room for the real you, know your True Self, and the sky is the limit to your writing success.

JUNE 27
Sway with Writing's Curveballs

*Convince yourself that you are working in clay,
not marble, on paper not eternal bronze: let
that first sentence be as stupid as it wishes.*

—Jacques Barzun

Tropical palms are sturdy trees. They survive because they're flexible enough to bend, swing, and sway with the force of the wind. Few of us writers have the fluidity of these wondrous trees, yet sometimes we are forced to swing and sway when the writing storms overpower us. Otherwise we would break.

It's our over-attachment to the outcomes of our writing careers that doom us. It's exhausting to force our rigid self-will against the giant writing world. When writing throws a curve, it's an opportunity to bend. Instead of resisting unwelcome outcomes, we can face them, find meaning and purpose, and learn from them—no matter how painful they are.

In the North Carolina mountains, we have a saying: "When treed by a bear, enjoy the view." Writers and philosophers have shared this wisdom for thousands of years: things change once we accept them *exactly* as they are, no matter how scary, frustrating, and heartbreaking. In the writing world, we have the choice of resisting and breaking or accepting and bending. What rigid habits can you break to write as if you're working with clay, not marble?

Today's Takeaway

Surrender to the unwanted writing circumstances over which you have no control, then decide what you can do to bend with the situation and make the best of it.

JUNE 28
Transcend the Past and Future Here and Now

*Odd that the future should be so difficult to
bring into focus when the past, uninvited,
offered itself up so easily for inspection.*
—Richard Russo

The business of writing can keep us up at night, thoughts going in many directions. When we get lost in past thoughts or future writing worries these out-of-the-moment episodes keep us disconnected from the present and become roadblocks to a peaceful mind.

Meditation takes us away from worrying about our writing being on the chopping block, bills piling up, or a relationship going down the toilet. It activates other areas of the brain that calm us down and leave us with a steady mind and calm heart.

Watching our thoughts, noticing where they go moment to moment, builds awareness of how often we leave our bodies. We can start to notice where our minds wander each moment of the day. As we notice them going off where we don't want them to, we gently bring them back into present time. When we transcend these mental events, we feel calmer, clearer, and more creative.

Today's Takeaway
In the next twenty-four hours, if you sense your mind drift to the past or future—even right now as you're reading—then gently bring it back and feel the tension lessen inside.

JUNE 29
Try a Round of Pilates

The Pilates Method of Body Conditioning
is gaining the mastery of your mind over
the complete control of your body.
—Joseph Pilates

Pilates is a system of strengthening and stretching exercises designed to develop the body's core, lengthen muscles, and raise body awareness. I grew an inch from 5'6" to 5'7" doing Pilates. Here's a Pilates position that can help stretch away your writing tightness.

On a mat, take the position lying on your back and bring your attention to your shoulder blades. Try to spread them out wide on your mat as if you're trying to flatten them to the floor. Easy now, you want a gentle stretch, not jerking or pulling. This position should make it feel like you're opening across your collarbone.

Gently slide your shoulder blades down toward your hips, away from your ears. Make sure you keep hip bones level. Now try to lengthen the back of your neck as if there's a string attached to the top of your head and someone is gently pulling on it. Lengthen your spine at the back of your neck, down between your shoulder blades, through the lower back all the way to your tailbone. You, too, might start to feel as if you've already grown an inch or two.

Today's Takeaway

Ask yourself how much time you devote to connecting with your body. If you're like many harried writers, your answer would be "not enough." If so, give Pilates a shot.

JUNE 30
Treat Failure as Your Best Friend

*Failure has been my best friend as a writer. It tests you
to see if you have what it takes to see it through.*

—Markus Zusak

How many of us have attended a signing to find an empty bookstore? Or checked the number of reviews on Amazon to discover there are only a handful? Or received a low total number of sales from our publisher on the first report? Perhaps we tell ourselves we've failed or beat ourselves up on the inside.

Failure is a frame of mind. When we call ourselves a failure, we start to feel, think, and behave like one. But as long as we're still trying and haven't quit, we haven't failed. We have failed only when we choose to put that label on ourselves.

The writer Neil Gaiman said, "Go and make mistakes, make amazing mistakes, make glorious and fantastic mistakes. Break the rules. Leave the world more interesting for you being here." We can redefine failure and permit ourselves to break the writing rules. Think of failure as your personal trainer. By raising the exercise bar, it gives you physical stamina and emotional resilience to face the next zinger the writing world throws.

Today's Takeaway

Refrain from labeling yourself as a "failure"; treat it as a best friend teaching you that you have what it takes to see things through, despite the hard knocks.

JULY

JULY 1
Celebrate Your Fought and Won Battles

Your battles inspired me—not the
obvious material battles but those that were
fought and won behind your forehead.
—James Joyce

How many battles have we fought and won inside ourselves that no one else knows about? What about the insecurities, self-doubts, inadequacies, and hopelessness that we've whipped? Too often we place more importance on winning the outside battles to determine our worth: the accolades, the awards, the reviews, and fat paychecks.

What about the inner battles we've won? Overcoming huge internal struggles, looking at a negative situation with fresh eyes, persevering through meteoric challenges, believing in ourselves when no one else did, and never letting go of our dreams?

We don't have to broadcast these victories to others, but it's important to recognize and acknowledge and applaud the writing battles we've fought and won within ourselves. When all is said and done, these are the most important of all. Meditate on the inside battles you've fought and won then give yourself the credit you deserve—high-fives, special treat, or a silent yes!

Today's Takeaway

Recognize the battles you have fought and won behind your forehead, then celebrate and inspire yourself with your victories.

JULY 2
Navigate "Facedown" Moments

Rising strong requires us to recognize that
we're experiencing a "facedown in the arena"
moment—an emotional reaction.
—Brené Brown

When we make ourselves vulnerable by putting our writing out for public scrutiny, we expose ourselves to potshots. After our manuscripts are shot down so many times, we can feel gun-shy. It can become more and more difficult to rebound and get back up.

All writers have facedown moments. When we're knocked down in the writing arena, the heartbreak slams the wind out of us. With our faces marred by dust and sweat and blood, we push ourselves up on our scabby knees, stagger to our feet, and summon the courage to try again.

Being able to struggle and overcome the hard times is just as valuable as having the courage to show up and be willing to face the challenge. We first realize the smackdown has activated our "lizard brain" and thrown our rational brain offline. We learn to give our emotions time to settle and our prefrontal cortex time to come back online before going straight to self-judgment: "I'm a miserable failure." Being brave and showing up is an admirable trait, but licking our wounds and getting back up after a writing smackdown is even more inspiring. How are you doing?

Today's Takeaway

Get through writing smackdowns by paying attention to your emotional struggling and navigating the hurt with self-compassion, then you'll rise up strong at your writing desk.

JULY 3
Discern When to Accept Criticism

Criticisms at the wrong time, even if its
legitimate criticism can be seriously damaging
and make the writer lose faith in what he's doing.
It's the timing that's all-important.
—Donna Tartt

We must be able to receive criticism in order to be good writers, but the timing of when we open ourselves to feedback is critical. Even if we want a second opinion, it can be disastrous having people tell us what to add, cut, or change before the piece is finished.

We may be eager to get an objective perspective of how we're doing—even if we know it's going to get us in trouble. But if we're premature in asking for constructive feedback on our writing, it can shut our creative juices down. We can lose heart and energy—even lose faith in the piece altogether.

Writing a creative story and editing it simultaneously requires the use of two competing sides of the brain and put our work on a collision course. This ill-timed strategy tends to bring in our critical thinking, which often leads to dry-well syndrome, sophomore slump, and writer's block. Sometimes the timing to receive criticism must be made from the heart instead of the head, and that requires patience and faith in our abilities. What have you learned about the best time and worst time for you to receive feedback on your writing? Are you able to stick with that knowledge?

Today's Takeaway

Discern the best time for you to receive constructive criticism about your work and don't let your impulsivity or someone else determine the timing for you.

JULY 4
Break Free from Second Zingers

Between stimulus and response there is a space. In that space is our power to choose our response. In our response lies our growth and our freedom.

—Viktor Frankl

Ever have an itch and the more you scratch it, the more it itches? Maybe you can't do anything about the itch, but you can do something about the scratch. When a bad writing outcome zings us and we react with frustration, we add insult to injury and make the suffering worse. A negative writing event is the first zinger, and our frustration is the second zinger—the one with which we impale ourselves. The first zinger is unpleasant for sure, but sometimes the real distress comes from our second-zinger reactions.

When we notice ourselves in an unpleasant emotional state—such as worry, anger, frustration—we can hold it at arm's length and observe it impartially as a separate part. Think of it much as we might notice and consider a blemish on our hand, then get curious about where it came from. Instead of pushing away the unpleasant feeling, ignoring it, or steamrolling over it, the key is to acknowledge it with something like, "Hello frustration, I see you're active today."

This simple recognition gets second zingers to relax and calm down so we can face the real roadblock—the first zinger—with more clarity and ease.

Today's Takeaway
Welcome, observe, and befriend stressors that pop up in your writing life with curiosity instead of judgment until discomfort subsides.

JULY 5
Unchain Yourself from the Desk

They intoxicate themselves with work so
they won't see how they really are.

—Aldous Huxley

Every year July fifth marks National Workaholics Day—dedicated to workers chained to their desks. You know the ones (maybe you're one). They start early, skip lunch, and stay late writing around the clock. Work takes top priority over everything else in life: family relationships, play, important social events, and self-care.

How many scribes among us use writing as an escape at the expense of a healthy work-life balance? If that sounds like you, today is a time to step back and take it easy. Consider taking an afternoon nap, read a book for fun, or spend some time watching videos on YouTube. Your writing will be waiting for you at your computer tomorrow.

For those of us who aren't workaholics, today is an opportunity to celebrate the workaholics in our lives and recognize all they have accomplished. To celebrate National Workaholics Day, we can arrive at our writing stations a little earlier than usual and tackle the writing project we've been avoiding. Which side of the coin are you on?

Today's Takeaway

If you're a workaholic, ask what you're using your writing to escape from; if you're not a workaholic, ask if you've avoided working on a writing project that needs your attention.

JULY 6
Kick More Butt and Take More Names

Assertiveness is not what you do, it's who you are!
—Shakti Gawain

Many of us say yes when we'd like to say no. We agree with other people when we actually disagree. Or we go along with the tastes of others without asserting our preferences.

When we put our preferences behind others, our needs rarely get met. Reluctance to disagree or say no comes from fear of rejection. But the fear of rejection— allowing others to thrust their needs and rights upon us—causes us to reject ourselves. When we learn to speak up, the self-acceptance far outweighs the loss from rejection. Those around us might reel from our assertions, but we don't have to let their discomfort cause us to back down.

Being assertive means relating to others on an equal basis and keeping our self-respect while opening ourselves to other opinions. We can surrender our combative attitudes without submitting to domination or mistreatment—yielding sometimes, holding our ground other times. Part of taking back our lives is letting go of other people's opinions and living our lives to suit our own requirements. Contemplate where you are on the spectrum between yielding and holding your ground, then ask yourself if you need to move the needle in one direction.

Today's Takeaway

Assert your beliefs and desires and you will find that you like yourself and your writing better and others do, too, because this is who you genuinely are.

JULY 7
Let the World Know You as You Are

*You can keep running and hiding and blaming the
world for your problems, or you can stand up for
yourself and decide to be somebody important.*
—Sidney Sheldon

Being who we are is one of the biggest challenges we face. There are costs to being strong and remaining true to ourselves. Some people call us names, disagree and challenge us, or get upset with our perspectives. But in the end the benefits outweigh the costs. We remain consistent with who we are and the self-satisfaction feels good as we live with ourselves inside our skin.

The writer/activist/lawyer, Bella Abzug said, "I've been described as a tough and noisy woman, a prizefighter, a man-hater, you name it. They call me Battling Bella, Mother Courage, and a Jewish mother with more complaints than Portnoy."

We can be sassy and tough or anything else we wish. We can speak our mind and stand our ground. If we modify ourselves to suit everyone else, we soon whittle ourselves away. And ultimately, the truth will out us. Here's a challenge. If you could be an action hero, who would it be? What would your outfit look like? What special powers that you already possess would you use to perform good deeds?

Today's Takeaway
Let the world see you as you are and give yourself permission to be sassy and tough or anything else that is truly you.

JULY 8
Set Lifelines Instead of Deadlines

I love deadlines. I love the whooshing
noise they make as they go by.
—Douglas Adams

Think about it. There's a reason why we call them deadlines. Sometimes we set the bar so high it's as if we require ourselves to change tires going eighty miles an hour. Out-of-reach deadlines can be toxic. They can make us sick, debilitate us—even kill us. And if we're dead, we can't write.

So let's consider lifelines that, paradoxically, make us more productive and effective in our writing. When we set lifelines, we don't over-schedule ourselves, we slow down, and we put time cushions between writing tasks. Time cushions give us time to breathe, eat a snack, go to the bathroom, or just look out the window.

When we have lifelines instead of deadlines, we are less likely to hear that whooshing sound as deadlines go by or feel the sick feeling in the pit of our stomachs for "always" being behind. Our literary days become less hurried and harried, and we enjoy the writing process more. What about you? Do you hear that whooshing sound? Or not?

Today's Takeaway

Consider setting lifelines with writing projects by slowing down and scheduling time cushions between tasks so that your writing life is more creative, fun, and productive.

JULY 9
Humble Yourself as a Writer

Humility is not thinking less of yourself;
it's thinking of yourself less.
—C. S. Lewis

Humility as a writer is a valuable asset. We put ourselves on a level plane with fellow writers by admitting we have the same human fallibilities as everyone else. We don't put ourselves down or devalue ourselves in any way. But we don't glorify our accomplishments to impress or compete with fellow writers for status, either. We're not preoccupied with ourselves and, in fact, we highlight the successes of other authors, even our "competitors."

There's something terribly expansive and satisfying when we put humility over pride. Close your eyes and contemplate the idea that you're a grain of sand in the universe. Then spend a few minutes noticing all the space, all the room that you have to expand. Whisper to yourself that you don't stand in the way of anything, you don't overcrowd, and you don't possess or obstruct anything. Take a few minutes to savor the feelings that emerge.

The irony is that humility attracts readers to our work. Self-aggrandizement turns them away. It's simply a matter of thinking of ourselves less and others more. As writers we don't have to grandstand our virtues. When deserved, our readers will do that for us.

Today's Takeaway

Humble yourself with the writing community and fans, and it will contribute to your overall success and fulfillment as a writer.

JULY 10
Protect Your Flame of Inspiration

The flame of inspiration needs to be encouraged.
Put a glass around that small candle and protect
it from discouragement or ridicule.
—Mary Higgins Clark

"What is an antagonist?" I asked myself many moons ago when I read a book on writing. Okay, go ahead and laugh. When I started writing, people made fun of my naïve questions and the short stories I penned as a child. They laughed at me, and they might laugh at you. Perhaps they already have. But remember this: they laughed at Thomas Edison and Janis Joplin. Many of the greats have been ridiculed for their early creative ambitions. I'm no Edison or Joplin, but I refused to allow discouragement to smother my inspiration flame and persevered. And you can, too.

The novelist James A. Michener said, "I know so many people who want to be writers. They wish they had a book in print. They don't want to go through the work of getting the damn book out." Never be afraid to ask questions, no matter how dumb they seem. Never belittle yourself or allow others to mock you as you learn the tricks of the trade. For unlike those laughing, you already have started the hard work of getting the damn book out! Name as many things as you can do to protect your flame of inspiration—such as caution who you let read your unfinished work. That's for starters. Now what else?

Today's Takeaway

Protect your flame of inspiration from discouragement and ridicule so that it can burn bright on your way to writing success.

JULY 11
Start from Wherever You Are

It doesn't matter if it takes a long time getting
there; the point is to have a destination.
—Eudora Welty

There are many starting points on our journeys as writers, and there's no designated starting line. Each of us begins at a different place—some in childhood, some as young students, and others in adulthood. It might take a while for us to get to our destination. We cannot snap our fingers and be somewhere we're not. As long as we have the love for writing and the destination of honing our craft, we can allow ourselves to be where we work best on the writing path. This pays off in droves.

Let's ask where we are starting from. Wherever that is, are we able to accept it? Or do we compare ourselves to others and whisper inside that we should be farther along? We need to ask what would happen if we were to contemplate accepting where we are: beginner, intermediate, or advanced.

Is it possible for you to be nowhere else on the path other than where you are? Starting now, what do you need to do to gain that acceptance? Take a minute to close your eyes and go within. Imagine accepting exactly where you are on your writing path with openheartedness and gratitude. After spending a few minutes in this exercise, notice what happens.

Today's Takeaway

Start writing wherever you are, accept your starting point, and never be ashamed or allow others to shame you for the starting line on which you're standing.

JULY 12
Get It Wrong as Much as You Like

You're allowed to get it wrong, as many times as you
need to; you only need to get it right once.
—Tana French

When driving through the Great Smoky Mountains, tourists encounter many unlit tunnels that cut through the mountains. Although dark inside, the tunnels always bring passengers into the light on the other side. Sometimes the writing journey can take us through dark passages as well. It can be frustrating, perhaps even a bit scary, when we feel lost from one sentence to the next.

When in the dark, the best action is to remember that the darkness is not final or fatal, that it can be a rewarding part of the process. Instead of fighting the dark, accept it, relax into it, and keep hammering away at a sentence or paragraph, giving yourself permission to get it wrong as often as necessary.

Here's the irony: giving ourselves permission to take wrong turns and get lost on our writing journey relaxes the critic and opens the floodgate to creativity. Once we have comfort in the darkness and trust the process, just as passing through a tunnel, it brings us into the light on the other side.

Today's Takeaway

Give yourself permission to make as many wrong turns as needed on your writing journey; keep plugging away in the dark without frustration or discouragement, and eventually you will end up where you want to be.

JULY 13
Grab the Handle of Hope

*Every problem has two handles. You can grab it
by the handle of fear or the handle of hope.*

—Margaret Mitchell

As we grow our craft of writing, we can also mature in the way we look at lost challenges. The writing and publishing worlds are under no obligation to give us what we expect, so holding our expectations at arm's length is one way to grab the handle of hope. The second grab is to learn that real blessings for writers often appear in the shape of pains, losses, and disappointments.

As we grow, we have the power to change our mental outlooks and see more gains than losses, more hope than despair. We learn to see blessings and constructive outcomes even in loss and disappointment. The key to a happy and hopeful writing trajectory is to change what we're looking for. We have a choice. We don't have to let little things become overblown and overwhelm us.

We can separate big concerns from small ones and focus on what matters. This small grain of knowledge—that each of us has the power to choose our outlook—can empower us to change our whole writing existence from hopelessness to hopefulness. What fresh new perspective can you bring to your writing that will help you soar?

Today's Takeaway

Persist in the face of opposition and bring different perspectives of hope and optimism to writing challenges until a path is cleared for you.

JULY 14
Dispense with Playing Small

*Your playing small does not serve the world. There
is nothing enlightened about shrinking so that
other people won't feel insecure around you.*
—Marianne Williamson

Some of us are not always aware that we go about our days shrinking ourselves so others feel tall. Perhaps we are more comfortable living small instead of large because we don't want others to feel insecure around us. We spend our days collecting evidence of our self-worth like butterflies in a net. At the end of the day, we sort and classify our collection of negative comments, defeats, and mistakes.

Had we aimed our net in another direction, we might have illuminated the blind spots and netted a collection of compliments, successes, and joys. We can ask ourselves what kinds of evidence about ourselves are we collecting today and if we need to look in another direction.

Contemplate what kinds of specimens you collect in your net. Flaws and mistakes? Or successes and compliments? Then scrutinize for blind spots where you shrink-wrapped yourself and ask if you need to aim your net in a different direction.

Today's Takeaway

Avoid playing small with yourself or others, watch out for blind spots, and wear your writing accomplishments as a badge of honor.

JULY 15
Loosen Your Stress Triangle

Exercises are like prose, whereas yoga is the poetry of movements. Once you understand the grammar of yoga, you can write your poetry of movements.

—Amit Ray

The most common area of the body where writers hold stress is in the stress triangle, the top of our shoulders and back of the neck. During writing jags, our shoulders lift up toward our ears in a shrug. If you notice this unconscious habit, as I often do, you can try the following stretch at your writing desk.

- Sitting or standing, lower your right ear to your right shoulder. Hold for ten seconds.

- Continue by reaching your left arm away from your body. Hold for ten seconds.

- Then reach your right arm to the left side of your forehead and gently pull the stretch a little further. Hold for the final thirty seconds.

- Release everything slowly in the reverse order and repeat on your left side.

Today's Takeaway

Your stress triangle is just one area of the body that carries writing stress. Take an inventory of the rest of your body and use gentle stretching movements that bring you relief.

JULY 16
Hold Animosity at a Cattle Prod's Distance

Life appears to me too short to be spent in
nursing animosity, or registering wrongs.
—Charlotte Brontë

In case you haven't noticed, our writing journeys provide plenty of opportunities to register wrongs and nurse animosity. Chances are we have lots to be resentful about—from the way others treat us to our own reactions to that treatment—but what we do with animosity is the key. If we nurse it, it poisons us and interferes with the energy and creativity required for writing. It clouds our thinking and keeps our thoughts stuck on the negative.

Writing doesn't come with a lifetime guarantee. Animosity can suck the life energy out of us. Or we can use that energy for a higher purpose. In the words of author J. K. Rowling, "We've all got both light and dark inside us. What matters is the part we choose to act on. That's who we really are."

We can stay a cattle prod's distance from animosity, refuse to let it dominate the front lines of our writing lives, and maturely express our feelings and views. Ask yourself if you harbor any animosity and if so, how it has served you. Then reflect on the possibility of harnessing that energy for a higher purpose to take you farther in your writing.

Today's Takeaway

Take an inventory of how you might be nursing animosity then note some mature ways of dealing with it in order to keep your writing path clear of obstacles.

JULY 17
Prospect with the Three P's

*Patience, persistence, and perspiration make
an unbeatable combination for success.*
—Napoleon Hill

Prospectors are explorers, usually sifting through mineral deposits, panning for gold. Writers are somewhat like prospectors, panning for writing success, sifting through rejection after rejection. Our pens and keypads serve as pickaxes and shovels. To stake our claim, we show up at the mine and sift through endless wrong turns and setbacks if we want to strike pay dirt. After all the hard work, some of us never do.

The three P's are the best mental preparation for prospecting: patience, persistence, and perspiration. Prospectors expect the probability of coming up empty-handed, refusing to give up when they pull back an empty pan. If we give up, we close down and can't move forward, eliminating future possibilities. The three P's equip us with the prospect of a disappointing outcome so we're not crestfallen when we come up empty-handed.

Those of us who want to be good writers have the three P's at our disposal and within our reach. All we have to do is look inside and utilize them, keep panning through the sediment, and hold the vision before us until we hit pay dirt. Let's ask, "Which of my three P's is the strongest? Weakest? And which ones can I sharpen?"

Today's Takeaway

Prospect with the three P's, and you won't be sidelined with setbacks and rejections; keep sifting and use them as maps to help you strike golden writing opportunities.

JULY 18
Stick Out Like a Rusty Nail

Perseverance ... keeps honor bright: to have
done, is to hang quite out of fashion, like a
rusty nail in monumental mockery.
—Shakespeare

To be successful, all writers need their tough and soft sides. As author James Patterson reveals: "Am I tough? Am I hard-core? Absolutely. Did I whimper with pathetic delight when I sank my teeth into my hot fried-chicken sandwich? You betcha."

Many writers begin with their softer sides—their love for writing. But as we progress into rougher seas, we must summon our tough sides, not our whimpers. Hard publishing knocks are not personal vendettas; they come with the territory. When unrealized expectations knock us down, it's easy to get mired in frustration and hopelessness and walk away from our dreams. But no one can steal our fierce determination without our consent.

When we stick out like a rusty nail, we valiantly meet obstacles with the same force they bring to us. We don't crumble, and we don't slither silently away into the dark. We grow thicker skin by standing our ground, holding our heads up, and exploring other avenues for writing success.

Today's Takeaway

Grow thicker skin in the face of disappointments and rejections, and you'll be around for quite a while sticking out like a rusty nail.

JULY 19
Renew Your Hope Each Day

*Hope is a renewable option: If you run out of it at the
end of the day, you get to start over in the morning.*
—Barbara Kingsolver

Have you lost hope so many times that you feel like you have no more
left? If so, you're not alone. It happens to many writers. Believe me,
there will be times when hopelessness takes over, blends with us, and
becomes us. It's okay, perhaps even essential, to welcome hopelessness
and set a place at the table for it.

The best approach is to welcome it in, ask it to pull up a chair, and
have a cup of tea. Look it in the face and get to know it. Then ask yourself who invited hopelessness in. And you will see that you're not mired
in hopelessness and that it's separate from you—nothing more than a
part of you that comes and goes from time to time.

Just because hopelessness is visiting doesn't mean it has to move in.
After tea, we can wish it safe travels and usher it on its way. As it leaves,
we feel renewed as hope takes its place. Next time hopelessness visits
you, go within and acknowledge it. Welcome it at your table, and ask it
to pull up a chair. Without trying to convert it, talk to it and get to know
it then watch what happens.

Today's Takeaway
Remember that just because things feel hopeless doesn't mean they are;
hope is a renewable commodity that is accessible to us at all times, each
moment, each day.

JULY 20
Stretch Yourself

Courage is not the absence of fear but the ability
to carry on with dignity in spite of it.
—Scott Turow

One of the greatest emotional risks writers must take is stepping into the unknown. The writing path is filled with one uncertainty after another. The best antidote to emotional risk-taking is called *stretching*—taking a different action than we would normally take, such as feeling fear and jumping in anyway. The stretch takes a certain amount of courage, but it also takes us to a completely different—usually better—place.

Facing the pleasure and avoiding pain is an easy one for most of us. But to be successful writers, we must also let ourselves stretch into the unfamiliar, the unknown, the unpredictable. If we're afraid, we must go ahead anyway instead of recoiling from fear. The ability to stretch and face *everything* in the writing world, without judging it as *scary* or *safe*, builds courage and joy.

Stretching into unpredictable situations strengthens our emotional beliefs in ourselves as well as enriches our creative juices and writing. The paradox is the more we accept fear and safety equally, the more strength we have to face hurdles. In your writing, how willing are you to stretch yourself, surprise yourself—even to embarrass yourself to hone your craft?

Today's Takeaway

Stretch into some aspect of your writing—perhaps something you've avoided or been afraid to face—that can carry you forward with dignity in spite of the fear.

JULY 21
Gauge Your Writing Resilience Needle

I used to ask for an easy life, now I ask to be strong.
—William Kent Krueger

How resilient are you in your writing goals? Are you able to face opposition with a positive attitude and physical stamina? Can you keep going no matter how frequent and difficult the obstacles? If you could gauge your resilience needle, where would it fall?

One way to check your resilient zone is to see where the needle falls on a 10-point scale. You can rate yourself from 0 to 3 (low resilience), 4 to 7 (moderate resilience), 8 to 10 (the highest resilience you can imagine). If it's lower than you want, write down some actions you can take to tilt it higher, such as thinking more positive thoughts, carving out more time to write, or joining a writing class.

Over time, our resilience needle rises and falls depending on our writing conditions. Mapping that progression gives us a clearer measure of the conditions under which we are most and least resilient. It helps us to see where we are currently, compared to other times in our writing trajectory and where we want to be. In discouraging times when the needle is low, we can use that understanding to get back in our resilient zone. What about now? Where does your writing resilience needle fall? Contemplate actions you can take to tilt the needle higher on the scale.

Today's Takeaway

Reflect on the writing obstacles you've overcome, point to the lessons you've learned, and gauge the ways in which you have grown stronger through writing's hard knocks.

JULY 22
Listen to the Sounds of Silence

Learn to listen to silence. Listen to the world around you.
And the silence will sing you a beautiful song.
—Melody Beattie

The sounds of silence are often ones many of us never get to hear. We might have a radio, TV, or iPod blasting, the vacuum cleaner roaring, or an iPhone and computer whirring and dinging. The dog is barking, the children are arguing. Everyday stuff can muffle life's healing sounds around us: a chorus of crickets, tweeting birds, the drip of water, or the rush of wind through leaves of trees.

If we were to turn off the mechanical objects around us and listen to what's there, we would discover another world of sounds that we often don't hear. Silence stirs our creative juices and gives our ideas time to hatch. We can find peace and serenity as the silence sings its beautiful song and replenishes our spirit with nature's music.

It is here that we find a stillness and sanctuary to which we can retreat anytime. As we reflect on the quiet, answers to writing blocks and solutions to literary problems bubble up automatically. Give it a shot and meditate on what you learn from the experiment.

Today's Takeaway

Welcome the sounds of silence, listen with curiosity, and discover another auditory world that refreshes, relaxes, and recharges and fertilizes the growth of your writing.

JULY 23
Practice Mindful Awareness

*We do not believe in ourselves until someone reveals that
deep inside us something is valuable, worth listening to,
worthy of our trust, sacred to our touch.*

—e. e. cummings

When we fail at a writing task, make a mistake, or experience a loss or letdown, how many of us kick ourselves while we're down? The way we treat ourselves inside when things fall apart determines the intensity of our suffering.

If we pay attention to our feelings with curiosity and loving-kindness, we may still feel hurt or pain. But if we pay attention with judgment and criticism ("I'm a lousy writer"), the hurt or pain is magnified. The latter is an example of being aware while the former is an example of being *mindfully aware.*

The ability to experience writing's hardships with impartiality and openhearted kindness keeps us in mindful awareness, allows us to feel appropriate feelings, and reduces the intensity of the loss. This mindful awareness is a form of self-relationship, an internal form of self-attunement that creates states of mental wellbeing and medical health. How are you doing? Go inside and see if you can find that *something* that is valuable and worth listening to, worthy of your trust, and sacred to your touch.

Today's Takeaway

When you're down and out, love, affirm, and respect yourself; enjoy your own company, be your own best friend, and do for yourself what you would do for those you love most.

JULY 24
Tell Yourself You're a Rewriter

Books aren't written—they're rewritten. Including your own. It is one of the hardest things to accept, especially after the seventh rewrite hasn't quite done it.
—Michael Crichton

One of the biggest misunderstandings of aspiring scribes is that rewrite after rewrite is usually necessary before we have a finished product. For some writers, the road to hell is paved with rewriting and stagnating hours of agony. The need for rewriting often makes new writers think they're not up to the challenge, but that's usually untrue.

In order to be good writers, we must be good rewriters. The willingness to write and rewrite is often the mark of a great writer. So don't feel inadequate if you're displeased with what you write. That's actually a good and necessary thing. After you have a draft, plan to spend three to four weeks away from the manuscript. You'll be amazed to see what needs revising when you return. Your fresh new look will give your work the kind of bird's-eye view that readers might have.

Next time you find yourself rewriting for the umpteenth time, don't get too discouraged. Remind yourself that you're doing exactly what all great writers have done. Writing isn't a one-shot deal, because books aren't simply written; they're rewritten.

Today's Takeaway

Think of yourself as a rewriter instead of a writer; know that's what it takes to pen successful literature, and you won't feel so discouraged when it's time to rewrite.

JULY 25
Exercise Your Writing Worth

*You don't get to choose how you're going to die, or
when. You can only decide how you're going to live. Now.*

—Joan Baez

Ask yourself what you think of your writing worth. Are you making free choices when it comes to your writing life? Or do you feel like a prisoner of publishers and critics? Are you condemned to unhappiness because of the hand the publishing world has dealt you? If you discover that your life conditions are controlling your writing worth instead of you controlling it, you might feel as though you're in an emotional prison.

Although we writers have the power to choose our writing worth, we frequently and unwittingly give that authority away. We allow negative circumstances to dictate our thoughts, feelings, and actions surrounding a rejection or failure.

Sometimes we forget that no matter the outcome of our submissions, we always have the freedom to choose how we deal with it. The power of choice is within all of us. When you exercise your conscious choice, it increases your value. Your writing worth is more important than wealth. The more you spend it, the more you gain. Name one conscious choice you can take in your writing life to raise your worth.

Today's Takeaway

Notice the choices you make (or don't make) about your writing worth, and don't let the writing world dictate your wellbeing as an author.

JULY 26
Forget About How Much the Fall Will Hurt

*If you put your energy into thinking about how much
the fall would hurt, you're already halfway down.*

—Tana French

Sometimes it's the voice in our mind's echo chamber that tells us we're defeated before we even begin. When we let that voice take over, we're already halfway down, and we haven't even started the journey.

Next time a discouraging voice blinks in our mind like a neon sign, we can listen to it as a separate part of ourselves. Listening to our mind's echo chamber with impartiality gives us distance and keeps us from attacking ourselves. This kind of detachment helps us notice an ease in seeing what's there—it's merely the mind's chatter, nothing more.

This conscious separation from the mind's activity alleviates suffering and helps us become more self-attuned in gentler and kinder ways. And ultimately, this mindful approach aids in us becoming better writers. Take a few minutes now and listen to your mind's chatter with curiosity and without judgment. Try listening with the detachment of an outsider and see if you can organically feel the unblending of the chatter from yourself followed by an ease inside.

Today's Takeaway

With an open heart and mind, listen to your mind's harsh chatter with healthy detachment that keeps you from believing it, taking it personally, or avoiding a writing challenge.

JULY 27
Remove Your Blinders

Where we go depends on what we know,
and what we know depends on where we go.

—Tess Gerritsen

Many of us enter the writing world like a horse wearing blinders, and we focus straight ahead, setting our sights on the future, perhaps jumping at the first offer handed to us. Rushing forward, we can miss some very important considerations along the way. In the words of novelist Tess Gerritsen, "The heart makes its choices without weighing the consequences."

It's possible to keep our sights on future consequences *and* consider all options before jumping at the first opportunity that comes along. Removing our blinders, we can pause to weigh critical outcomes we might ordinarily miss. We owe it to ourselves to remain fully awake and aware on our writing journeys, weighing our options and their consequences before making hasty decisions.

We can ask ourselves where are our blind spots. What or who have we overlooked? What blinders do you need to remove before making further decisions about your writing?

Today's Takeaway

Remove your blinders, pause to notice potential blind spots, and arm yourself with information that will allow you to weigh your options openly and fully from every angle.

JULY 28
Realize One Is a Whole Number

*All my life I've thought I needed someone to complete
me. Now I know I need to belong to myself.*
—Sue Monk Kidd

There's no greater pain than feeling ill at ease in our own skin, believing we need another human to make us complete, searching outside for someone to make us whole. Novelist Sue Monk Kidd isn't the only author who has said this. Other writers look for someone or something to belong to—to complete them. When we feel broken and pin our hopes on another person, it binds us to them in such a way that keeps us from making decisions in our own best interests, an impediment to our literary success.

One is a whole number. Each of us is already complete exactly as we are. Although we need love and support, we don't have to lose ourselves in other people. We are all works-in-progress, but nothing and no one outside of ourselves can complete us. That's our job.

We have our own separate thoughts, feelings, and actions—and they matter. It's important to keep them separate, value them, and complete ourselves with self-love first, giving ourselves the same respect we give to others. What are some actions you can take today to underscore that you belong to yourself?

Today's Takeaway

Celebrate your wholeness, remembering you're whole exactly as you are and don't need another person or writing project to complete you; you only need *you* to complete you.

JULY 29
Sacrifice for Your Higher Purpose

*What do you want? What are you willing to give
up to get it? Writing requires you make sacrifices.
Be prepared to work hard to be a writer.*

—Sandra Brown

Sandra Brown hit the nail on the head. Not only must we be willing to work hard to become writers, we must be willing to sacrifice to get there. That doesn't make "sacrifice" a dirty word. It doesn't mean we have to live miserable, poverty-stricken lives to get what we want. It means we must be willing to devote, commit, and dedicate our time to writing: daily.

To sacrifice is to give up something for a higher purpose. If writing is truly a higher purpose, we must make it a priority above everything else. It requires that we move other desires, goals, events, perhaps even relationships, below our higher purpose.

How many of us are prepared to make the necessary sacrifice to make writing a successful vocation? What are some experiences you love that you're willing to forgo to pursue your love for writing. Hanging out with the gang? A hobby? A relationship? Alone time?

Today's Takeaway

Plan on sacrificing something you really love and enjoy for the sake of a better cause or higher purpose: your deep love of writing.

JULY 30
Promote Yourself to Boss or Hire One

I have a rigid self-accountability. You have to work hard.
—Elizabeth Gilbert

No matter how devoted we are to writing, there are times when we don't feel like penning words, and that unfinished manuscript stretches before us like a hike up Mount Everest. When no one is breathing down our necks to get it done, it's easy to vacuum the house, text a friend, listen to music on our iPod, or pay bills.

The best way to get on with it is to be accountable to ourselves. If that doesn't work, we can find someone to hold us accountable and prompt us to complete that manuscript: a writing class, an editor, an agent, or a close friend.

For those among us who are self-accountable, it's helpful to break down the writing into small concrete goals that we can work toward— smaller targets that give us immediate payoffs. Upon completion of each small goal, we give ourselves a well-deserved reward.

For those of us who find it hard to be our own boss and continue putting off our writing, we might need to fire ourselves and get another boss. Being accountable to someone other than ourselves often helps us reach our writing goals.

Today's Takeaway
Be your own boss in order to reach your writing goals, or fire yourself and hire someone who will hold your feet to the fire in order to get your manuscript completed.

JULY 31
Write Today

A writer is someone who has written today. If you want to be a writer, ask yourself if you've written today. That's the first mark of a true writer.

—J. A. Jance

The first mark of a true writer is that we have to write today and every day, not for glory or money but because we have ink in our blood and can't not write. We love it so much that we're drawn to it. Novelist Sara Gruen said, "The only thing that makes me crazier than writing is not writing." What is the first mark of the writer's life? The simple answer: we write today.

If we don't have natural fire in our fingertips, we might be able to cultivate it by getting into the habit of writing each day, even if it's only for fifteen or twenty minutes, even if we don't have a specific project in mind. After a while, the discipline of everyday writing grows on us, even if you don't have ink in your blood.

Have you written today? If not, why not take time right now to pen a few words just for a short amount of time, and watch what happens. Every time you take an opportunity to write during your spare time, you prove to yourself that you're indeed a writer. Have you written today? Will you write today?

Today's Takeaway

If you want to be a writer, ask yourself if you've written today, and if you haven't, sit down and write; you'll have fulfilled your dream.

AUGUST

AUGUST 1
Enjoy the Ride In-Between

It's not the beginning or the destination
that counts. It's the ride in between.
—David Baldacci

Every writer I know has had a setback or two, but it's not the setback as much as what we do afterward that matters. Studies show when we condemn ourselves after a setback, it's more difficult to bounce back, and anxiety and depression undermine our capacity to write. Pep talks and positive self-talk after a setback help us get back in the saddle and enjoy the ride.

Sometimes not seeing the light at the end of the tunnel can be the bliss of getting to it. When we're feeling frustrated and hopeless, floundering with uncertainty in our writing, we can remind ourselves that we're "in the meantime"—that place in-between where there's no land in sight in front or behind. But land is still there. All we do in that moment is keep plugging away until we reach our destination.

The next time you have a setback, get comfortable with being "in the meantime." Relax, be kind and gentle with yourself instead of attacking yourself, and the setback will be a more enjoyable and successful ride.

Today's Takeaway

Next time you have a writing setback, be compassionate with yourself and remember you're having the ride in-between that all writers have and nothing more.

AUGUST 2
Quit Looking for Approval

I've never had anyone's approval,
so I've learned to live without it.

—Pat Conroy

Approval was a privilege novelist Pat Conroy never got in his boyhood, so he learned not to seek it. That strategy turned out to be a curse as a child but a blessing as an author. Unlike Conroy, many of us seek approval for our writing efforts as a gauge for how well we've mastered the craft. We seek the approval of agents, editors, critics, and writing buddies for the encouragement to continue. Are we good enough? Will others want to read our work? Can we be successful?

Seasoned writers learn to live without approval of their literary work. The sage advice of author Sue Grafton addresses this point: "Learn to evaluate your own work with a dispassionate eye. The lessons you acquire will be all the more valuable because you've mastered your craft from within."

The more successful writers become, the more negative scrutiny follows them. With so many mixed messages from reviewers and fans, it becomes difficult to maintain an objective perspective. Whether we attain the level of success of Conroy or Grafton, the goal is to write without approval and to evaluate the merits of our own work. It grows us as masters of our craft. Take time now to reflect on how you're doing in this regard. Are you comfortable evaluating the merits of your own writing? If not, what actions can you take to master your craft from within?

Today's Takeaway

Stop relying on approval from outside sources and learn to master your craft from within by evaluating the merits of your writing with a dispassionate eye.

AUGUST 3
Resist Nothing

Everything happens for you, not to you.
Everything happens at exactly the right
moment, neither too soon nor too late. You
don't have to like it ... it's just easier if you do.

—Byron Katie

No writer with a sound mind would leap off a ledge into the Grand Canyon because we obey the law of gravity. Yet we leap off the cliff of our writing lives moment-to-moment by resisting, forcing, and clinging to the way we want our work to be received instead of letting life happen on its terms.

One of our greatest difficulties is the expectation that our literary path should lead in a certain direction. Another is the mental resistance that arises because of our underlying assumptions that they shouldn't. Here is the bitter pill to swallow: the more we *resist* painful writing consequences—letdown, rejection, disappointment—the more heartbreaking they become. The more we *accept* disappointing outcomes, the less pain and suffering.

Complete acceptance of a difficult situation simultaneously lets it go. When bad things happen, we can remember that everything happens *for* us, not *to* us. Then we can nail down what the *for* is. Recall a writing disappointment and contemplate how in retrospect it might've happened *for* you instead of *to* you and notice the difference inside.

Today's Takeaway

With an open heart, have the courage to let things happen *for* you; then after a big loss, wait patiently, look for the blessings, and they will come. That's a promise.

AUGUST 4
Outlast the Blank Page

*It doesn't matter how many words you wrote the
day before … every day you start fresh again with the
same blank page, or that same blank screen.*
—Lincoln Child

We sit in front of blank paper or a blank screen. It can be either terrifying or exhilarating, and there's a fine line between the two. While there is no consensus among writers about mindset, no one doubts that the blank page is hard work. Some authors say it never gets easier, no matter how accomplished you are as a writer. Others say sitting down in front of a blank screen or page is bliss.

What mindset do you bring to the blank page? Dread or delight? A perspective of dread brings closed energy to our craft. Dread is a form of resistance that activates the stress response and can interfere with creative ideas, sometimes leading to "blank page syndrome." Delight brings open energy to the page—a form of curiosity which activates the rest and digest response and opens the floodgates for creativity.

Today's Takeaway

The next time before you face a blank page or screen, meditate on bringing excitement, curiosity, or delight to the experience. This open mindset will encourage your creative juices to flow freely.

AUGUST 5
Shun "Wannabe Writer Syndrome"

I was far too self-absorbed, and now I realize I was writing
for others, so that they'd applaud me, see my genius, tell
me how wonderful I am, or be jealous of my success.

—Louise Penny

I don't have enough fingers on both hands to count the number of times I've been cornered by a wannabe writer at a social gathering. "Someday I'm gonna write a book," they say, "I've got a story for a great novel." They just know Hollywood will break their door down to film it—one both they *and* I know will never see the light of day because one day isn't a day of the week.

Swept up in the glamour of what they imagine it would be like to have a published book, wannabes have no clue about the gritty and grimy work, time, and sacrifice it entails. So don't become a writer if you're looking for fame, money, and approval. On the other hand, if you like to dig ditches, you'll love writing.

The most successful writers are those who get a satisfying payoff simply from their love of writing. The inner fulfillment dwarfs all else: the material trappings of money and fame, the sweaty work, sacrifices, and disappointments. So make sure you research the ins-and-outs of writing *before* the fantasy carries you away into "wannabe land." And if you're already there, ask yourself if you're writing for the right reasons or if there's something you need to change.

Today's Takeaway

Shun being a wannabe writer and do the grunt work of writing the book first then wait for interested people to ask you about it before talking it up at parties and social events.

AUGUST 6
Put the Skids on Multitasking

I'm a person of whim and easily distracted.
I don't like multitasking. When I'm doing
one thing, I like to do just that.
—Margaret Atwood

In some ways, the writing and publishing worlds make it necessary for us to be multitaskers—to change tires going eighty miles an hour in order to get everything done. And some writers consider bouncing between several writing tasks to be the ticket to productivity.

But experts claim multitasking isn't what it's cracked up to be. Juggling e-mails, phone calls, and text messages actually fatigues the brain, undermines our ability to focus, and diminishes productivity. When we're multitasking, we're actually forcing the brain to refocus with each rebound, reducing productivity by up to 40 percent. Multitaskers with fractured thinking and lack of concentration take longer to switch among tasks and are less efficient at balancing problems than non-multitaskers.

Once in a while we have to balance several activities, but when we're in the middle of a writing project, we can avoid letting our e-mail or texting ping interrupt us, engage in fewer tasks at once, and finish one big writing project before revving up another. What habits could you break to be more productive? And what can you do to change them?

Today's Takeaway

Put the skids on multitasking, do one thing at a time, and you'll feel less overwhelmed plus you'll be more focused, efficient, productive, energetic, and creative.

AUGUST 7
Backpedal from the Negative "Ism's"

I don't have concrete plans for the future. I just
think of success and keep a successful attitude.
—Peter James

A successful attitude is paramount for writing success. Ism's—forms of revolt against undesirable situations—can be beneficial in changing cultural wrongs, such as sexism or racism, or upending dangerous political movements, such as fascism or communism. Some isms such as alcoholism or workaholism imbue our fictional characters with rich personality traits.

But certain negative-isms poison our attitudes and work against writing progress. Cynicism, fatalism, and pessimism can undermine our writing aspirations, kill our creative spirits, and erode any possibilities we might have for future success.

The writer Hurston Smith said, "All isms end up in schisms." Our isms can make us so oppositional that they pit us (writers) against "them" (the powers that be). After a big letdown, any of us could feel the onslaught of a negative-ism, but with continued mindfulness, we can hold it at arms length and replace it with "optim-ism."

Ask yourself what negative isms you can ditch today so that schisms don't impede your writing trajectory. Then make a mental list of the positive isms you can put in their place.

Today's Takeaway
Back off from any negative-isms that could poison your attitude or sabotage your writing success and embrace the positive isms that contain faith, hope, and promise.

AUGUST 8
Unearth Your Eight C's

We all carry it within us; supreme strength,
the fullness of wisdom, unquenchable joy. It is
never thwarted and cannot be destroyed.
—Huston Smith

There are eight "C words"—qualities that psychologists associate with resilience—that can rev all our cylinders to face writing challenges. Read down the list of "C words" then contemplate each one. Check off the ones you have mastered and star the ones that need more attention:

1. A satisfying **connectedness** with fellow writers, editors, and ourselves

2. An overwhelming sense of **clear-mindedness** and direction

3. An unmistakable feeling of **calm** and loss of the ability to worry

4. More **curiosity** with less interest in judging writing colleagues and ourselves

5. A heightened ability to act from **confidence** instead of past hurts or future fears

6. An increased susceptibility for **compassion** for other authors and ourselves

7. Greater **courage** to let unknown situations happen instead of making them happen

8. Frequent bursts of **creativity** and unrestrained joy

Once you have identified the "C words" that need attention, write down some ways you can apply them to the craft of writing. For example, when you catch yourself judging something you've written, replace your self-judgment with one of the "C words." Then ask yourself what are some other ways you might write the piece that would make it better.

Today's Takeaway

Always remember that you have the eight C's within reach to be a successful writer—even when you feel like you don't—and all you need do is utilize them to persevere.

AUGUST 9
Inject Humor into Tense Hours

Humor—I see it as a survival skill.
—Jill McCorkle

As writers, we put ourselves through many tense hours waiting to see the outcome of our efforts. Will my manuscript get accepted? Will I get on a panel at the writing conference? Will my work be recognized with an award? Will anyone show up at the book signing?

During these tense hours, humor can be an effective tool to lighten our concerns, bringing balance to intense feelings. Fear is not preparation; it doesn't make the waiting better, but humor does. Too many of us approach writing with such seriousness that it can straightjacket us. We have forgotten how to have fun.

The lighter side of life brings relief from writing pressures. Living life honestly requires us writers to be as open to humor and amusement as we are to worry and fear. Ask yourself when the last time you cackled at yourself or at one incredulous defeat after another.

Today's Takeaway

During tense hours, make a special effort to lighten up by inviting humor and silliness to be your writing companions.

AUGUST 10
Hang Out on the Fringes

*Writers are first and foremost observers. Often we feel
on the fringes, in the margins of life. And that's where we
belong. What you are a part of, you cannot observe.*

—Lisa Unger

Most writers have personal war stories about writing struggles and the horrible manner in which agents or publishers betrayed us. When we reminisce over these stories and put ourselves in the position of the actor—the one on the receiving end of the hurt—we can victimize ourselves. But if we treat our personal setbacks like we do our characters, we place ourselves as the witness or narrator of hurtful situations, taking us out of the receiving end, providing us a wide-angle view with a dispassionate lens.

The writer and teacher Ram Dass said, "Everything changes once we identify with being the witness to the story instead of the actor in it." As we replay personal rejections, disappointments, and letdowns on our writing journeys, it helps to put ourselves in the observation role instead of the one on the receiving end of the hurt. It prevents us from being re-traumatized, lessens the sting of being a victim, and makes us feel empowered. This big-picture strategy gives us a larger perspective and potential insight into our own value and worth.

Today's Takeaway

Stay on the sidelines of your writing traumas as a dispassionate-eyed witness instead of putting yourself in the vulnerable position of the actor on the receiving end of the hurt.

AUGUST 11
Don't Get Hoodwinked

The brain can be hoodwinked but not the stomach.
—Rex Stout

As many of us veteran authors have learned, writing is an impersonal world where many have an uphill struggle. Getting our work recognized can be a monumental goal. For aspiring writers, frustration can turn into desperation to get your work out, leaving you vulnerable to getting hoodwinked. A publisher dangles a contract in your face, you sign over the book to them. They charge you a fee to edit it, slap it together, and throw it online. The only sales are your mother, her bridge club, and a few family members.

Don't be fooled by vanity presses masquerading as bona fide publishing houses that will take any book, charge the writer, and conduct no marketing. They might look impressive on the surface, but don't judge a book by its cover. It's important to ask several questions before you make a final decision: What marketing do you offer? Do you charge authors a fee? What editing do you provide for the book? How do you get books into bookstores? Do you deal with a distributor? What are your success stories?

Today's Takeaway

Follow your brain as well as your gut so you don't get hoodwinked by a publisher—whose main goal is to make money for themselves, not you—offering what looks like an alluring book deal that is really a scam.

AUGUST 12
Unbutton Yourself Wisely

We're all in this together—when one writer succeeds, all writers succeed...I think we need to take care of each other and talk about craft and nurture talent.
—Lisa Gardner

In the isolating and lonely writing world, it's important to have a place where we don't have to stay buttoned up, where we can be ourselves and have emotionally honest talks about our craft, where we can bounce off ideas—a spouse, friend, writing class, writing group, or writing organization. And it's important to choose wisely where we unbutton ourselves. Drawn to people of like minds, the relationship can feel like a heartfelt connection of finally meeting fellow tribe members who really know who we are at our core.

It's key to choose a sounding board that understands the ins-and-outs of the writing and publishing industry—someone we feel safe and comfortable opening up to and whose advice we trust. Some writing groups or classes—composed of other unpublished, perhaps wannabe writers— know less about the craft than we do, a collection of people unschooled on how to write a publishable book but happy to comment on ours. Instead, think carefully about the kind of people who can best help and guide you before asking them to be your sounding board and guide.

Today's Takeaway
Unbutton yourself with like-minded writers with whom you feel safe and comfortable opening up and whose knowledge about the writing and publishing worlds you trust.

AUGUST 13
Meditation Practice: Learn How to Fall

The most important thing in life is learning how to fall.
—Jeanette Walls

Our self-judgment about a loss of an agent or rejection of our writing creates more stress for us than the situations themselves. The judgment magnifies the bad news, causing us to suffer inside with worry, anxiety, or self-flagellation.

Judgmental thoughts can easily overtake us no matter where we are—walking hand-in-hand at the seashore or contemplating our next writing idea. We might not understand we're caught up in a thought stream, although we know we're miserable. In these instances, our minds are using us and we don't realize it.

When we practice mindfulness, we use our minds to reclaim our emotional reactions. Now as you practice this technique, close your eyes and remember a writing experience when you berated yourself for making a mistake or failing at something. Stay with that episode for a few minutes and recall how you felt. Now substitute compassionate heart speak for a few minutes and notice the difference you feel inside.

It's amazing how much better we feel when we stop judging ourselves and start loving ourselves. And how much better our writing becomes.

Today's Takeaway

When bad news comes knocking and you stumble on your writing path, be mindful of how you fall and cushion yourself with compassionate, nonjudgmental self-talk.

AUGUST 14
Stay Open to Second Chances

*To give up too easily leads to regret, yet trying and
then failing can lead us to second chances if we do
not accept it as failure, but a chance to learn.*
—Karen White

"I really screwed up the plot in my short story. I'm such a loser. I'll never get published." We make a sweeping conclusion about our capabilities or worth on the basis of one negative event.

We believe that if something's true the first time, it will always be true in all others. This unreliable mind trap is called *overgeneralization*, but we rely on it because it's what we think at the time.

After one negative situation, we always have a second chance to turn things around. When we catch ourselves looking at a negative consequence as a never-ending pattern of defeat, we can search for the proof. We won't find evidence for the exaggeration, and then we see that there are two separate events with two different possibilities. We accept the negative situation as a chance to learn, and we hang on until the miracle happens.

Today's Takeaway

Keep your mind open to second chances because trying again after failing can lead to success.

AUGUST 15
Broaden Your Positivity Scope

To me the glass is half empty some days and half-full on others. Sometimes it's bone dry. Or overflowing.
—Mary Alice Monroe

Two things we know about our power as writers: one is that we have the ability to change our outlook; two is that a positive outlook leads us toward more possibilities than a negative one.

When we're dealing with stressful writing situations, positivity unlocks the range of possibilities. It helps us focus on an encouraging outcome that negativity hides from view. Simply put, negativity keeps us targeted on the writing problem, whereas positivity helps us discover solutions to it. When we intentionally widen our scope, we see the big picture of possible solutions and more potential for success instead of staying mired in the problem.

Known as the broaden-and-build effect, this strategy expands our worldview and allows us to take more in so we can see many more solutions to writing woes. The more we take in, the more ideas and actions we add to our literary toolbox.

Contemplate your writing woes. Be willing to widen old points of view and let your imagination roam. "I'll never be a writer" becomes "I'm still learning how to become the best writer I can be."

Today's Takeaway

Step back from your negative beliefs and broaden your positivity scope by brainstorming a wide range of possibilities that can build an arsenal for your writing success.

AUGUST 16
Mobilize the Courage to Continue

Success is not final, failure is not fatal:
It is the courage to continue that counts.
—Winston Churchill

Perhaps we know how to stand strong in defense of someone we love. We know how to assert ourselves. We might even know how to take safety risks. But how many of us have the greatest courage of all: to stay the course defeat after defeat with our writing? The statistics say more of us have the stamina to continue taking safety risks after a car crash than to continue after a series of psychological defeats.

Courage is the gateway to many attributes: confidence, perseverance, self-worth, inner peace, and success. And courage exists deep within all of us. When we're down and out, courage gives us the energy to get up and take one more step. It teaches us that failure is not fatal and success is not final, that we will stumble into both off and on as we travel our literary journeys.

In the words of novelist Jenny Milchman, "Writing is a marathon, not a sprint. Sometimes it's a slow walk or crawl, but keep moving because so long as you're not dead anything can happen." It's important to always remember that failure is not final. It's simply a guidepost on our way to success.

Today's Takeaway

When writing knocks you to the ground, let courage pick you up, push you through daily daggers of relentless steel, and help you make decisions that bring peace and fulfillment.

AUGUST 17
Boycott Pessimism and Despair

No horse named Morbid ever won a race.

—Ernest Hemingway

Some writing days are full of anxiety, frustration, and irritability. These difficult times test us, strain us, and deplete us, often leaving us without hope. Feeling lonely, sad, and hopeless are normal human emotions that most of us have from time to time. It's important not to push the feelings away or ignore them but to let them be there until they ease. Sometimes we have to take three steps backward before leaping ten steps forward, but falling back is part of moving forward.

The dark feelings are not our final destination. They're valleys practically all writers visit on route to their writing summits. Always remember that optimism is on the horizon. When you're passing through an emotional valley, remind yourself that you're on a beaten path that was blazed by successful writers before you. It will give you strength to endure today.

Today's Takeaway

When you feel like giving up, remember the dark days are just part of the writing roadmap that we all pass through on our writing journeys.

AUGUST 18
Breathe with the Labor Pains

Writing books is the closest
men ever come to childbearing.
—Norman Mailer

We are a curious breed, we writers. We're attracted to one of the toughest jobs on the planet: putting words together in a unique, comprehensible yet interesting way. Our pregnant ideas excite us and make aborting them unthinkable, but we must endure months and months of discomfort, frustration, and misery along the way.

Our love and passion for writing give us the determination to see the work in progress through to the end, no matter what. We continue the pursuit despite discomfort, pain, and incessant struggles. Sometimes our temperaments make us cranky—even throw temper tantrums.

Perhaps we marvel at how easily other writers deliver their works. We brood and pine and draw into ourselves. We rebuff sympathy from someone who assures us that everything will turn out okay. Still, our passion fuels the pursuit until we bear the fruits of our labor.

After the delivery of my first novel, I cuddled it in my arms and slept with it all night as if it were my firstborn. In some ways it was—given the blood, sweat, and tears I put into it. Rest assured, in the end, the misery is worth the struggle.

Today's Takeaway

Stick with the pain and misery of your manuscript's gestation until the end, and once it's delivered, you will feel every minute of the struggle was worth it.

AUGUST 19
Scoff at Shillyshallying and Keep at It

The only lesson is you gotta keep at it.
—R. L. Stine

Writing might not be the most dangerous career, but it sure can scare the pants off us. And the mind's natural response is to avoid any source of fear. Faced with writing fears, how many of us walk away? When we walk away, fear wins out over us. But when we face fear with self-compassion, we automatically achieve success—regardless of the outcome. This action builds courage, perseverance, resilience and ultimately accomplishments.

Success is built on failure. Avoidance of failure turns into avoidance of success. Once we start to accept failure as an essential stepping stone to writing success, we can give ourselves permission to make the mistakes necessary to get where we want to go.

What if you identified a fear that has crippled or prevented you from fully embracing your writing aspirations? It could be as small as shillyshallying around and procrastinating over a deadline or as big as refusing to allow someone to read something you wrote. Once you find just one action you've avoided to risk failure, see if you can bring courage and compassion to the fear and move through it. And you will stretch one lap closer to the success you've been avoiding.

Today's Takeaway

As you face your writing fears with self-compassion, you'll unearth greater courage and find yourself one lap closer to the writing life you have been avoiding.

AUGUST 20
Stop Being a Worrywart Writer

Worrying is like paying a debt that may never come due.
—Will Rogers

Raise your hand if you've worried about your writing—either that it's not good enough, that it won't be accepted, or that no one will take the time to read it. Hey, that's just about everybody in the room.

Writing and worry go hand in hand, but stop and think about it. Worry doesn't prepare us for anything, and most of what we worry about never happens. In fact, worry can sabotage the very thing we're worried about: our writing. It consumes us, drains our energy, keeps us on edge, and interferes with concentration.

Although most worry is unnecessary, our minds and bodies go through the mental and physical toll anyway, even when things turn out okay, and we end up paying a debt that never came due. The best policy is to make a pact with our inner worrywart to wait for the outcome and then worry if necessary. That way we're not wasting our valuable writing assets for nothing, and we have more resources to spend on penning our best work.

Today's Takeaway

Let go of unnecessary worry so you have more energy and concentration and less stress to focus on what you love most: your best writing.

AUGUST 21
Employ Artful Waiting

Your life is already artful-waiting,
just waiting for you to make it art.
—Toni Morrison

Those of us who are beginning writers might underestimate the long lead times and snail-like movement of the writing process. We wait months, maybe years, to complete a manuscript, two or three more months to try and snag an agent (if ever), then another several months to get a publisher. Or not. Then another long stretch to hold the piece in our impatient little hands. In the age of "instant everything," patience isn't something we're accustomed to.

The glacial pace of the writing world is an excruciating challenge for most of us. Sometimes it takes years for us to scribble our creative art into words. Then our chance comes to turn passion into patience so that editors and publishers can make our writing sparkle in full form. During the long waits, we don't have to hold our breath and twiddle our thumbs. Patience is about how and the attitude with which we wait.

A writer's job doesn't end with a finished product. While waiting, we can devise a plan to market, promote, and sell the piece of work. We could sequester ourselves and scribble our next project. Or we might replenish the areas of our lives we neglected while immersed in writing moments.

Today's Takeaway

Employ artful waiting during the long lags on getting your writing from page to print, start your next project, and develop a marketing plan for the project in production.

AUGUST 22
Indulge in a Restorative Activity

*There must be quite a few things that a hot bath
won't cure, but I don't know many of them.*
—Sylvia Plath

When was the last time you took the time to soak in a hot bath or indulge yourself in a restorative activity? A restorative activity can be any action that energizes us and restores our creative juices. After we get back to writing, the activity rejuvenates our bodies and minds.

Think of a restorative activity that you enjoy, one that helps you unwind. Recall the last time you did it. Was it a day, week, month, or year ago? Then think of something you've always wanted to do but never made time for. It could be something you're not good at but that you'd like to explore. It doesn't have to culminate in a tangible product.

It could be something you deliberately do imperfectly. After you've thought of something you really like or think you'd like, dive into it. Whatever you choose, let it engulf you, take you away, lift your spirits, and rest your mind. Then notice the benefits: greater clarity, sharper concentration, and a more relaxed state.

Today's Takeaway

Indulge in a restorative activity that helps you let go of built-up tension and unwind, and then notice afterward how much more creative and productive your writing becomes.

AUGUST 23
Bow to Those Who Accept You

When you're different, sometimes you don't see the millions of people who accept you for what you are. All you notice is the person who doesn't.

—Jodi Picoult

Do you blush when someone praises your writing? Do you feel discomfort when you're applauded for a kind deed? Do you feel awkward when someone compliments you on your looks?

Our negative thoughts are more automatic than positive ones, and we tend to believe one negative thought or situation over three positive ones. Although our negative tilt hardwires us for safety, it creates unnecessary stress, limits our possibilities, and keeps us from believing in ourselves. But we don't have to let our wiring lives dominate our writing lives.

We have to be more intentional about underscoring the positive situations instead of letting them roll over our heads. We can learn to accept affirming comments and validations more easily and feel more comfortable with praise than criticism. We can overestimate exciting possibilities and underestimate negative feedback. We can pay attention to gains contained in losses. And we can refuse to allow one bad outcome to rule future outlooks. Is your glass half full or half empty? Meditate on focusing on positive aspects instead of the negative ones.

Today's Takeaway

Your job is to go beyond survival thinking, to avoid taking the bait as negative thoughts or situations clobber you, and to acknowledge those who see you for who you are.

AUGUST 24
Make Rejections Work for You

I received rejection letters for ten years…I had all my rejection notices stored in a box. When the box was finally full, I took it to the curb and set it on fire.

—Janet Evanovich

When rejections flash on the computer screen, our hearts sink, heads drop, and disappointments howl. But the most important thing is what we do in the aftermath of the letdown. How many of us join ranks with those who reject us by attacking or putting ourselves down? Just because someone gives up on us doesn't mean we have to give up on ourselves.

Rejection of ourselves keeps us stuck, and the bad feelings permeate our writing. A better course of action is to make a writing rejection work in our favor instead of betraying ourselves or becoming a victim of it. We determine our own destinies, not publishing honchos or booksellers or critics.

Ask how rejection can improve your work. Perhaps it can teach us to be kinder, more compassionate, and supportive of ourselves during down times. It can remind us to slow down, give ourselves pep talks, and allow time to work through the loss. After we rebound from the defeated feelings, we can continue our writing agendas with more determination, perseverance, and resilience. Contemplate on how you can turn a writing rejection into a boon then name specific ways to use rejection to improve your craft.

Today's Takeaway

Use rejections to toughen you up by joining ranks with yourself instead of beating yourself up and joining in with those who reject your work.

AUGUST 25
Don't Bite the Hook

I have been through some terrible things in
my life, some of which actually happened.
—Mark Twain

Imagine someone scolding you and you holding the cell phone away from your ear. In the same way you can hold a negative thought away from you and watch it from afar without believing it or blending with it.

Think of a negative thought you've been carrying around about a situation, another person, or yourself. It could be something like, "I can't make headway with my manuscript" or "Getting published is the last thing that will happen."

Then position yourself in a comfortable place, close your eyes, and watch the negative thought for a few minutes. With curiosity instead of judgment, observe it as a part of you. As you watch the thought, see if you can understand that it's not you, it is separate from you, and it's not necessarily true.

You can observe your negative thoughts this way with a dispassionate eye without believing they are true or that everything they say is true. Let them come and go without personalizing them, resisting, or identifying with them, and eventually they float away.

Today's Takeaway

Don't bite the hook of every negative thought just because you think it; welcome the thought with curiosity instead of judgment; and observe it from a bird's eye view.

AUGUST 26
Ban Fighting Your Inner Bully

*When it comes to your inner critic, my advice
is to not take advice from someone who doesn't
like you. That's like returning to the perpetrator
for healing after you've been abused.*
—Patrick Califia

Every writer I know has an inner critic that bullies us with harsh words. It calls us names like lazy, rigid, stupid, selfish, and unattractive. It tells us we can't, that we should, ought, or must. It judges us mercilessly saying we're not good enough, we didn't do it right or quick enough. The list goes on and on.

There's no use fighting the inner bully, because it only gets stronger over time, and we cannot get rid of it. Next time your inner bully pipes up, realize it's speaking to you. Listen to the critical voice as a separate part of you, not all of you. Avoid arguing or trying to reason with your bully because it always has a comeback and always wins.

Think of yourself as the CEO in charge of your mind's boardroom, and your inner critic as a stockholder. You can let it have an opinion without agreeing with everything it has to say. Then use your kinder voice to run the boardroom and encourage and nurture yourself.

Today's Takeaway

When your inner bully overshadows you, instead of arguing with it, remember that it's a stockholder but you're the "CEO," then let it blab without believing everything it says.

AUGUST 27
Give Your Body the Fingers

The emotional, psychological, and spiritual
stresses present in our minds travel, like
oxygen, to every part of our bodies.
—Caroline Myss

Our bodies have minds of their own, tensing and tightening in reaction to the daily grind. The human body is wired to "think" for us while we manage the big picture of our lives—like paying bills, managing our portfolio, or burning the midnight oil to meet a writing deadline.

The body constantly responds to stressors while we're busy with writing pursuits. My shoulders hunched up to my ears in reaction to writing pressures before I was even aware of it. Now when I'm under the gun and my shoulders contract, I make a concerted effort to keep the muscles relaxed. When we don't listen to our bodies, they grab our attention by speaking to us in a stern voice: headaches, indigestion, muscle pain, or clenched jaw.

Self-massage techniques at your desk bring quick body relief:

1. **Head**: Use your fingertips to gently massage the area around your temples, forehead, and ears.

2. **Eyes**: Close your eyes and place your ring finger directly under your eyebrows near the bridge of your nose. Slowly increase the pressure for five to ten seconds, gently release, then repeat as needed.

3. **Shoulders**: Reach one arm across the front of your body to your opposite shoulder. Use a circular motion to press firmly on the muscle above your shoulder blade. Repeat on the other side.

Today's Takeaway

As you're writing, become better acquainted with your body's reaction to pressure, listen to what it says, attend to it, and you'll notice a big drop in your stress level.

AUGUST 28
Spend Time Outdoors in Nature

The winds will blow their own freshness
into you, and the storms their energy,
while cares will drop off like autumn leaves.
—John Muir

Many of us writers spend an inordinate amount of time inside in front of our computers. While this is often necessary, scientists say getting outdoors is the ticket to reducing stress and revitalizing our health.

Studies show that spending twenty minutes a day outside can make us peppier. Taking a brisk ten-minute walk raises and sustains our energy level and recalibrates a fatigued brain. And we perform better after a walk in the woods than after a walk along a busy street.

So take a break from scribbling and find a park or natural setting. Feel the breeze on your face, notice the colors and smells of leaves and flowers, and pay attention to the sounds of chirping crickets, warbling birds, or rushing water.

Today's Takeaway

Spend time letting nature transport you out of the artificial world of social media and machines, calm and relax you, and infuse you with mental clarity to replace your cares as they drop off like autumn leaves.

AUGUST 29
Evict the Literary World from Your Heart

The reward for conformity is that
everyone likes you but yourself.
—Rita Mae Brown

Some of us think doing "right"—conforming to what others want—is more important than being who we really are. We become chameleons, change colors to fit in with whomever we encounter, and mold our attitudes, emotions, and behaviors around everybody else's wishes. Somewhere in our pursuit to measure up outwardly we lose touch with ourselves on the inside because the views of others occupy that space.

What about you? Have you sold out to the approval of other writers or publishers by penning what's popular instead of what you know and feel? Have you leased your heart and soul, allowing the writing world to rent that space?

Nobody has squatter's rights in our heads and hearts unless we grant it, and that's a choice we make every day. When our writing changes with the wind, we lose our self-respect. We can reclaim our writing space by standing firm in who we are and in what we believe, and penning what suits us, not what agents are seeking or publishers are selling.

Today's Takeaway

Take possession of *your* writing life and carve out *your* opinions, *your* writing passions, and write about what's in *your* heart and soul and you'll come closer to that bestseller.

AUGUST 30
Lighten Up Your Writing Life

I had the epiphany that laughter was light, and light was laughter, and that this was the secret of the universe.

—Gillian Flynn

Some of us take writing's challenges with grim, humorless determination and think it has to be all work and no play. We believe we must toil and sweat before earning the right to have fun. We might even feel guilty laughing and smiling because we feel we haven't earned it.

Truth be told, a lighthearted literary life can contribute to our eventual success. We become recipients of our own joy and elation or frustration or rage. Uplifting moods have positive physical effects while dark moods have harmful effects on the body. Laughter is good medicine, creating body chemistry that heals and sustains us.

Almost anything can be taken as an opportunity to lighten up. The potential for having fun and seeing the humorous side of life is all around us: the funny things children say, a joke someone tells, something silly we do. The prescription for a happy and lengthy writing life is one or more big belly laughs per day.

Today's Takeaway

Make it a point to take your writing life more lightly and look at the humorous side of situations whenever possible.

AUGUST 31
Watch for the Invasion of the Balance Snatchers

In all my years of counseling those near death,
I've yet to hear anyone say they wish
they had spent more time at the office.
—Harold S. Kushner

Watch out. They're everywhere: the balance snatchers invade your writing life, debilitating you, making you less efficient in your craft. Are you stretching days into the wee night hours to juggle more tasks, leashing yourself to electronic devices, giving up much-needed vacation time, making yourself available to everyone else but yourself 24/7?

Studies show that work stress turns us into more disgruntled, less effective writers. Those of us who work longer hours suffer greater depression, anxiety, and burnout and have twice the number of health-related problems. All of us writers must take steps to prevent the balance snatchers from overtaking our lives.

Arrange to power down and clock out from your desk at a certain time and follow the adage "Work smarter, not longer." Stay fit and think of your writing days as the Olympics, where your physical and mental endurance hinges on being in good shape. Then prime yourself with good nutrition and vigorous exercise, avoid nicotine, and if you drink, use alcohol in moderation. Make a fifteen or twenty minute appointment with yourself and schedule personal time to keep the balance snatchers at bay.

Today's Takeaway

Repel the balance snatchers and build writing resilience by scheduling something fun once in a while—a hobby, hot bath, manicure, yoga, facial, reading, a sport, or meditation.

SEPTEMBER

SEPTEMBER 1
Remember That Grass Grows Through Concrete

*You're BRAVER than you believe, STRONGER
than you seem, and SMARTER than you think.*

—A. A. Milne

Each of us is more resilient than we realize. In the face of turbulence, we have the ability to anticipate risk, limit impact, and bounce back rapidly through survival and adaptability. We also have the ability to tap into and reset the natural balance of our nervous system.

One tool that harnesses the body's innate ability to override reactions to fear and threat is called "resourcing"—anything that helps us feel better or provides comfort. An *internal resource* is something positive inside of us such as a talent, a trait, or ability. An *external resource* is something outside of us such as a loved one, a place, a memory, or a pet. Resourcing puts the brakes on our fight-or-flight response and shifts us into a rest-or-digest state.

The first step is to bring to mind something that sustains and nurtures you—a positive memory, a person, place, pet, or spiritual guide. Or a talent or trait inside that you value. Then redirect your attention to the accompanying pleasant or calming sensations felt inside, and focus on those sensations for a minute or two.

Today's Takeaway

In turbulent writing times, you can reset your nervous system by 1.) bringing to mind a person, place, pet, or strong personal quality that gives you strength or joy 2.) holding that resource in your mind's eye while paying attention to the pleasant sensations 3.) and noticing your slowed breath, heart rate, and muscle tension.

SEPTEMBER 2
Take the Risk to Bloom

And the day came when the risk to remain tight in a bud
was more painful than the risk it took to bloom.

—Anaïs Nin

Although growth can be painful (that's why we call them growing pains), it can be even more painful to remain tight in our little security holes. Taking the risk to bloom determines whether we become the writers we want to be and whether we attain the things of value and achieve the goals we set.

Even in distressful times when we come short of our writing goals, we must refuse to view risk and effort as actions that might reveal our inadequacies or show that we're not up to the task. We continue to take risks, confront challenges, and keep working at our craft. Instead of hiding our writing deficiencies, we identify and overcome them. Rather than attaching to fellow writers who pat us on the head and boost our insecurities, we connect with those who challenge us to grow. We don't seek out the tried and true, we search for challenging writing experiences that help us bloom.

We need to ask ourselves, "Where in my writing journey do I need to take the risk to bloom?" Then we take it. What is your answer to this question? And what will you do about it?

Today's Takeaway

Exercise your ability to identify your strengths and weaknesses by seeking out risky writing experiences that help you bloom instead of low-risk experiences that hold you tight.

SEPTEMBER 3
Be a Card-Carrying Optimist

Twixt the optimist and pessimist
the difference is droll: The optimist sees the
doughnut but the pessimist sees the hole.
—McLandburgh Wilson

To be optimistic, you don't have to possess some magical joy juice. You don't have to be a smiley-face romantic looking through rose-colored glasses, either. Optimists are realists who take positive steps to cope with challenges rather than succumb to them.

Being able to see the positive side of a negative situation can arm you with the hope of overcoming writing obstacles. Studies show that optimism literally expands our peripheral vision and lets us see more than we usually do. Because of a broadened scope, optimists have lower stress levels, move faster up the career ladder, have fewer health complaints, and live longer than pessimists.

Who wouldn't want that? All we have to do is practice seeing the gains in our losses, the beginnings contained in endings. When we enter a rose garden, we savor the beauty and fragrance of the flowers instead of focusing on the thorns. When we hit forty, we think of half a life left instead of half a life over. We can always find a granule of good in the negative when we practice looking for it. Make it a practice to identify your pessimistic thoughts, turn them inside out, and look for granules of optimism.

Today's Takeaway

Surround yourself with optimists, instead of pessimists who pull you down, and make a commitment to bring a positive attitude to your writing and personal relationships.

SEPTEMBER 4
Underscore What You've Overcome

*Being a successful person is not necessarily defined by
what you have achieved, but by what you have overcome.*

—Fannie Flagg

Damn! Today, I received another rejection. I feel a deep sense of loss, like giving up, like burning the manuscript in front of my house—to proclaim that I'm done, that I have nothing more to give to the craft. I'm a total failure.

Sound familiar? It's normal to have these feelings. Most writers have them. But feelings are not facts. Let's look at what we're saying to ourselves: I'm a failure because of the rejections. First of all, the only fact here is that I've had rejections like all successful writers. I'm not a failure as long as I keep going. Suppose I get a publisher's rejection on a Friday and another publisher accepts the same piece on Monday. How can I be a failure on Friday and a success on Monday with the same literary work?

The hurdles we overcome define our successes: the numerous rejections, our own negative feelings about our writing ability, people who tell us that the bar is high for acceptance nowadays. And our refusals to turn on ourselves, burn the manuscript, and side with those who reject our work. Wow! Come to think about it, we're pretty damn successful!

Today's Takeaway

Avoid labeling yourself as a failure. Separate your feelings from facts, make a list of all the writing obstacles you've overcome, and recognize how accomplished you really are.

SEPTEMBER 5
Pick Calm over Chaos

Freedom means choosing your burdens.
—Hephzibah Menuhin

Sometimes we get so used to living with stress and chaos that it can become a habit. We find ourselves adding stress to our lives, even when we don't have to. But we are free to refuse crisis and chaos and choose stillness within ourselves, even when stress swirls around us.

How often do we turn a simple situation into a crisis without even thinking about it? Why do we feel as if we're constantly putting out fires? Could it be that we're creating them? We can ask ourselves what we gain from crises. Comfort? Success? Importance?

Once we become mindful of what we're doing, we can find more constructive ways of getting the same satisfactions without distressing others or ourselves. When someone in front of us drives too slowly, we can slow down. If our writing goals don't materialize as expected, we can let them materialize in a different way. When someone is inconsiderate or rude, we can always choose calm over chaos. When we do this, we emancipate ourselves from the emotional bondage that robs us of our freedom to decide.

Today's Takeaway
Pick your moods instead of letting them pick you, and choose calm over chaos no matter the existing circumstances.

SEPTEMBER 6
Regulate Your Sizzlers

*Let us not look back in anger, nor forward
in fear, but around in awareness.*
—James Thurber

On some days it can feel like disappointments and letdowns are coming at us from all angles and at lightning speed. Pressures and deadlines, rejections, unreachable expectations, and unfinished projects can feel like bullets pummeling us. Then the breakdown of our technology sends us over the edge. The printer doesn't work or we forgot to back up our manuscripts then lose them in a blackout. And we sizzle.

It's a fact of life that people will push your buttons, but what remains to be seen is how you respond to them. What buttons make you sizzle? To find out, pay close attention to when your sizzlers pop up and emotionally hijack you, throwing your executive functioning (reasoning mind) off line.

Instead of automatically reacting, start to notice a pattern of people and situations that cause you to sizzle. Then see if you can regulate your sizzlers. After all, your sizzlers belong to you, and mine belong to me. So it's our individual responsibilities to regulate them.

Today's Takeaway

Recognize the people and situations that make you sizzle, separate your sizzlers from present circumstances, and then regulate them for a happier and more productive writing journey.

SEPTEMBER 7
Put a Supportive Arm Around Your Shoulder

If you're self-compassionate, you'll tend to have higher self-esteem than if you're endlessly self-critical.
—David D. Burns

When we're hit with bad news, there's nothing more soothing than an arm around our shoulder. I don't mean someone else's arm. I mean our own arm. It's called self-soothing, and it's a huge Rx for setbacks and letdowns.

We know that a direct link exists between self-compassion, self-esteem, and creative output. After a setback or discouraging situation, we bounce back to our writing selves quicker if we self-soothe with kind words and compassionate feelings.

Self-compassion is associated with less anxiety and depression as well as more happiness, optimism, and creative productivity. As we embrace negative feelings—such as disappointment or hopelessness—with compassion, new positive emotions rise up within us. We liberate ourselves from negativity's grip, and that open space fills up with more positive emotions such as hope, courage, and confidence, which in turn fuel our creativity and productivity.

Today's Takeaway
Use your own shoulder to cry on and put a supportive arm around yourself when you have a loss or receive bad news to soothe and calm your troubled mind.

SEPTEMBER 8
Keep on Going

Make your mistakes, take your chances, look silly, but keep on going. Don't freeze up.
—Thomas Wolfe

A couple arrived in England on their way to visit relatives in Scotland and discovered the country had come to a transportation standstill because of a national rail strike. There were no trains, rental cars, buses, or boat tickets. Their only recourse was to hitchhike along the motorway, which they did with some trepidation.

The experience turned out to be the best vacation of their lives. They met interesting people, learned about the politics and customs firsthand, and got to see more of the countryside than they would have by train.

There is a difference between stubbornness and persistence. Stubbornness is an expression of self-will—to have things the way we want them to be, not as they are. We are persistent when we are open to new alternative ways to achieve our purpose. Don't let stubborn resistance clutter your path. Instead, take a personal inventory of your stubborn self-will versus your openhearted persistence and note which quality leads your writing life.

Today's Takeaway

Persist in the face of opposition with openheartedness to the many different approaches to writing challenges, and move forward calmly and consistently on the path that is cleared for you.

SEPTEMBER 9
Embrace Your Stumbling

We chew on yesterday's and tomorrow's sorrows...
We add an unnecessary layer of rumination and
resistance to life, and this creates suffering.
—Jeff Foster

When something unpleasant happens on our writing journey, it isn't necessarily the situation that upsets us, but the way we think, feel, and react to it. The event or action isn't good or bad, and it isn't personal. It just *is*.

The minute we judge situations based on our subjective thoughts and feelings, we are emotionally involved in them. Negative thoughts keep us isolated from our higher selves. On the flip side, if we notice our judgmental thoughts without reacting to them, they won't trap us.

In the words of Jeff Foster, "Be humbled by the journey rather than trying to be perfect. Doubt, disappointment, and disillusionment will be constant friends along this pathless path." It helps for us to remember that true joy isn't the absence of upset or disappointment but the willingness to embrace it all. Directly experiencing each day's events as they arrive, instead of ruminating about the past, is the hallmark of daily writing resilience.

What feelings can you open your arms to that you avoided? Embrace your doubts and frustrations, and they will rescind to make way for hope and joy.

Today's Takeaway
Greet unpleasant writing situations without rumination or resistance but with kindness and curiosity, and you will cut your suffering in half.

SEPTEMBER 10
Break Bad Writing Habits

*I'm a full-time believer in writing habits ... this [talent] is
something that has to be assisted all the time by physical
and mental habits or it dries up and blows away.*

—Flannery O'Connor

Our writing habits slowly mount up over time to support our success or impede it, much like brooks make rivers and rivers make oceans. Many of us get so caught up in the process of penning a piece that we don't pay attention to bad habits that could be holding us back: procrastination, distraction, self-sabotage, lack of sleep, little exercise, or poor nutrition.

We can ask ourselves: are our habits taking us into rough waters or are they carrying us into calm seas? The habits we've made can be broken. Each opportunity we have to break a bad habit puts us further along on our writing journey.

In the words of Mark Twain, "You can't break a bad habit by throwing it out the window. You've got to walk it slowly down the stairs." Decide on one bad writing habit that needs breaking and commit to break it the same way you built it, slowly and one step at a time. Then assess which ones you want to keep.

Today's Takeaway

Constantly monitor your writing habits, thinning out the ones that become obsolete and adding new ones that foster your growth as a writer.

SEPTEMBER 11
Tie Up Loose Ends

It is the loose ends with which men hang themselves.
—Zelda Fitzgerald

If we want to advance on our writing journeys, we need to complete the task of tying up loose ends. What projects or actions have we left unattended that need completion? This could be a writing project or resolving a relationship that is still uncertain. It's also worth contemplating why we left things hanging to begin with.

One approach to resolving past incompletions is to make a list of the projects and persons with whom we have unfinished business and put them in order of priority. Then we start with the most important one or the one we can complete in a short period of time. Taking it one task at a time, we can check off each one and shed the burden of loose ends.

Wiping the slate clean gives us more energy to put into our creative productivity. What in your writing life needs tying up? Do you need to shed long-held feelings of guilt, clear the air of misunderstandings, or complete a long-postponed writing commitment? Take action with whatever they are now.

Today's Takeaway

Resolve old loose ends that have stockpiled instead of leaving them for the future so they don't hang you up on your writing path.

SEPTEMBER 12
Chill Your Faultfinder

*The ego is the great faultfinder. It presents
the most subtle and insidious arguments for
casting other people out of our hearts.*
—Marianne Williamson

Most people are doing the best they can most of the time even when they push our buttons. If we look beneath the surface of our frustrations and stretch to understand the motives of those who upset us, it softens our reactions and leads to self-understanding.

Maintaining inner peace when things fall apart is a huge boon for our writing success. If we want to find more peace within ourselves, one of the great paradoxes is to develop an understanding that people and situations that upset us the most offer the greatest opportunity for growth. They give us a chance to open our hearts, if we're willing to look at it that way.

Seeing people's faults as part of their human condition instead of as a "bad" person helps us cope in otherwise intolerable situations. Plus, focusing on someone's intentions, instead of their surface behaviors, makes a big difference in how we respond to them.

Today's Takeaway

For one day try replacing your "faultfinder" with your "favorfinder" (especially toward people who bug you, including yourself) and notice the difference in what you see and feel and how much more you learn about yourself as a writer.

SEPTEMBER 13
Renounce Who You Are Not

Fuck Hemingway, Plath, Fitzgerald, and the rest. Discover the writer you can be and the writer you want to be.

—William Kent Krueger

The demands of writing can crash over us like a huge wave and suck us under. But as we hit bottom, we can kick against it, float to the surface, and breathe again. We are more powerful than we give ourselves credit as long as we embrace who we really are.

Sometimes there's a womp on the side of our head that wakes us into seeing who we are, instead of who we are not. Once we let go of who we are not and what we don't need, we realize we have everything to be successful at our craft.

Author Richard Rohr said, "All great spirituality teaches about letting go of what you don't need and who you are not. Then … you'll find that the little place where you really are is ironically more than enough and is all you need."

We don't have to push, beg, crawl, force, or resist. There's nothing to prove and nothing to protect. The realization that we are enough exactly as we are frees us to be the best writers we can be. Spend a moment meditating on the idea that you are enough exactly as you are. Then let that liberation free your writing voice to soar and pen what only you can say.

Today's Takeaway

Reflect on who you are *not* as a writer then focus on who you *are* as a writer, and tell yourself that you don't have to prove anything, that the writer you are is enough.

SEPTEMBER 14
Be a Mindful Writer

When we pause, allow a gap and breathe deeply,
we can experience instant refreshment. Suddenly
we slow down, look out, and there's the world
—Pema Chödrön

What exactly does it mean to be a mindful writer? And how can we put it into practice? We know it's about being in a state of calm and present-moment awareness—one in which compassion dwarfs judgment. But how do we put it into our everyday writing?

One way to practice mindful writing is to contemplate three questions. First, what does our body need? Food, sleep, exercise? Then make sure we get nutritious meals, good sleep, and a brisk walk around the block or some yoga exercises.

Second, what does our mind need? Before we sit to write, we can pause, breathe deeply, and pay attention to our thoughts and feelings. Perhaps urgency to get a manuscript to the publisher, worry that today's writing won't meet the mark, or feelings of inadequacy that the right words won't come. With compassion, acknowledge the thoughts and feelings with "I see you're here with me today," then watch them float away like a leaf swept downstream.

Third, what does your writing space need? More quiet, additional light, less clutter. Then take action to prepare a writing environment that nurtures you and fosters your best writing.

Today's Takeaway

Before you begin your writing day, treat your mind and body with compassion, providing them what they need and arranging your writing environment for optimal writing success.

SEPTEMBER 15
Don't Squander Time

You meet people who say, "Oh, I'd like to do such-and-such, but I don't have the time." But it always seemed to me like you make the time.

—David Sedaris

How many times a day do we hear the refrain, "I don't have time" or "There's not enough time in the day"? I hear writers say it a lot, even though it's untrue. Few writers have the time to write, but productive writers *make* the time that's already there.

Novelist Cassandra King said, "Do be a miser with time: hoard it, treasure it, don't squander a single minute of it." The question we writers must ask ourselves is what do we do with the time that we have? Do we squander it away with worry or frivolous tasks? Do we distract ourselves to avoid our fear that our ideas won't be good enough? We can never recover the time lost.

Truth be told, there's plenty of time in the day—twenty-four hours. We don't need more time to write; we don't even have to *make* time to write. We just need to *take* time and do it. We can ask ourselves, "What is it that keeps me from taking time to write?"

Today's Takeaway

Ask what keeps you from taking time to write and if you squander time by watching too much TV, oversleeping, or surfing on Facebook; then consider taking a chunk of time to jot down your thoughts.

SEPTEMBER 16
Explore All Your Selves

There are so many selves in everybody,
and just to explore one is wrong, dead
wrong, for the creative person.

—James Dickey

As writers, we are not just one personality; we are multi-dimensional with many different sides or parts. How many times have you been torn over making a decision? A part of you wants to go hiking but another part of you wants to be a couch potato. Just as a cake is a combination of ingredients, we are a combination of sub-personalities.

As multi-dimensional creatures, we have a treasure trove to explore and mine as resources for our writing. We can be forceful at times and yielding at others. Sometimes we're in the mood for a burger; other times we prefer a salad. Whether we write fiction or nonfiction, these many selves give us various perspectives to explore and write about.

Contemplate the many sides to your personality—smart, dishonest, affectionate, lazy, impatient, competent, controlling, angry—and note which ones you would like to explore in your writing, either for self-understanding or as a potential composite character or perhaps both.

Today's Takeaway

Explore your many selves as you contemplate your multidimensionality as a writer and mine those parts for self-understanding and/or content in your writing as pen hits paper.

SEPTEMBER 17
Call Out Your Blurts

The past was always there, lived inside you, and it helped to make you who you are. But it had to be placed in perspective. The past could not dominate the future.

—Barbara Taylor Bradford

Those of us writers who grew up in dysfunctional families (didn't we all?), and who have been made to believe that we're unworthy or doomed to fail, will take those past thoughts with us into our everyday lives and treat them as facts. We superimpose past negative beliefs on current-day situations and filter today through yesterday. These beliefs—called *blurts*—pop up, preventing us from seeing current situations clearly as they really are and from recognizing the best in ourselves. As a result, we react to present circumstances based on past events.

But instead of automatically reacting, we can start to notice the past event that the current situation triggers within us. Why keep living the old circumstances over and over? As we call out these blurts and separate past from present perspectives, negative history will no longer dominate our lives. We see that it's usually an inner filter that causes a negative reaction in us, not the present person or circumstance.

Give this strategy a shot and see if it doesn't help you to separate the past from the present, see current moments with clarity, and handle them in a more positive way.

Today's Takeaway

Place into perspective past people or situations that cause present-day blurts, separate them from the current situation, and you'll have a happier, more productive writing journey.

SEPTEMBER 18
Practice Acts of Kindness

*Practice kindness all day to everybody and
you will realize you're already in heaven now.*

—Jack Kerouac

It might sound odd, but helping others has a boomerang effect commonly known as the "helper's high." Performing good deeds boosts our moods, calms us down, and relieves us of stress-related illnesses. The bursts of euphoria come from dopamine and endorphin squirts released in the brain.

Medical studies show that the saliva of compassionate people contains more immunoglobulin A—an antibody that fights infection. Brain scans of benevolent people show that generosity gives them a calmer disposition, less stress, better emotional health, and higher self-worth.

"So what does kindness have to do with writing resilience?" you ask. Everything. When we help others in need, it takes us away from our own writing burdens, gives our immune systems an extra boost, and makes us feel better. And it gives us an appreciation for our own lot in life. In short, caring for others boosts our writing resilience. Now are you sold on the old adage that it's better to give than to receive?

Today's Takeaway

Perform an act of kindness not only because it makes a difference in someone else's life but also because it makes a difference in yours and benefits you as a writer.

SEPTEMBER 19
Monitor Your Pick-Me-Ups

*Never get so focused on what you're looking for
that you overlook the thing you actually find.*
—Ann Patchett

Many authors use pick-me-ups to relieve writing pressures—a cup of coffee, beer, chocolate, Red Bull, bowl of ice cream, or a shopping trip. And chances are that you're no exception. Most of us have our guilty pleasures that bring us down after writing jags or lift us up before them. To maintain resilience, it's important that our pick-me-ups contribute to our craft, not detract from it.

Think about what you reach for and how often. Is it booze, pills, or sugar? Is it occasional or regular? Do you routinely overindulge in alcohol or food? Do you drown yourself in compulsive behaviors such as gambling, overspending, sex, or working?

If we're not careful, the remedy we use to relieve writing stress can become the problem instead of the relief. Pick-me-ups are only temporary solutions. We return to them again the next time we're under the gun. If they stop relieving stress, we up the ante and look for stronger ways to feel good. To keep from getting into this unhealthy cycle, monitor your pick-me-ups and make sure you use them in moderation. And don't forget that less is more.

Today's Takeaway

Monitor your pick-me-ups so that your temporary stress reliever doesn't become the stressor that sabotages your writing resilience and productivity.

SEPTEMBER 20
Switch Channels During a Downturn

*We gain tremendous confidence when we are
suddenly faced with a painful situation or memory
and are able to sustain our positive focus.*
—Fredric Luskin

When struggling with words consumes more of your time than your productivity, it's natural to become agitated and bewildered. Hit with devastating news about your writing, frustration might block your way. Switching channels can help you feel gratitude and underscore what's good and beautiful in your life.

Switching channels is much like switching TV programs. The first switch is to remind ourselves we were made for these discouraging times. The elegant design of our nervous system prewired us to surmount the harshest challenges and land on our feet. The second switch is to remember we're not alone and to be inspired by the thousands of successful writers who visited this place and on whose shoulders we stand. The third switch is to change our channel from a grievance to something we're grateful for, a person or pet we love, a thing of beauty, such as a flower, or forgive someone for a small offense.

Practicing this technique can keep you from losing heart and feeling defeat. It can restore your stamina and propel you forward with your craft.

Today's Takeaway

In difficult times, tune in to these three channels and notice what happens. Usually you will have shifts in body sensations such as lowered heart rate, slowed breathing, or loosened muscles, more peace of mind, and greater stamina.

SEPTEMBER 21
Pendulate Your Body Stress

Adopting the right attitude can convert
a negative stress into a positive one.
—Hans Selye

The pendulum exercise refers to the natural swing of your nervous system between sensations of wellbeing and stress. The exercise brings your attention to the presence of natural relaxation that often gets eclipsed by stressful body sensations during around-the-clock writing.

With your eyes closed, notice a place in your body where you feel stress. It can show up as pain, an ache, or a constriction. Then swing your attention to a place inside where you feel less stress or no stress. Focus there on the absence of stress, noticing your bodily sensations: steady heartbeat, slowed breathing, softened jaw, relaxed muscles. Remain focused there and note the sensation for ten seconds. Then visualize that sensation spreading to other parts of your body for another ten seconds.

Now shift back to the place where you originally felt stress. If it has changed, focus on the sensation of the change. Continue moving your attention back and forth between what is left of the stress and the relaxed parts of your body. As you shift, note where stress has lessened and savor the lessening so it can spread to other parts of your body.

Nothing erases unpleasant body stress more effectively than conscious concentration on the pleasant body sensations.

Today's Takeaway

When you have unpleasant body sensations, get in the habit of pendulating to the parts of your body where you have pleasant sensations and spend time there to offset the unpleasantness.

SEPTEMBER 22
Topple Thoughts That Jerk You Around

Watch your thoughts; they become words.
Watch your words; they become actions.
Watch your habits; they become character.
Watch your character; it becomes your destiny.

—Eleanor Roosevelt

Ultimately, what we believe about our writing capabilities determines our literary destiny. Thoughts have no real power over us unless we give in to them. They are nothing more than synapses firing in our brains, but we can be way too quick to believe them. Although they have very little to do with truth, thoughts jerk us around and whip us into shape so much so that *we don't have thoughts; thoughts have us.*

Once we believe them, they become real and powerful. They overtake and dominate us, calling the shots in our lives. They cause us to feel and act in ways consistent with them—ways not always in keeping with our writing goals or best interests. Entrapped by them, we live at their mercy. Don't believe everything you think.

It's important for us writers not to believe everything we think about our literary potential. As thoughts stream through your mind, keep a bead on them, making conscious choices about which ones you believe and which ones you don't.

Today's Takeaway

Watch your thoughts, but be careful which ones you turn your power over to, for once you do so they become your destiny.

SEPTEMBER 23
Begin with "Yes"

We begin with "yes," ready to receive reality
just as it is and ready to let it teach us.
—Richard Rohr

Our success starts with the mantra, "yes," not "no." We might hear "no" reverberating in our mental echo chambers from past rejections, disappointments, and letdowns. But our refrain is "yes" to the moment, to the pushbacks, to all the self-doubts, and to all the negative outcomes in the literary world.

We don't have to like the consequences of our writing efforts. We don't have to compare our accomplishments to another writer's successes. It helps to accept our lot instead of preferring it to be different. And we don't need to know where our writing takes us every step of the way. Sometimes we writers find our way by losing it first. When we can say yes to losing our way, our writing becomes an adventure, instead of a problem to solve. That acceptance helps us find out where we are and blooms our creativity.

We need to accept the outcome for what it is, not what our heart wants it to be. When we say yes to the outcome instead of no, it allows space for the question, "What does this writing outcome say to me and what does it have to teach me?"

Today's Takeaway

Begin your day with "yes" to the outcomes in your writing, no matter how challenging or disappointing, in order to build your inner fortitude and to keep moving forward.

SEPTEMBER 24
Stow Away the Power of Positivity

You must not under any pretense allow
your mind to dwell on any thought that is
not positive, constructive, optimistic, kind.

—Emmet Fox

If you're like many writers, you automatically highlight the aspects of your writing that make you hot under the collar: there are the same lousy rejections, the usual inconsiderate publisher, or the writing conference wasn't anything to write home about. You build your resentment list and filter your writing practice through a negative lens.

Studies show that a positive outlook can undo the damage that writing stress and negative attitudes do to the mind and body, making us more stress resilient. You can trump your negative lens by learning to see and underscore the upside.

Don't let pleasantness slip by without highlighting it. Start pinpointing the positive aspects of your writing world, no matter how small they seem: you love the way you feel when you write about a great plot. You love the smell of the flowers at your writing station or the breeze against your face when you write outside. You appreciate the high fives your writing group gave you on your last reading. Taking time to dwell on your constructive thoughts creates positive feelings and pleasant sensations that offset negative attitudes and boost writing resiliency.

Today's Takeaway

Release your negative thoughts one by one and fill that opened space with positive thoughts that are more likely to propel you further along your writing trajectory.

SEPTEMBER 25
Reboot Your Lighter Side

Life is a drama full of tragedy and comedy. You should
learn to enjoy the comic episodes a little more.
—Jeanette Walls

The road to successful writing and publication has plenty of its own tragedy, but it doesn't have to be all grim determination. It is paved with light-heartedness, too, if we choose to focus on it. But sometimes with our noses to the grind, we become so determined, persistent, and goal oriented that we consider lighter moments to be frivolous or irresponsible.

Too many of us have forgotten how to have fun. Writing involves both tragedy and comedy. The lighter side gives us elbowroom and breathing space from daily writing pressures. All of us have a playful child inside longing to emerge. Taking time to let out that playful part of ourselves fortifies our resilience and perseverance. And that allows us to handle the difficult moments more easily.

Make it a habit to get in touch with your lighter side and explore it thoroughly at least once a day, ideally before sitting at your writing desk.

Today's Takeaway
Make a special effort to lighten up and reboot your lighter side, inviting fun and play as your writing companions.

SEPTEMBER 26
Throw Down Your Crutches

For me, a happy ending is … more coming
to a place where a person has a clear vision of
his or her own life in a way that enables them
to throw down their crutches and walk.

—Jill McCorkle

You have renewed moments of ecstasy when, after many rejections, you win a writing award or your manuscript is finally accepted. Your confidence swells. Success has arrived, and you are high as a kite. You're on your way. What great things are next?

Months later a magazine sends you a form e-mail rejecting your short story. Bad news continues to stare you down. Your next three submissions are all met with rejections, hurling you into a deep depression. What happened to the success you tasted? Things are not working out as you had expected. Your dream evaporates.

There are very few happy endings with a red bow tied around them. How many of us put our emotional well being at the mercy of one or a series of writing incidents? The writing life is full of frustrations and disappointments. Instead of depending on external situations to determine our happiness, we can throw down our crutches and walk. We can use past successes as a source of inner strength. We can remove our necks from the chopping block and experience each letdown as a lesson to build our inner fortitude. Meditate on how you can use a writing letdown to build inner fortitude so that it benefits you in your future literary life.

Today's Takeaway

Draw upon your inner strength, keep your feet firmly planted on the ground, and walk on your own when disappointments threaten to uproot your confidence.

SEPTEMBER 27
Stop Banging Your Head Against the Wall

Resisting pain truly is banging your head against the wall of reality ... you are piling on feelings of anger, frustration, and stress on top of the pain.
—Kristin Neff

If you have written for any length of time, you have suffered. There's a formula that says suffering occurs when we resist emotional pain: Suffering = Pain X Resistance. When a writing outcome matches our wants and desires, we're happy and satisfied. But when a writing consequence doesn't fit with our expectation, we suffer because we want it to be different.

It's the resistance of wanting the outcome to be different on top of the painful situation itself that creates our suffering. We suffer when we prefer a different outcome, turn against ourselves, or reject the consequences of our writing in any way.

Practically all writers experience the pain of self-doubt, rejection, or agony of endless waiting. But if we accept the outcome of a situation *exactly* as it is, we don't have to suffer. We have the option of banging our heads against the wall (suffering) or not, depending upon whether we accept or reject the tough outcomes of our efforts.

Meditate on accepting a part of your writing life that has challenged you. If you can't change it, accept it fully in your heart and soul then bring self-compassion to your disappointment.

Today's Takeaway

When writing disappointments stare you down, let the heartbreak of your suffering stir your acceptance and self-compassion into action to reduce the suffering.

SEPTEMBER 28
Fire and Wire Together

Brain cells that fire together wire together.
—Carla Schatz

When we receive an e-mail rejection of a manuscript (Ugh! And we will receive more than one), we might want to tell the agent or editor to stick the S.A.S.E. where the sun doesn't shine. After all, we have spent months or years perfecting our craft. To have it dissed in one fell swoop of an e-mail can be maddening! It's okay to be pissed off, but we don't have to stay there.

Along those lines, when we are in states of anger and resentment, our brain fires then wires with those negative emotional reactions. Over time it becomes a pattern that can sabotage our writing success. But we can literally change the neural connections in our central nervous system by acting instead of reacting. The timing of this activity is critical to determine which neural connections are strengthened and retained and which ones are weakened and eliminated.

If we want to rid ourselves of sustained anger and resentment, we can change our response in the heat of the moment. Calming ourselves when bad news stares us down can change the firing and wiring that causes us prolonged distress.

Today's Takeaway

Instead of doing the same thing and expecting different results when you get upset about your writing, calm yourself with self-compassion in order to alter negative patterns of defeat.

SEPTEMBER 29
Abstain from Sticking Pencils in Your Eyes

What I've become convinced makes a writer
are the days you hate it, the days you'd
rather stick those pencils in your eyes.
—Ron Rash

We've all had those days, the days we hate writing. Beautiful weather beckons, and the last thing we want to do is sequester ourselves at our writing stations. Call me old fashioned, but I don't think we have to stick pencils in our eyes to cope. And I don't think we have to deprive ourselves of a beautiful day, either.

It's important for us to write even at times when we don't want to. Disciplining ourselves in this way can make us better writers. But it's also important to treat ourselves the way we would our best friends or loved ones. It's called positive reinforcement.

After a regimen of writing, we can treat ourselves to a favorite food or activity. If the weather beckons, a walk in the park or around the neighborhood can be a positive reward for a round of disciplined writing. Instead of punishing ourselves, we get better results if we reward ourselves for a job well done.

Today's Takeaway

On days you don't want to write, instead of sticking pencils in your eyes, discipline yourself to pen something for a period of time then reward yourself for a job well done.

SEPTEMBER 30
Look What's Happening—Seriously

If you take a deep breath and look around,
"Look what's happening to me!"
can become "Look what's happening!"
—Sylvia Boorstein

So look what's happening! The incredible drama of a writing life, and we're in it—the good, bad, and ugly. It's not happening *to* us. It's happening *for* us, and we're active participants in it, not victims of it.

When a bad thing happens beyond our control in our literary world, we can surrender to it by not demanding that it be different. We can think of ourselves as survivors and accept the painful things without crumbling. When we think of ourselves as survivors instead of victims—no matter what happens—we are empowered. Then we can consider how the unwelcome event is happening *for* us to become stronger.

If we use writing letdowns to improve our thoughts, feelings, and actions, we create a positive experience out of a negative one. This mindset teaches us that the control over our writing lives comes from inside, not from outside. It deepens our resilience and gives us fortitude for the next unforeseen event that can make us want to flip our lid. Take a deep breath and contemplate a writing disappointment that you can turn into a neutral or positive one. Then look what's happening!

Today's Takeaway
Become an active participant in your writing dramas, not a victim of them, so that the bad and ugly will be easier to swallow and your resilient zone will grow stronger.

OCTOBER

OCTOBER 1
Use Natural Abdominal Breathing

Breathing in, I calm body and mind.
Breathing out, I smile. Dwelling in the present
moment, I know this is the only moment.
—Thich Nhat Hanh

Much of the time when we're writing—trying so hard to get the words just right—we forget to breathe naturally. We either hold our breath, or we take shallow breaths. When we breathe naturally, the way we did as newborns, our abdomens expand as we inhale, and contract as we exhale. By practicing natural abdominal breathing, we can achieve a state of deep relaxation. And it only takes five minutes to practice. Here's how it works:

Place one hand on your chest, the other on your belly. Keeping your upper chest still, gently and slowly inhale a normal amount of air through your nose, and slowly count to four on the in-breath. As you bring the air into the lowest part of your lungs, notice your abdomen rise on the in-breath and fall on the out-breath. Your chest will barely move in abdominal breathing. After each inhalation, hold your breath briefly then exhale slowly and gently, again counting to four, letting your entire body go limp.

Repeat these steps for five minutes each day or several five-minute sets per day. In a short while, you'll notice a reduction in your stress level.

Today's Takeaway

The more you take time to practice natural abdominal breathing, the more moments of calm you'll have, and your ability to relax will increase along with your best writing ever.

OCTOBER 2
Let Go of Control

Some of us think holding on makes us
strong, but sometimes it is letting go.

—Hermann Hesse

There are times that it takes more strength to let go of control rather than hold on to it. One of the bitter pills we must swallow is that we have no control over our literary lives once projects are submitted. And this is not necessarily a bad thing if we keep it in mind. In fact, it can serve us in many ways. Fretting, worrying, and ruminating don't prepare us for anything; they just zap our energies and distract us from present concerns. Once we have persevered through the hard part of writing and rewrite after rewrite and submit the manuscript, we're powerless over the outcome.

In the words of novelist E. M. Forster, "We must be willing to let go of the life we have planned, so as to have the life that is waiting for us." Surrender and letting go—the opposites of giving up or giving in—are actions of personal power, not defeat. They contribute to perseverance and inner peace, allowing us to focus on the things we can control and move forward with our writing lives.

What attitudes, feelings, or actions do you need to let go of to unblock your path, develop resilience, and propel you forward in your writing life? Write them down and contemplate each one.

Today's Takeaway

Once you've done all you can do toward your writing plans, release your willfulness, let go of control, and welcome the serenity and calm waiting for you.

OCTOBER 3
Treat the Highs and Lows Equally

*Celebrate the highs but don't take them
anymore seriously than the lows, and don't take
the lows anymore seriously than the highs.*
—Wendy Tyson

Despite the agonizing heartache we face, there's a tremendous upside to getting our work published. It's an accomplishment that few aspiring scribes achieve. It's euphoric, worthy of celebration. But when the lows come, we tend to treat them more seriously than the highs.

Because of the mind-body connection, the cells of our bodies eavesdrop on our thoughts from the wings of our minds. When we're disappointed about our writing, our bodies go with the downturn of our feelings, making us feel worse. We might hold our heads down or slump when we walk.

The good news is if we change our posture, breathing patterns, facial expressions, gestures, movements, words, and tone, we automatically change our internal state. For example, making the facial expression of a smile can make you happy. Training your body to position itself the way you want to think and feel adjusts your thoughts and feelings to the way you want them to be. Making body adjustments—pulling your shoulders back, standing or sitting up straight, walking in a more expansive way—can pull you out of a letdown.

Today's Takeaway
When writing challenges hang over you, position your body in a powerful way or make strong gestures to jumpstart your positive mental scope that stretches the span of writing possibilities.

OCTOBER 4
Back Off from Overwhelming Yourself

Just one step. One step at a time.
You don't have to do them all at once.
—Jennifer Niven

No matter how tough the writing challenges get, we don't have to do it all at once. And we can live by the phrases "one word at a time" and "easy does it." When the burdens are too much to bear, when we struggle with heartache and indecision, or when the waves of writing seem to drown us, these two phrases can help navigate us through the sea of emotional turmoil.

These simple phrases release us from immobilization and provide solace. We take only this second, this moment, this hour. We live our lives now, making it through each day, one by one. When we are able to work through writing burdens with ease step-by-step, it breaks down large tasks into small steps, and we don't feel overwhelmed with the big picture. As we take each step at a steady pace, we can trust that all is well, we're on course, and we will arrive in good stead.

Today's Takeaway
When writing obstacles overwhelm you, find solace in the mottoes "one word at a time" and "easy does it"; these simple reminders will help you get through writing tasks and any literary woes that befall you.

OCTOBER 5
High-Five Your Local Bookstore

Bookstores, like libraries, are the physical manifestation of the wide world's longest, most thrilling conversation.
—Richard Russo

My local bookstore, Malaprop's Bookstore and Café, is a unique gathering spot where locals browse and drink lattes and aspiring scribes hunch over laptops tapping in what they hope will be the next bestseller. Patrons are tantalized by pungent smells of fresh-ground coffee, commingled with a just-off-the-press scent of new ink and the musty aroma and seductive invitations from the bookshelves—thrillers, mysteries, memoir, histories, broken secrets, and sage advice on life.

Sometimes we authors forget that bookstores are alive, that they have feelings, and we take them for granted. We prance in and check the shelves to see if they stock our books. If you're like me, you're damned if they do and damned if they don't. When my books are missing from the stacks, I assume the store isn't stocking them. When the books are on the shelves, I conclude the store isn't promoting them.

The relationship between authors and bookstores is a two-way street. We expect bookstores to support our work but forget that they also need our support, especially independent bookstores. If you haven't already, visit your local bookstores and let them know of your work. Most local independents like to promote local authors, but they also appreciate local authors supporting them.

Today's Takeaway

Frequent your local independent bookstores, purchase books from them, participate in their events, and encourage others to do the same.

OCTOBER 6
Diminish Your Wants

I cried because I had no shoes.
Then I met a man who had no feet.

—Saadi

When we think of happiness in terms of what we want, we operate from a position of loss and discontent. We focus on what's missing from our lives—a short story published in a magazine, paid book tour around the country, award for best fiction—and fool our minds into thinking more of *something* or *someone* will fill the void.

Whatever we focus on expands; wanting increases the feeling that our lives are lacking. Then we want and need more and more to satisfy the hunger. The best way to reach contentment is to want and feel grateful for what we already have. How many times a day do we stop to appreciate what we have—food on the table, shelter over our heads, our health, and special people who touch our lives?

A wounded vet who lost his leg climbed to the summit of Mount Everest, persevering on one limb. Let's be mindful of the wonderful gifts that perhaps we have overlooked, forgot, or taken for granted. Counting our blessings for all we have turns an outlook of dissatisfaction into abundance and the desire to share with others.

Today's Takeaway

Diminish your wants by *wanting what you have instead of having what you want* and abundance and fulfillment are yours forever.

OCTOBER 7
Use the "F" Word in Difficult Situations

Flow with whatever may happen
and let your mind be free.
—Chuang Tzu

Flow. What a great "F" word: the ability to roll with whatever our writing lives send our way! The ability to fit into any unexpected situation instead of trying to force the situation to fit our specifications is a wonderful asset to our writing.

When we think we're lost or not in control, flowing can help things turn out okay in the end. Sometimes penning words can be like a river flowing to the sea, and we don't even have to swim. We can relax and flow with it. Flowing with faith gets us through difficult writing situations without the oppositional reactions of frustration and anger.

See if you can identify one person or situation that challenges your ability to flow. Close your eyes and imagine that you're in the presence of that person or situation. Try using the "F" word inside your mind's eye and flow. Notice what happens in your body, how much freer and looser you feel, and how much using the "F" word reduces your tension.

Today's Takeaway

Notice how practicing the "F" words of fluidity, flexibility, and flowing brings you more lightness, happiness, and peace of mind over the long haul.

OCTOBER 8
Enter the Great Shadows

The cave you fear to enter holds the treasure you seek.
—Joseph Campbell

One night Nasreddin lost his house key on the way home. A stranger passed by and saw Nasreddin on all fours under a streetlight searching for his key. Perplexed, the stranger asked Nasreddin why he was on his hands and knees. When Nasreddin told the stranger his dilemma, the kind man helped search for the key. After hours of futile searching, the stranger asked, "Are you sure you dropped the key in this spot?" Then pointing toward a small alleyway, Nasreddin said, "Oh, no. I dropped it over there in the dark." Frustrated, the stranger exploded, "Then why are we looking for it under this lamppost?" "Because the light's better here," Nasreddin replied.

The moral to this ancient tale is that we often seek familiar places for answers due to fear of venturing into the shadows where solutions actually lie. The mind doesn't like the unfamiliar, preferring instead to cling to what it knows and where it's comfortable, often putting us at odds with writing demands. French author and poet Antoine de Saint-Exupéry said, "We are afraid to let go of our petty reality in order to grasp at a great shadow." However, we often find the key to creative resilience in the shadows where we fear to tread.

Today's Takeaway

Eliminate petty reality and grasp at a great shadow in some area of your writing life, no matter how small, then stand back and watch the light switch on.

OCTOBER 9
Ignore Cutthroat Critics

Who knew paper and ink could be so vicious.
—Kathryn Stockett

The literary world is full of critics. If we want to write something of value, certain critics will scrutinize it. Call these particular reviewers haters, trolls, or just downright cutthroats, but they are inescapable.

When we get an eviscerating review, we want to retaliate. An Amazon reader writes a scathing rant of your book, describing it as vapid and lifeless. Feeling your blood boil, your first inclination is to plop down in front of the computer and whip off an equally scathing response. Or a critic rips into your debut novel, saying you would be better off flipping burgers. Instead, you flip your lid and start to respond.

But don't. One of the cardinal rules for authors is never to respond publically to a critic's belligerent rant. It only makes us look defensive (which we are) and gives more attention to the critic's initial review. The best course of action is to leave the review alone until it fades away. Then we remind ourselves that it's only one person's subjective perspective, that harsh reviews have slammed the best writers of our time.

It's not the cutthroat critic—the one who has never written anything of importance—who matters anyway. It's those of us who put in the hours, whose faces are marred by blood, sweat and tears along the way.

Today's Takeaway
Avoid giving power to cutthroat critics who are more interested in tearing your work to shreds than adding constructive feedback by simply moving on to your next project.

OCTOBER 10
Dislodge the Relentless Complainer

*It is humbling to realize that the voice giving the
controlling demands and criticisms was not really
as intelligent as the one receiving them!*
—W. Timothy Gallwey

We all have a relentless complainer who lives inside us. And we might
not know how to act without it. If we met this critical companion face-to-
face at a social event, our eyebrows would jump at the cruel and cutting
remarks, wondering what the hell is wrong with this merciless judge. We
would assume that some terrible thing had happened, that this person
lives in the fallout of some terrible event to cause such negative rants.
Although correct, we would put immediate distance between us.

Stepping back, it's obvious that our relentless complainer doesn't
tell the truth, whittles us down to a stub, and undermines our writing
resilience and perseverance. We can loosen the tyrannical grip by not
believing or agreeing with anything it screams at us.

Try watching your relentless complainer with dispassion without
arguing, fighting, or debating. You'll realize it's not as wise as you are
and that it's only a tiny part of your mind. As you watch your complainer from afar and without judgment, pay attention to what you're
like without this chronic part of you.

Today's Takeaway

Refuse to allow your relentless complainer to dominate your thinking;
maintain your separation from it and stay true to yourself as you persevere with your writing.

OCTOBER 11
Keep Chipping Away

A book must be the ax for the frozen sea inside us.

—Franz Kafka

"Where's the ticker tape?" I wondered, after the release of my debut murder mystery. To my dismay, I didn't even make the evening news. I couldn't find it on the *New York Times* bestseller list, either. I got a decent size check but not enough to pay off the mortgage. What's the deal?

Welcome to my writing world. Writing is hard work—years of revising, pitching ideas to agents and publishers, editing, then marketing. Plagued by self-doubt and uncertainty, we writers sacrifice our personal lives—holidays and birthdays—and in some cases our health. Despite the hard work and low pay, there's something tremendously satisfying about this insane process—more than money and fame.

For those of us who keep writing, there's no such thing as enough. We're drawn by the pull of what we love because it's a journey of self-discovery. It takes us deeper into our inner workings—that unmapped landscape—where we search for answers to the mystery of the world and ourselves. We chip away at the frozen sea inside until the amorphous entity takes form, slowly revealing itself with a wink.

Aside from your enjoyment of writing and a completed product, what deeper ore are you mining? Meditate on what it is that you keep chipping away. What form has it taken so far? And what are you learning about you?

Today's Takeaway

Keep chipping away at the frozen sea inside you until a fully formed writing self is revealed, winking its small clear eye.

OCTOBER 12
Press the Flesh

Above all, a query letter is a sales pitch
and it is the single most important page
an unpublished writer will ever write.
—Nicholas Sparks

Perhaps you don't ride elevators much. But you still need an elevator pitch—a quick and catchy summary of your writing idea that could be told in an elevator. Imagine people stepping into an elevator with you, asking, "What's it about?" You want to grab them before reaching the fifth floor.

Many authors say crafting the pitch is harder than writing the entire manuscript because it must contain appeal, brevity, and a hook. And the pitch is necessary to snag agents, publishers, and publicists who have limited time to give your projects—not to mention potential readers who have thousands of reading choices.

Take time to craft a brief to-the-point summary of your work so you can make a great first impression to whoever shows interest in your project. Whether you present it as a query letter or an elevator pitch, it's the single most important piece an unpublished writer will ever pen. Keep the pitch in your virtual hip pocket so you can easily let people know who you are and what you've written.

Today's Takeaway
Rehearse your sales pitch and carry it in your virtual hip pocket wherever you go to promote your writing off the cuff, and hook interested parties when they inquire.

OCTOBER 13
Weigh Your Commitment to the Craft

*The good news is that going blind is not
going to make you as unhappy as you
think it will. The bad news is that winning the
lottery will not make you as happy as you expect.*
—Daniel Gilbert

How committed are you to writing? On a scale from 0 to 10, how committed would you say you are to honing your craft? What specific actions can you take to raise your commitment score a point or two?

It's an intriguing exercise to consider how devoted we are to our craft. What would you do if you won the lottery and had access to unlimited funds for life. Would you quit writing altogether? Or would you eliminate the other activities and commitments that interfere with your writing agendas and write more often?

Honest answers to these questions reveal a lot about our devotion to the craft. Do we write to make money in hopes of someday getting rich? Or do we work another job to pay bills so we can write for our deep love for the craft?

Of course, there's nothing wrong with making money. But if writing brings you true joy and happiness then all the money in the world won't make you any happier. Since you've already hit the jackpot, it's important to remember why you write to begin with so that losses and disappointments won't be as painful.

Today's Takeaway

Ask yourself what you would do if you won the lottery, then contemplate what your answers mean to you as a writer. If you want to up the ante, think of ways to renew your dedication to writing.

OCTOBER 14
Slow Down, You Move Too Fast

Some days the writing pressure is impossibly relentless,
but every time I allow my brain to relax, I get a
good idea. And I'm writing from joy again.
—Hank Phillippi Ryan

Each of us writers respond to high-pressured situations in different ways. Some of us get energized, ratchet up our inner resources, and thrive. Others muddle through or succumb to pressure, watching our dreams blow up in smoke. What about you? Is your stomach in knots? Do you drag yourself through the day? Do you grind your teeth or clench your hands into fists? And did you swear at the car that cut you off in traffic?

We writers on the fast track need to make elbowroom for downtime. A five-minute slowing down meditation can help. Start with a deep breath, step back from your writing station and social media to reset your pace. Once you're feeling somewhat relaxed, visualize going through your day at a slow pace. Take yourself through your routines, all the while slowing down. See yourself eating slower, driving slower, writing slower, and doing one thing at a time. Imagine the smallest details of the day. Release any images that pop up of hurrying. Notice how you feel as your routines wind down to a slower pace.

Moving at a steady pace puts us at the finish line before those in a frantic race against the clock. And we get to enjoy life as it's happening. Remember, the tortoise won the race.

Today's Takeaway
Make a conscious effort to slow down and let the downtime quiet your mind. You'll get there quicker, healthier, and in one calm piece.

OCTOBER 15
Do Some Soul Searching

Any kind of creative activity is likely to be stressful.
Easiness, relaxation, comfort—these are not conditions
that usually accompany serious work.
—Joyce Carol Oates

From time to time we writers must do some soul searching to discover what's producing our stress by checking in with our thoughts periodically, and always with compassion. Once we question our stressful thoughts, we are no longer victims in our heads.

If we're constantly arguing with family members or squabbling with coworkers, we might gently ask, "What's the common denominator?" Could stress come from forcing our way of doing things or resisting someone else's point of view? What if we've sunk into a worry rut as a coping mechanism, not realizing that it doesn't help and only makes matters worse? Or we might've gotten into a habit of negative thinking that causes us to see the glass as half empty instead of half full.

Take time now to evaluate the answers to what's underneath your stressful reactions. Is it fear of failure? Urgency to complete a project? Or frustration that the words won't come? Once you find the common denominator(s), see if you can calm the concerns.

Today's Takeaway

Make it a habit to do some soul searching on a regular basis to discover the sources of your writing stressors in order to create more harmony and productivity in your literary life.

OCTOBER 16
Forgive What Disturbs Your Tranquility

Forgiveness must encompass all those things which
disturb the tranquility of our soul: the barking dog that
robs you of sleep, the heat of summer, the cold of winter.
—Barbara Wood

Learning to forgive others and ourselves for wrongdoings is a major accomplishment. We writers are not perfect. But when we can absolve our shortcomings, our negative self-doubts, and our harsh judgments and envy, it's a true measure of human success.

What if we could forgive everything that disturbs the tranquility of our writing spirit: the mosquito bites up and down our legs, the party-hardy neighbor, the ringing cell phone, the cranky child, the sulking spouse, the ingrown toenail, the air conditioning on the blink in the summer heat, the roaring motorcycle, the itchy shirt, the aching back, the offline computer, writing deadlines, demanding editors, book clubs that buy our second-hand books, and the barking dog that crapped in the living room floor.

Forgiveness is not just a gift for others it's a gift for us. It neutralizes frustration, irritation, anger, and worry—all the attributes that get in the way of our concentration and creative writing. Go inside right now and take an inventory of all the things that have disturbed your tranquility lately without judging yourself. Then take a moment to forgive every single one.

Today's Takeaway
Forgive the things that come between you and your writing and learn that it isn't those things but your own annoyance that interferes then forgive yourself.

OCTOBER 17
Stand Somewhere Else

*From where we stand, the rain seems random. If we could
stand somewhere else, we would see the order in it.*

—Tony Hillerman

Our thoughts and actions depend on the angle from which we're looking at things. How many of us go through life using only our own standpoint? When we do this, we don't see the whole picture. We only see life
as we think it is. Such a twisted view causes us to miss opportunities to
learn, understand, and love. And it limits our writing experiences.

When we take the viewpoint of someone else, something magical happens. We realize there are so many ways to look at life. Along with changed
perspectives, we usually gain a renewed outlook on life. Our writing
becomes more stimulating, and our landscapes and characters spring into
life. We see something wondrous in everything—beauty in the ordinary,
elegance in the simple, wisdom in the shallow, excitement in the dull.

We have the power to change our daily world simply by standing in
a different place. We can rediscover the world that we have known for
so long and see it with new insight and greater clarity. This flexibility
to look at life from different angles will cultivate more self-confidence,
hope, and inner peace. As you shift your belief system from time to
time, it will move you further along your literary path.

Today's Takeaway

Stand somewhere different and look at the world through fresh eyes—
in multidimensional ways to get the fuller picture instead of just one
slice of it.

OCTOBER 18
See Your Judgments as Mirrors of Yourself

Everything that irritates us about others
can lead us to an understanding of ourselves.

—Carl Jung

Our judgments of others are like automobile headlights—they always seem more glaring than our own. As writers, our criticisms, judgments, and complaints of others keep the spotlight on them and prevent us from seeing our own side of the street. We see our own faults in people who annoy us instead of in ourselves. But an honest scrutiny of our judgments is more self-revealing than we think. When we criticize someone else, it's usually about something we don't like about ourselves.

Understanding this can be a valuable asset informing us about our own faults that we project onto others—flaws that we could work on within ourselves. The secret is to catch ourselves when we judge another person and instead ask what the criticism says about us. Then we can harness the energy we use to criticize others and put it to good use on ourselves.

Once we've mastered this strategy, we can practice self-change and notice how much better it feels to correct our own faults and focus more on ourselves and not on tearing down others.

Today's Takeaway

When we objectively assess our judgments, it gives us insight into what we think about ourselves and helps us identify traits and habits that we'd like to change.

OCTOBER 19
Loosen the Grip of Fear

Of all the liars in the world
sometimes the worst are our fears.
—Rudyard Kipling

Some writers have deep-seated fears of inadequacy, failure, rejection, and abandonment. That's why many of us started writing to begin with: to find acceptance. Of course, that's a slippery slope because the literary world can easily activate those qualities in the mentally healthiest and best writers among us.

When fear rules our lives, it leaves us with a twisted view of our writing capabilities. It makes us hyper vigilant and super sensitive in situations where we need thick skin. And it makes it difficult to connect with others.

Truth be told, fears have no grip on us. They exist only in our minds, not in the outside world. We just think they do. If we think Pinocchio was a compulsive liar, he didn't hold a candle to the lies our fears tell us on a daily basis. Once we realize our writing fears cannot be trusted, we learn that they have no power over us and that they exist only in our heads, not in the real world.

Today's Takeaway

Pinpoint a writing fear that has held you back—embarking on a big writing project, penning something totally different from what you've done before, or speaking in front of a writing group—then try it and realize it isn't nearly as bad as your fear made you think.

OCTOBER 20
Discover What's Beyond the Barrier

*... as soon as we come up against the least edge of
pain, we're gong to run; we'll never know what's beyond
that particular barrier or wall or fearful thing.*
—Pema Chödrön

Ouch! My aching back, the stiffness in my shoulders. Chances are that after sitting at the computer for long writing jags, you start to feel pain in your body. And you know what to do about it. Stretch. Walk around the block. Hop on the treadmill. Pop an aspirin. But what do we do about the other pain—the fear of failure, the hurt of rejection, the heartbreak of disappointment?

Our natural tendency is to deal with the physical pain after sitting for long periods. But as we come up against emotional or psychological pain, we tend to avoid it at all costs. We run in the other direction. When we do this, we rob ourselves because we never know what missed opportunities lay beyond the barrier.

If we ditch the desire for comfort and step into emotional pain, instead of running away from it, it won't kill us. It makes us more resilient and allows us to discover the exciting opportunities before us. Go to the edge of your pain, be fully present with what lays beyond the barrier, and notice the emotional pain subside.

Today's Takeaway

Commit yourself to the emotional growth pains that all writers bump up against by facing them head-on and discovering the gifts that await you beyond the wall.

OCTOBER 21
Welcome Catastrophe

I welcomed catastrophe. It was material.
Missed planes, broken pipes...you name it.
If it was something gone horribly wrong,
it was worth banging out 600 words about.
—Linwood Barclay

Let me share something that happened to me. After scanning my twenty dollars worth of groceries, the checkout clerk looked up at me and said, "That'll be one hundred forty-five dollars and thirty-five cents." Astonished, I looked down at the conveyer belt and noticed the woman in line behind me hadn't put the separating stick between our groceries. Although the mix-up took an extra twenty minutes to straighten out, I didn't flip my lid. Instead, I saw it as grist for the mill. I couldn't wait to get to my computer and bang out this scene in the novel I'd been working on, using it to describe how a couple met.

None of us is powerful enough to fend off unwelcome events in our lives. They will happen no matter what. So we might as well use them to our advantage. Catastrophe can be a huge boon. Mishaps are going to happen, so our best option is to be grateful, use them as rich writing material, and keep our blood pressure from blasting through the roof.

Think of an unwelcomed situation that upset you. Then see if you can turn it into a writing benefit.

Today's Takeaway
Welcoming catastrophe as fodder for your writing helps you accept life on its terms, turn a negative situation into a positive one, and neutralize an otherwise annoying event.

OCTOBER 22
Enhance Your Wellbeing

We may not be able to imagine a life in which we don't
spend... time criticizing ourselves and others; but we
should keep in mind the self-love that is always in play.
—Adam Phillips

Many of us have been taught that self-sacrifice is a great virtue, and it is. But always putting ourselves last is not virtuous and can be just as detrimental to the soul as always putting ourselves first.

When we accept deep within ourselves that we are our own best friends who deserve life's best, we will love and write more fully. When we treat ourselves with the same love and respect, kindness and consideration we give those we care about, we treat ourselves to the grand prize rather than the consolation prize.

Self-love is a difficult concept, often confused with selfishness. Self-sacrifice and self-centeredness keep us stuck. Self-love propels us forward. Human compassion and kindness are natural byproducts of self-love, which spill over into our goodwill toward everyone in our lives. Self-love allows us to extend care for others and do kind deeds without the need for payoff or recognition.

If your self-love tank is running on empty, give yourself encouraging words of affirmation, a big hug, a special treat, free time to do whatever you want, or a genuine compliment.

Today's Takeaway
Enhance your wellbeing by treating yourself with the same love, consideration, and respect that you give to others and go for the grand prize instead of the consolation prize.

OCTOBER 23
Turn a Deaf Ear to Naysayers

*Don't give up. There are too many naysayers out there
who will try to discourage you. Don't listen to them.
The only one who can make you give up is yourself.*
—Sidney Sheldon

Writing success is built on lessons, which are built on failing. Success and failure go together like a hand and glove, milk and cookies. After a failure, we don't listen to naysayers, and we don't naysay to ourselves. We get up, brush ourselves off, and consider our failures or mistakes as lessons. Then we figure out what the mistakes can teach us about our writing selves.

Turning failures into well-learned lessons is a great way to build up instead of tear ourselves down. It's important to look upon naysayers as messengers or teachers who can help us learn more about how we might achieve writing success.

I know it's a hard sell, but think of those who discourage, embarrass, hurt or contradict you or even betray you as doing a great favor. Then meditate on the idea that naysayers can teach you lessons that make you wiser and stronger and better able to successfully meet the next writing challenge that comes your way. Notice what lessons emerge from your meditation.

Today's Takeaway

Turn a deaf ear to naysayers who discourage you because of their own self-inadequacies; use their discouragements as motivation, and never give up writing goals that you seek.

OCTOBER 24
Fix Your Mistakes and Move On

*It took me a long time to learn that
mistakes aren't good or bad; they're just
mistakes, and you clean them up and go on.*
—Kaye Gibbons

All writers make mistakes. Bummer. So what? We're all human. Sometimes when we make a mistake, shame and guilt elbow their way in. We tell ourselves we're bad. We berate ourselves, batter our insides out, and stay stuck there. We confuse our errors with who we are, jam the two together in our heads, and we feel we *are* the mistakes.

Mistakes aren't good or bad; they just are. When we do something wrong, instead of hammering ourselves, it behooves us to stay focused on polishing our craft, repairing the mistake, and moving on. The repair work entails admitting we made a mistake and remembering that mistakes aren't good or bad, they're part of the human condition.

When we refrain from self-condemnation and forgive ourselves, things have a way of working themselves out. Tomorrow is a new day. Our minds will be clearer, the mistakes won't look as bad, and we can move on with our writing for god's sake.

Today's Takeaway

Untangle yourself from your mistakes, admit your shortcomings without shame or guilt, then forgive yourself and move on with your writing.

OCTOBER 25
Don't Cripple Yourself with Protection

People should not be protected
from the world ... it cripples them.
—Josephine Humphreys

It's human nature to protect ourselves from opposition, and we're hard-wired to do so. We need our survival brain to protect us from danger, but it can hinder us when it comes to risking our necks with writing challenges. We cannot buy writing success, no matter how much money or power we have. Like all things of value, writing success is difficult to achieve. But we can attain it through hard work, persistence, and risky effort.

The only person who can achieve the success is me, myself, and I. We each have the desire and the skills, but we must put our noses to the grindstone. We cannot run and hide when the going gets rough. We cannot look for protection from the hard knocks under the rocks. We must face the writing world with courage and confidence so that we're strengthened instead of crippled.

We can boldly take positive action, perhaps breaking old and rigid rules by which we lived or taking a different approach to a recurring problem. Ask yourself, "What have I avoided or protected myself from that could cripple my writing? And what can I do differently to carry myself forward through opposition?"

Today's Takeaway

Persist in the face of opposition, instead of running away, and take many different approaches to writing challenges until a path is cleared for you.

OCTOBER 26
Train Your Self-Doubt

Your doubt can become a good quality if you train it.
—Rainer Maria Rilke

There's a common myth that successful writers don't have self-doubt. Truth be told, famous writers, perhaps more than other artists, are riddled with it. Self-doubt stalks us when we're glued to the computer screen and lurks over our shoulders when we're weaving a plot or scribbling a poem. Am I talented enough? Will people like my work? Will people like me?

Doubt is not a totally bad quality. It can keep us from becoming too complacent with our writing and settling into mediocrity. It keeps us on our toes and motivates us to do our best work. Once we see the benefits of self-doubt, we're empowered instead of intimidated by it.

Successful writers, like novelist Harlan Coben, have learned to live with it and train it to their advantage: "If a book starts going too well, I usually know there's a problem. I need to struggle. I need that self-doubt. I need to think it's not the best thing ever."

Taking this sage advice, identify a self-doubt that has cramped your writing style or crippled you from growing fully as a writer. Harness it—instead of running from it—and channel it into useful writing so it doesn't paralyze you.

Today's Takeaway

Capitalize on your self-doubt, harness it, and use it as encouragement to motivate your writing, and you will have conquered it.

OCTOBER 27
Neutralize Disharmony with Empathy

It's useful to go out of this world and see
it from the perspective of another one.
—Terry Pratchett

The ability to stand in someone's shoes and see their point of view increases our understanding and sensitivity and cultivates resilience. Empathy neutralizes disharmony and liberates our narrow and negative judgments. Plus it helps us respond to situations with more confidence and face difficult people and situations with more peace of mind.

Suppose you're having dinner with someone special in an expensive restaurant with candlelight, soft music, and intimate conversation. Your server is invasive, impatient, and short tempered. How would you feel? Most people would say annoyed or angry.

Then someone next to you mentions that the server's son was killed in a car wreck, that she's a single mom who has to work. Now how would you feel? Most people would say sympathetic.

What changed? She's still the same. Instead, something inside you switched from anger to compassion because you put yourself in her place. Chances are you feel kinder inside, and your actions toward her are more positive. Perhaps you even leave her a generous tip. We never know the burdens that people carry on a daily basis, but when we go deeper into our hearts, we live in a world with less fear, isolation, and loneliness.

Today's Takeaway

Suspend your point of view temporarily and walk in another person's shoes for a while in order to create more resilience and positive feelings for yourself.

OCTOBER 28
Surrender Your Attachments

Surrender means wisely accommodating
ourselves to what is beyond our control.
—Sylvia Boorstein

Most of us writers are attached to the results of our work and rightly so. Our vision is to see our writing reviewed in a good light and readers enjoying it. We want it to make us famous and earn lots of money until it hits the big screen in an Oscar worthy movie.

Getting overly attached to this vision dooms us to a writing life of worry, frustration, and insecurity. Once attachment grips us, we become obsessed with controlling the world around us, trying to make the outcome fit with our desires, leaving us feeling miserable and exhausted.

The literary world is unpredictable. An agent sends an e-mail offering to speak with us about representation, and we never hear another word from her (yes, that actually happened). A publisher offers a contract. Before signing it, they file for bankruptcy a month later and close shop.

The key to sanity is to write our best work, avoid tightly attaching to outcomes beyond our control, and make the best of what the literary world has to offer. Oftentimes situations actually turn out better than we expect when we surrender our attachments. Meditate on a pending writing attachment. Consider surrendering it to make room perhaps for something even better.

Today's Takeaway

Work hard toward achieving your writing goals without getting hung up on the results; once you've done the best you can, accept what the writing world has to offer.

OCTOBER 29
Be for Yourself

If you are not for yourself, who will be for you?
If you are only for yourself, what are you?
—Tony Hillerman

To achieve success as a writer, you must be for yourself, not against others but for yourself. If not, then who will be for you? That sounds simple enough, but some of us are not used to being for ourselves. We have more comfort with being for others, perhaps because we were told in subtle or not so subtle ways that we don't count. Or we got the idea from somewhere that we don't deserve to be happy.

Many of us are too quick to judge ourselves, to minimize our accomplishments, or to resign ourselves to being the underdog. Are you on your own side? Do you look out for your best interests? Can you advocate for what you need?

We can ask these questions each day on our writing journey. In our answers, we want to make sure we treat ourselves as well as we do our best friends. Take time to go inside and ask if you wish yourself well. Do you advocate for yourself? And do you nurture yourself on a regular basis? What other actions can you take to be on your own team?

Today's Takeaway

Be on your own side, wish yourself well, keep a lookout for your best interests, and be your own best advocate as you progress on your writing journey.

OCTOBER 30
Recreate Yourself

*I admire people who recreate themselves. And it seems
to me that what gives us all the opportunity to be heroic
is that we work to…be better than we were yesterday.*
—Robert Crais

When our goal is to become better writers than we were yesterday, we discover that our limitations are defined in the ways we use our minds. When we think the worst, it brings about the worst. On the flipside, thinking and expecting the best reaps positive results.

It's heroic to learn that the self-fulfilling prophecy is alive and well in our heads, and that we have the power to change our lives by changing our perspectives. Perhaps most importantly we learn that life isn't all misery, drudgery, and heartache.

We don't live in a fantasy world of wonder and magic, yet we need to look for the best in all situations. We don't let narrow-mindedness keep us from growing, and we stay open to new experiences with each new day. We become better writers today than we were yesterday when we look at our writing life through realistic but optimistic eyes, when we think positive thoughts, experience positive feelings, and expect positive outcomes.

Today's Takeaway

Recreate your literary life by taking a bird's-eye view of your perspective, noting what you need to change about your outlook today in order to fulfill your writing dreams of tomorrow.

OCTOBER 31
Preserve the Good Moments

It was a good moment, the kind you would like to press between the pages of a book, or hide in your sock drawer, so you could touch it again.
—Rick Bragg

We all have those good moments, rich writing memories, peak literary experiences—the kind we want to preserve forever that often get pushed into the backs of our minds to make more room for the bad ones.

The best way to preserve the good times is to be mindfully present as they happen and to underscore them in the moment. Instead of zipping through an important writing experience, it's important for us to savor and spend time with it. Being fully in the moment during positive events expands our peripheral vision and imprints the event in our mind, embedding our personal resources and opportunities for use under future possibly difficult conditions.

Arming ourselves with an arsenal of good moments provides us with the hope of overcoming future writing obstacles. Ask yourself if you were to choose a writing memory as a keepsake to press between the pages of a book or hide in your sock drawer so you could look at it again, what would it be?

Today's Takeaway

Remove your blinders and press the good writing moments between the pages of your mind so you have access to them when it's difficult to recall the personal resources you have at your disposal.

NOVEMBER

NOVEMBER 1
Build Your Life Around Writing

*I write as a way of keeping myself going. You build your
life around writing, and it's what gets you through.*
—Robert Morgan

If we put little rocks into a wide-mouthed jar and try to fit big rocks inside, there won't be room for the larger rocks. But if we put the big rocks in first, the small rocks will fall in around them. Some writers are more successful than others because they treat writing as a big rock. They put writing first and build their lives around it.

Some tasks are more important than others, so we must decide what comes first. We need to set priorities that are clear and practical. The clearer we are on what we want to accomplish and how we plan to achieve our goal, the more focused, efficient, and less stressed we are.

As writers, it's important to decide which aspects of the literary life are key. After we focus first on the things that require immediate attention, we put nonessentials on the back burner or farm them out to an assistant or family member. We build our lives around writing, not writing around our lives, and that's what gets us through. Ask yourself, "What do I need to do to give writing a higher priority in my life?"

Today's Takeaway

Ask yourself if writing really has a high enough priority in your life, then position it accordingly so it keeps you going and gets you through to your goals.

NOVEMBER 2
Listen to Your Body Talk

*We will be in tune with our bodies only
if we truly honor them. We can't be in good
communication with the enemy.*
—Harriet Lerner

For writers who sit for long stretches, listening to body talk is important. Chances are we spend so much time in our minds we forget to listen to the bodies that house and get us from place to place. We are so accustomed to living in our bodies that we ignore stored-up stiffness and soreness and don't realize when they have something to say.

You might notice that your chest muscles and those in front of your underarms are often tight from repeatedly reaching out in front. It's time to pay closer attention and give our bodies the nurturing they need.

Find a quiet place where you can sit or lie flat comfortably and relax as much as you can. Slowly start scanning at your feet, working your way up your body. As you move up each muscle, focus on each muscle group one at a time. Note areas where you're holding tension, tightness, or pain or places that are stiff, sore, or sensitive. Then stretch those areas with built-up stress, fully noticing where tension is held, followed by its release.

Today's Takeaway

Honor your body when it speaks to you with soreness or tightness and care for it so that it can continue to house and support you in productive and happy writing.

NOVEMBER 3
Unchain from Perfection

*I have not written a perfect sentence, in the
literary sense. It's a lot easier to throw a perfect
pass than to write a perfect sentence.*

—Greg Iles

Although we writers can be our own worst critics, few if any of us can scribble a perfect sentence. Many of us are such sticklers that nobody, not even ourselves, can meet our standards. We tell ourselves nothing we do is good enough, and the flaws stand out from the shine. Even when others don't demand perfection, we demand it. And it can stop us in our tracks.

Our main literary goal is to unchain ourselves from thoughts that we can never get a plot right or a sentence perfect enough. Authors chained to perfection in everything they hope to write cannot attain it in anything they actually pen. The first step is to accept that there's no such thing as perfection. Once we sidestep perfectionism and allow for mistakes, our creative juices start to flow again.

Does perfectionism shackle your writing? If so, unchain yourself with free writing where you forget everything your teachers taught you about grammar, spelling, and handwriting. Then write nonstop those first few stupid pages without judgment.

Today's Takeaway

Unchain yourself from the notion of perfection, do the best you can, and it will be enough to achieve excellence in your writing.

NOVEMBER 4
Reboot Your Physical/Psychological Space

If you let the temporary relief achieved by tidying up
your physical space deceive you, you will never recognize
the need to clean up your psychological space.
—Marie Kondo

Chances are, like many writers, you're not aware when your stress response is on high alert while you're writing. Getting swept up in the day-to-day minutiae can prevent us from realizing the toll—physical and psychological—writing stress takes on us. Even seemingly innocuous writing stations such as home offices can pose health risks. Occasionally, it's important to reboot our workspaces for optimal writing sustainability.

Does our workstation look like a tsunami struck? If so, give it a makeover. A disorganized or sloppy work area can raise tension. A tidy workspace can reduce stress and establish feelings of calm and control.

Be mindful of your surroundings. Take off your socks and shoes and feel your toes against the floor, paying close attention to how the floor feels against your feet: cold, warm, soft, hard? If you have an opened window, focus on the sounds of chirping birds or inhale the fragrance of a flower. Once in a while meditate or contemplate at your desk for just five minutes to help you unwind, clear your head, and refresh mind, body, and spirit.

Today's Takeaway

Toil by the adage of working smarter not longer, dial back on overtime, and recognize that good writing hinges on a healthy psychological space that fosters mental endurance.

NOVEMBER 5
Learn to Say No Instead of Yo

One does what one can, not what one cannot.
—Agatha Christie

Some of us want to accept every writing opportunity that comes along. Saying "yo" when we need to say no overwhelms us, hampering our writing agendas. Good writers learn to do what they can and say no to what they cannot. On the flip side, when someone tells us no, we must accept no, not push for yo.

When we say yes to everyone else, we automatically say no to ourselves, and that whittles us away until there's nothing left. Once we learn to accept our limitations, we develop strength of character, not weakness. We strive to stay away from people who drain our energy and surround ourselves with those who support, love, and affirm us.

When we're already overloaded and need self-time, we're in no position to take on more commitments. Every time we say yes when we mean no, we do others and ourselves an injustice. If we can't say no, we deprive ourselves of free choice, and our yeses are really noes in disguise. Until we can say no once in a while, we can never offer a genuine yes. What do you need to say no to?

Today's Takeaway

Develop a healthy attitude about what is humanly possible for you, then do what you can, not what you cannot, and say yes when you mean yes and no when you mean no.

NOVEMBER 6
Check Your Disgruntled Attitude

*If things are going well, if the writing's coming
along, I jump out of bed happy. And if the previous
day has been bad, I get out of bed disgruntled.*
—Robert Caro

Each day pay close attention to the attitude you bring to a writing regimen and keep it in check. Optimistic writers achieve higher career success than pessimists. Compared to their sunnier counterparts, disgruntled writers have trouble looking on the bright side, working as team players, thinking outside the box, and finding solutions to problems. Pessimistic writers more often suffer derailed careers because their negative attitudes mire them in writing stresses, whereas an optimistic attitude helps surmount stress.

We can modulate a disgruntled attitude by looking on the bright side and thinking of ourselves as winners instead of losers. We can remind ourselves of past challenges that we've overcome and of positive comments people made about our literary skills.

Even during stressful projects, we can find one or two positive things we enjoy and look forward to. We can hang out with optimistic writers instead of negative folks who pull us down and give ourselves pep talks as we would a best friend. Above all, instead of giving up, we can tell ourselves, "I can overcome anything I set my mind to."

Today's Takeaway

Avoid letting a disgruntled attitude metastasize into your daily writing so it doesn't derail writing success and prevent your best work from soaring to the top of the charts.

NOVEMBER 7
Walk down a Different Street

I walk down the same street. There is a
deep hole in the sidewalk. I walk around it.

—Portia Nelson

As writers, many of us walk down the same street day after day. We see that there is a hole in the sidewalk; we pretend we don't see it and fall in. We say it isn't our fault, that we're helpless, and it takes a long time to get out. Each time it happens, we say we can't believe we're in the same place.

When we get bad news about our writing, chances are that our immediate reactions are the same: frustration, anger, and hopelessness. But we don't have to keep falling into the same hole. We can change our perspective by asking different questions to find a different path.

What are some detours around the obstacle? Are there other avenues we can take to reach our destination? Do we need a new roadmap? No matter what writing hurdles, we must overcome, we can step over them, walk around them, or wiggle under them. Or we can even walk down a different street.

Today's Takeaway

Ask yourself what directions in your life you can change that will help you better reach your writing destination.

NOVEMBER 8
Test-Drive Challenge and Novelty

This is one of the many paradoxes of happiness: we seek to control our lives, but the unfamiliar and the unexpected are important sources of happiness.

—Gretchen Rubin

Gretchen Rubin's research shows that challenge and novelty are powerful sources to happiness. If we want to be happy writers, seeking sameness and avoiding challenges can get in the way and actually lead to boredom and unhappiness.

The human brain is stimulated by surprise, and being able to overcome an unexpected outcome gives us a powerful sense of satisfaction. When we take on new writing tasks, we're more apt to feel excited than if we stick to the familiar. Seeking opportunities for writing novelty and considering the unfamiliar and unexpected as challenges leads us to more satisfied lives as writers.

Creating novel situations evokes more emotional responses and makes the passage of time seem slower and richer. Let's ask ourselves what different path we can take today. It can be a new type of literary experience or an uncharacteristic way of responding to a surprise or negative event. Whatever the answer, give something new a try.

Today's Takeaway

Test-drive the idea that, as a writer, you can achieve greater rewards if you push through the frustration and irritation that novelty and challenge bring to your writing.

NOVEMBER 9
Travel the Longest Journey

You have to start knowing yourself so well
that you begin to know other people. A piece
of us is in every person we can ever meet.
—John D. MacDonald

The longest journey we will make is the eighteen inches between our head and heart. If we take this journey, it can shorten our misery in the literary world. Impatience, judgment, frustration, and anger reside in our heads. When we live in that place too long, it makes us unhappy. But when we take the journey from our heads to our hearts, something shifts inside.

What if we were able to love everything that gets in our way? What if we tried loving the shopper who unknowingly steps in front of us in line, the driver who cuts us off in traffic, the swimmer who splashes us with water during a belly dive, or the reader who pens a bad online review of our writing.

Every person who makes us miserable is like us—a human being, most likely doing the best they can, deeply loved by their parents, a child, or a friend. And how many times have we unwittingly stepped in front of someone in line? Cut someone off in traffic? Splashed someone in a pool? Or made a negative statement about something we've read? It helps to remember that a piece of us resides in every person we encounter.

Today's Takeaway

Take the longer journey with moments of impatience; bow in service to a bigger storyline where we're all unconscious characters, unaware of the plot, yet doing the best we can.

NOVEMBER 10
Savor Your Writing Ability as a Vintage Wine

If you're a singer, you lose your voice. A baseball player
loses his arm. A writer gets more knowledge, and if he's
good, the older he gets, the better he writes.
—Mickey Spillane

If I hear one more person say "I'm too old" or "It's too late for me to start writing," I'm going to scream! Comedy writer Joan Rivers said she didn't find her voice until she hit seventy. Famed folk artist Grandma Moses didn't start painting until seventy-eight. A client of mine wrote his first novel at eighty.

At eighty-two years old, novelist Tony Hillerman said he would keep on writing as long as anyone wanted to keep reading. Both Hillerman and Spillane pumped them out to the end of their lives. Whether we're eighteen or eighty, it's never too late to follow our dreams. Romance novelist Barbara Cartland said she planned to keep going until her face fell off. And she did—until the ripe age of ninety-nine.

It's never too late to start writing. Ask yourself, "What is it I want to write that I haven't?" And if you've already written, it's never too late to write something new and different than you've written before: a novel, a song, a screenplay, a short story, a letter to someone you love. All in the name of love.

Today's Takeaway

Think of your writing ability as a vintage wine that gets better and better with age; the more you practice your craft, the more you believe in yourself.

NOVEMBER 11
Go up the Stairs

The world is made of stairs, and there are
those who go up and those who go down.
—Ed McBain

The literary stairway goes up and down. Which way are you headed? The answer isn't determined by the actions of the publishing industry— the broken promises, rejections, and unexpected disappointments. It's determined by which way we choose to step, despite any negative outcomes of our writing attempts.

The stairs going up take us to writing success and fulfillment. The stairs going down take us to failure and disappointment. When our literary projects seem to be taking us down, we can still go up the stairs simply using our determination and fortitude.

Each day as you write, ask yourself in which direction you're moving. If you've been going downstairs, what mindset do you need to alter, what action do you need to take, or what habit do you need to break to change direction and head upstairs? If you've been going upstairs, which of these trends do you want to sustain? And what does that entail?

Today's Takeaway

Make sure you're moving up the stairs as you go through your writing day, and if you discover that you're headed down, consider what you need to do to make a U-turn.

NOVEMBER 12
Focus on the Task

*If you focus on the risks, they'll multiply in your mind and
eventually paralyze you. You want to focus on the task,
instead, on doing what needs to be done.*
—Barry Eisler

As writers, whatever we focus on multiplies and expands. When our
minds stay focused on obstacles, the tension grows larger than it actually is, and the very word *obstacle* becomes an obstacle. From the mind's
perspective, barriers to our writing swell, and we eventually become
paralyzed, unable to move beyond them.

Chances are that most of us realize—I sure do—that much of the
time we're jerked around by our passing fears that get bigger the more
we think about them. So much so that *we don't have feelings; feelings
have us*. Staying focused on the task allows us to stand guard and not let
our emotions and obsessive fears take control of our writing potential.
Once we focus on getting the job done, our progress multiplies, eventually helping us become more effective writers and complete our work.

Have you focused on a risk that has magnified and eclipsed you? If
so, what is your next step to retake the lead in future writing tasks?

Today's Takeaway
Stay focused on your writing tasks so your fears don't jerk you off course;
you will be more productive and can boast that you have emotions, not
that your emotions have you.

NOVEMBER 13
Ax Your Blame Thrower

There is an expiry date on blaming your parents for
steering you in the wrong direction; the moment you are
old enough to take the wheel, responsibility lies with you.

—J. K. Rowling

How often do we try to blame other people for our shortcomings? How many times have we unleashed our blame thrower on innocent bystanders? When things don't go the way we want, we must look within ourselves and check the expiration date for the reasons.

No matter how often or how much we blame others, it will not change us or make us better scribes. The only thing blame does is distract us from looking within ourselves because we're looking for external reasons to explain our discontent or frustration. Blame-throwing will never change whatever it is inside that makes us unhappy.

We can fail many times in our writing efforts, but we aren't failures until we begin to blame somebody else. As long as we blame other people or situations for our lot, we prevent ourselves from accepting responsibility for changing our literary lives for the better. When we take our lives in our own hands, suddenly there's no one to blame. Owning our actions and literary predicaments lifts us from literary adolescence to writing maturity.

Today's Takeaway

Control your own writing destiny by facing the consequences of your actions and taking ownership for your problems.

NOVEMBER 14
Starve Self-Doubt

Feed your faith and your doubts will starve to death.
—Debbie Macomber

When recognition for our writing efforts doesn't come soon enough, self-doubt bullies us into believing we're imposters—talentless nobodies trying to become someone we're not. It tells us to give up before we fail. At times we lose faith and believe that sense of doubt, don't we? Of course we do. We all do.

We believe it simply because we think self-doubt is us, but it isn't us at all. It's only one of the voices in our stadium. When doubt picks up the megaphone, we can imagine it's someone scolding us over a cell phone and we hold it away from our ear, listening from afar without believing it or blending with it.

In order to feed faith and starve self-doubt, we can regularly affirm ourselves along the literary journey. Perseverance comes as we learn to value and affirm our writing abilities, regardless of the messages self-doubt screams at us or the publishing industry hurls at us. That power to overcome resides within us.

Today's Takeaway

Feed your faith when you sit down to write by telling yourself you're one of the best writers in the world, then believe it until a starving self-doubt goes out for a burger.

NOVEMBER 15
Roll Up Your Sleeves

Wringin' your hands only stops
you from rollin' up your sleeves.

—James Rollins

How often do we get bummed out about something that went wrong or wigged out about something that hasn't even happened yet? Wringing our hands about the past or future interferes with rolling up our sleeves and addressing present writing needs. How often do we wait for the axe to fall or worry that something bad might happen, even though there's no good reason for it?

Some writers think of worry as an enemy infiltrator. They try to ignore it, get angry at it, or try to extinguish it. When we create an adversarial relationship with worry, it only leads to more internal frustration and anxiety. Although we think worry is working against us, it's actually trying to protect us, warning of a threatening writing challenge so we don't get our heads blown off in literary struggles.

Next time worry tries to prepare you for the next writing hurdle, acknowledge and befriend it as a separate part of you then turn your attention to the task at hand, roll up your sleeves, and dig in.

Today's Takeaway

Don't let wringing your hands over an upcoming writing challenge stop you from rolling up your sleeves and attacking head-on the task in front of you.

NOVEMBER 16
Widen Your Resilient Zone

*Mankind is resilient: the atrocities that horrified
us a week ago become acceptable tomorrow.*
—Joseph Heller

We're all genetically wired with what scientists call a "resilient zone." It's our safe zone—that place inside where we feel calm, cool, and collected. Studies show that we don't have to be trapped by the storms of our bodies (discomfort, anxiety, worry). In fact, we can widen our resilient zone simply by introducing a different behavior into our usual responses.

Here's how it works: write a brief statement to yourself that could strengthen your resolve to persevere and stay the course on your literary journey. It could be, "When I want to quit writing, I will remember why I started" or "I can accomplish most anything I set my mind to." Then, in a quiet place, read the statement to yourself several times. Close your eyes and pay attention to the sensations inside as you repeat the words. Focus your attention on the neutral or pleasant sensations in your body. Remember and contemplate these words if new beliefs, feelings, or meanings come up about your craft of writing.

Today's Takeaway

Reset your resilient zone by pairing a positive thought or action with a negative one so you are better equipped with the flexibility to adapt to writing stressors.

NOVEMBER 17
Refresh Your Writing Perspective

Leave home, leave the country, leave the familiar. Only then can routine experiences— buying bread, eating vegetables, even saying hello—become new all over again.

—Anthony Doerr

Rules, routines, and schedules. We need to keep our lives ordered, but how many creative experiences and exciting people do we exclude living our lives by the book? Clutching the familiar might feel comfortable and secure, but it limits the scope of our creative flow. No matter how hard we cling, change will eventually drag us kicking and screaming to discover new ways of writing sustainability.

Doing the same things day in and day out keeps us stuck on one track, from writing through fresh eyes. Novelist Tess Gerritsen advises, "Be curious...Go someplace you've never been before. Being in a foreign country makes you see new things, gives you a fresh perspective."

If we can't travel, we can renew the outlook on our lives. We can live each day as if it's a first-time experience and rediscover our routine world simply by the view we take of it: beauty in the ordinary, elegance in the simple, wisdom in the shallow, excitement in the humdrum. With curious eyes in a routine world, there's always more for us to see.

Today's Takeaway

Refresh your writing perspective and develop creative sustainability by eliminating sameness, traveling somewhere new, or turning daily routines into novel experiences.

NOVEMBER 18
Find Contentment

If you have a strong sense of contentment,
it doesn't matter whether you obtain the
object or not; either way you are still content.
—His Holiness the Dalai Lama

His Holiness the Dalai Lama says there are two ways to reach contentment. One is to acquire everything we want and desire: an expensive house, sporty car, perfect mate, gourmet foods, fashionable clothes, exotic trips, a perfectly toned body. The list is endless.

The problem with this approach is that this type of wanting is a bottomless pit. It fuels our work addiction to obtain external things to feel better inside. Sooner or later there will be something we want but can't have, no matter how many hours or how hard we work.

We can change this pattern with the second and more reliable approach to contentment, and that is to want and feel grateful for what we already possess. That way we are not driven beyond our capacity, and contentment and inner calm can be ours forever. We can practice an attitude of gratitude, make a list of the many things we're grateful for, that make life worth living, and visualize things we've taken for granted that if we didn't have them, would leave our lives empty and unfulfilled.

Today's Takeaway

In order to obtain contentment, practice intentional gratitude on a regular basis by naming all the abundant writing opportunities around you that you're already grateful for.

NOVEMBER 19
Set Healthy Writing Boundaries

If you're a lawyer or doctor, friends don't just stop by the office to chat or interrupt you from your work ... But for some reason, people think writing is different.

—Douglas Preston

One major difference sets writers apart from plumbers. Most of us work at home, which makes writing sustainability dependent on the respect family and friends have for our private writing spaces.

Most authors (myself included) report that well-intended loved ones often intrude into private writing zones. To find solace, some authors write outside the home, but that's not always possible. Home writers can define a space, away from common areas, off limits to housemates, designated only for writing as if it's an attorney's office across town.

When we set boundaries, everyone benefits. Family and friends learn that our craft isn't any different from that of an electrician or dentist. It prevents precious writing time from being compromised and allows us to get work done while teaching others respect for our private writing space. What boundaries can you set that will aid you in your writing agenda?

Today's Takeaway

Set writing boundaries so you're more productive and others understand that the craft of writing is no different from any other profession requiring privacy and concentration.

NOVEMBER 20
Pause to Give Thanks

Thanksgiving dinners take eighteen hours to prepare.
They are consumed in twelve minutes. Half-times
take twelve minutes. This is not coincidence.
—Erma Bombeck

It's important for us to take time out from the ballgames, parades, and the turkey and stuffing to contemplate all that we are thankful for. Most of us already have all the abundance we need to be happy.

As our feet touch the floor each morning of Thanksgiving week, we can be mindful of everything and everyone we encounter that we appreciate. This is especially important for us writers who overly focus on what we haven't achieved instead of what we have accomplished, no matter how small it seems.

Heartfelt thankfulness for our blessings slows us down and fills us up. This is a time to be aware of all the blessings that we might have forgotten about or taken for granted instead of complaining about what we still need. Express thankfulness for the riches in your life and notice how contented you feel inside.

Today's Takeaway

Spend each morning Thanksgiving week naming everyone and everything for which you are thankful; feel the abundance fill your horn of plenty then go watch the game!

NOVEMBER 21
Cultivate Open-Mindedness

The trouble with having an open mind,
of course, is that people will insist on
coming along and trying to put things in it.
—Terry Pratchett

A narrow mind doesn't have room to grow. It keeps us self-centered, cut off from creative invention, the mysteries of life, and seeing the world from the perspective of others. Close-mindedness is a consequence of fear and insecurity, which most of us writers have to some degree.

But we don't have to let our fears and insecurities eclipse the majestic gifts our writing lives have to offer. We can cultivate open minds and screen what we choose to let in so that just anyone can't come along and try to put things in it against our will. Whatever we choose to let in should move us farther along our literary journeys.

Take an inventory of your writing life. After assessing what external factors you have closed out of your life, ask yourself, "What can I open up to more in order to enrich my daily writing and grow as an author?"

Today's Takeaway

Stay open-minded to new experiences each day and be selective about the feelings you let in so narrow-mindedness doesn't keep you from growing as a writer.

NOVEMBER 22
Nudge Yourself

*In order to have more success, I needed
to be willing to accept more failure.*
—Gretchen Rubin

Success and failure are flipsides of the same coin—twins, not enemies. Once I had a graduate student who never learned to swim because she was afraid she wouldn't stay afloat on her first try. If she had tried, she would've succeeded to some degree, but she didn't and never learned to swim.

How many of us writers are afraid to push ourselves because we're afraid of failing? How many aspiring scribes remain secluded at desks, manuscripts hidden away in a drawer, too fearful of joining a writer's group or sharing their words in some way? How many seasoned writers still carry that reluctance to nudge themselves?

Failure is an important ingredient for success, just as flour is an important ingredient for a cake. We need a certain amount of failure in order to have more success. The ability to turn failure to an advantage is the mark of a great writer, as evidenced by the words of someone who should know—J. K. Rowling: "Failure is so important. We speak of success all the time. It is the ability to resist failure or use failure that often leads to greater success." Reflect on some ways you can use your failures to built future successes.

Today's Takeaway

Nudge yourself out of your comfort zone, be willing to accept more failure, and you will have tons more writing success.

NOVEMBER 23
Go to New and Unexpected Shores

*You come finally to the irreducible thing, and there's
nothing left to do but pick it up and hold it. Then, at
last, you can enter the severe mercy of acceptance.*
—Sue Monk Kidd

Sometimes we're forced to go to new places when old ways of thinking and behaving no longer work, and it might feel like things are falling apart. We resist, tightening our control, willing to do anything to hold on to old patterns. Letting go feels threatening and unsafe. But surrendering to experiences that we can't control is often the freedom the soul seeks. Patience and trust are key elements when our writing world seems to be crumbling under our feet.

Sometimes these changes yield exciting, unexpected gifts, and we don't realize it at first. With patience and faith, we can find new meaning in situations over which we have no control. After waiting for the outcome, we pick up the gift and embrace it then receive the mercy of acceptance. Think about what you need to let go of, surrender to, or accept to lessen your writing struggles. Then allow yourself to be spit up on a new and unexpected shore.

Today's Takeaway

Accept the natural transformations that occur in the literary world and as the anguish settles and you are able to accept the situation, look for the gifts that change brings.

NOVEMBER 24
Shear Your Expectations

*You can't let something that'll probably
never happen ruin your life. You're only
helping to make it a self-fulfilling prophecy.*
—Raymond Khoury

Why doesn't the universe listen to us? Why isn't our writing destiny going the way we planned? When things don't work out according to expectations, how often do we flip our lids? Whether it's expecting what we want to happen or don't want to happen, we create suffering when we carry demands that our expectations be different from the actual outcome. And we discover the self-fulfilling prophecy alive and well in our heads.

There's an old saying that expectations are premeditated resentments. When something happens, it's not the situation that upsets us (the first zinger), but the way we think and feel about it (the second zinger). As soon as we pass judgment based on our subjective thoughts and feelings, we are emotionally involved in it.

Much of what we demand won't occur because other forces that we cannot see are at play. Falling into anger, resentment, or despair, we create the very misery we tried to avoid. The following wise message, based on the serenity prayer, brings comfort and peace of mind to writing frustrations, disappointments, and rejections: change what you can, accept what you can't, and be smart enough to know the difference

Today's Takeaway

Shear your writing expectations by doing the best you can, changing what you can, making the best of what you can't control, and being wise enough to know the difference.

NOVEMBER 25
Fasten Your Seat Belt

*Catch me on a good day, I think half of
my books aren't too bad. Catch me on a
bad day, I think I've never written a good line.*

—Dennis Lehane

Our financial planners advise us against overreacting to stock market volatility. "It's nothing new," they say. "It's the nature of the market to bounce up and down, moderate dips or steep dives. What matters is how we respond."

The same can be said of the literary field. After we take a seat on the writing roller coaster, we must fasten our seat belts for a bumpy ride. Our writing lives can seem so out of control we feel like a trapeze artist flying though space. One day is a good writing day, the next a bad one. We are popping with creative ideas then go blank. We constantly spend enormous amounts of time and energy trying to get our feet back on the ground.

Our writing lives aren't out of control. The key is to not freak out over built-in writing volatility but view current downturns as part of a pattern, not as permanent events. We remind ourselves that we agreed to the ups-and-downs before we plopped down to write. We don't have to panic at the first disappointment; we simply take a breath and hold steady for more highs and lows to come.

Today's Takeaway

Fasten your seat belt for writing's bumpy ride, avoid overreacting to writing volatility, think long-term, hold steady but most of all—enjoy the ride.

NOVEMBER 26
Extract the Gains from Your Losses

*If you constantly think of illness, you eventually become
ill; if you believe yourself to be beautiful, you become so.*
—Shakti Gawain

Everything that happens is a thought before it's an action. Writers create
their masterpieces in their minds before putting them on paper. Artists and musicians envision their compositions before they put them on
canvas or play them on their instruments.

When we think negative thoughts about a situation, we're already
creating the tone the experience will take. When we visualize positive
thoughts, we create positive possibilities for future situations. We can
see more beauty than flaws, more hope than despair. We see blessings
and potential even in loss and disappointment.

For every loss there is a gain, even though we can get so blinded
by the loss it's hard to see anything else. When we can open our eyes
to blind spots and extract the gains from the losses, we're empowered.
Think of a loss you've encountered then see if you can extract a gain
upon which you can build or grow as a writer.

Today's Takeaway
When writing days are bleak, don't let loss and disappointments blind
you to the positive gifts, extract the gains from losses, and keep an optimistic outlook in your writing efforts.

NOVEMBER 27
Stop Cursing Your Autocorrect

"DAMN YOU, AUTOCORRECT!" If you
own a smartphone, there's a good chance
you've screamed that phrase at least once.
—Jillian Madison

While the automatic features on our mobile devices are meant to be blessings, they can be a curse. The autocorrect features on our computers and smartphones attempt to correct common typos on the fly by guessing the word we're trying to write. The purpose of autocorrect is to save writers time, but it often makes us want to pull our hair out.

Any device that starts with "auto" has a mind of its own. It can take over our writing and turn it into something other than what we intended. When we're flying high with a great idea, banging the keyboard hard and fast, autocorrect can take us in another direction. In her funny book, *Damn You, Autocorrect!,* Pop-culture blogger Jillian Madison gives an X-rated example of how autocorrect seems to be preoccupied with sex: Maybe you sent a text to your spouse that you "f——d the dog" (fed) or fired off a note to a coworker about your "bad case of manboobs" (Mondays).

Autocorrect means well although it changes words without rhyme or reason. So don't hit send too fast. You might forward your agent, publicist, or publisher an embarrassing message that could cause the rejection of your manuscript! By the way, I just laid (I mean paid) my publicist. See what I mean?

Today's Takeaway
Reserve cautious optimism for your autocorrect and remember that it means well even when it makes you want to pull your hair out.

NOVEMBER 28
Unshackle Your Limitations

---

*The chains that bind you are not held in place by a ruling
class, a "superior" race, by society, the state, or a leader.
They are held in place by none other than yourself.*

—W. Timothy Gallwey

It's amazing how many of us get trapped by the way we use our minds and yet we're not even aware of it. Although our writing capabilities are endless, our minds often put bars on that potential. The need for security causes us to become attached to negativity and perceive limitations as real. Truth be told, the limitations we writers have are defined by the way we use our minds.

When we have writing setbacks, it looks and feels as if life is treating us badly. It's possible that we can become so accustomed to seeing ourselves as losers that self-victimization and self-pity become habitual ways of thinking. We imprison ourselves by putting these bars around us.

It's important for us to understand that it's our limited view of ourselves that limits our writing success, not the objective situation. Once we discover that we have the key to the chains that bind us, our writing lives change for the better.

Today's Takeaway

Unlock the shackles you've put on yourself and don't let bad writing outcomes imprison your thoughts and feelings about yourself and your writing ability.

NOVEMBER 29
Hang On for a Second Wind

The thing with giving up is you never know.
You never know whether you could have done
the job, and I'm sick of not knowing about my life.
—Sophie Kinsella

Rejection and disappointment can nibble away at us until it feels like death from half a million cuts. After a while, it feels as if we're bleeding to death and can't tolerate one more slash.

But I'm here to tell you that we can. The acclaimed thriller writer, Steve Berry, rose to success after twelve years and eighty-five rejections. After constant rejection and disillusionment, many successful writers describe a second wind, as if they're running a marathon, just before they're ready to give up. A sudden jolt of electricity sizzles through us, and we're filled with renewed energy and determination.

When you're ready to give up, remember you always have more resilience inside than you realize. If you give up, you'll never know if you had it in you to pull it off. Are you sick about not knowing about your life? That's a tough question to live with. Are you prepared to always wonder if you could've done the job? Can you hang in for a second wind and learn how much more you're capable of?

Today's Takeaway

Don't despair of your writing goals, no matter how improbable they might seem because never giving up is how wordsmiths, just like Olympian champions, reach the top.

NOVEMBER 30
Write Outside the Lines

*Put down the pen someone else gave you. No
one ever drafted a line worth living on borrowed ink.*

—Jack Kerouac

When Gillian Flynn's novel *Gone Girl* broke the glass ceiling on unlikeable female leads, it triggered a flood of books with "girl" in the title—each novel riding the trending train, written on borrowed ink—some successful, some not so much. At an international writing conference, top publishers and agents said if they see another submission with "girl" in the title, it goes in the trash.

The key to successful writing is genuine and authentic words. Instead of jumping on the bandwagon and writing what's trending, we must find our own new forms that force us to write fresh, more truthful narratives. We write what *we* know, what *we* feel. *Gone Girl* was a success because it was original.

Albert Einstein said, "You have to color outside the lines once in a while if you want to make your life a masterpiece." If we want to write our masterpiece, we pen the words outside the lines, instead of inside them where everybody else scribbles. We are sincere, true to who we are, and genuine in our styles. Let's ask ourselves, "Are we writing with borrowed ink or using our own original signature?"

Today's Takeaway

Pick up *your* own pen, craft *your* own manuscript in original ink, and shine for *your* own creative endeavors.

DECEMBER

DECEMBER 1
Weather Writing Frustrations

I spent all morning removing a comma
and all afternoon putting it back.
—Oscar Wilde

The road to successful writing is paved with frustration: dried up ideas, perpetual works-in-progress, and drawer novels. Some days we face bad news or a fried brain. Tired and discouraged and reluctant to sit at our writing stations, we drag ourselves anyway moaning and complaining to the computer screen.

Sometimes it feels as if writing refuses to give us the time of day, yet we can't resist the chase. We move words around, adding a comma or removing a comma, but nothing seems to fit. We write another sentence then turn it upside down, inside out, and backward. We examine and rewrite it again, think about the sentence during lunch, then come back in the afternoon, delete the entire paragraph and start from scratch.

Welcome to the world of writing. When we remind ourselves that seasoned writers said there'd be days like this, it helps. We realize frustration is part of the process, not personal nor unique to our inability to find the right words. When we allow ourselves to be frustrated and learn from it—instead of fighting it or trying to push through it—it can work in our favor, bringing clarity and calm, sometimes even increased productivity.

Today's Takeaway

Accept instead of resist days of writing frustrations, don't take them personally, and remind yourself that the road to writing success is paved with days like this.

DECEMBER 2
Designate a Stress-Free Zone

Never let stress shape your strategy.
Most women think better after a brisk walk,
a light meal, a massage, and a nap.
—Barbara Taylor Bradford

No matter how frantic our schedules, we can always take time out to decompress. Having a special place to relax makes us more likely to hit the pause button. We can assign a getaway in our homes where we're not allowed to think about, feel, or deal with stressful writing issues.

This stress-free zone can be a place of solitude where we have quiet and serenity. It contains no electronic devices, no work tools, no hassles, and no scheduling boards. And getting carried into a thought stream of worry, rumination, and pressure is off-limits in this special place.

It can be a special room for meditation, prayer, or contemplation. If we don't have a room, we can designate an area with minimum traffic flow—a garage or basement. We can make an altar containing special mementos and favorite photographs that inspire pleasant memories and peaceful feelings. A corner of a den or bedroom can work as a getaway, where we wear earphones and listen to relaxing music. Or a screened porch is a place where we listen to nature sounds and watch mother nature conduct her magic.

Today's Takeaway
Find a place where you can unwind and decompress from the strains of writing demands and go to it often so clarity instead of stress shapes your writing strategies.

DECEMBER 3
Galvanize Your Self-Esteem

There are so many more important things to worry about than how you're perceived by strangers.
—Dennis Lehane

It's an interesting question: "Why is it more important what others think about us than what we think about ourselves?" Approval seeking comes from not fully appreciating who we are and not affirming our own talents and skills. Many of us spend our writing lives figuring out what others—strangers even—want us to be like or to write about. In that case, our interests and goals change with the wind to match what others want.

However, we must never demote ourselves—even when bad news comes or unexpected events clog our literary path. Self-esteem comes from within. We must believe we count for something, affirm and like ourselves, and treat ourselves with respect. Then we're able to mount the literary challenges, frustrations, and disappointments.

To galvanize your self-esteem, ask yourself a few questions: Am I magnifying the disappointment? If so, what can I say to myself to put it in perspective? Can I look at the upside of the situation? Or is there any silver lining in the downside? Am I focused on the problem or the solution? How can I brainstorm possible solutions? Can I pinpoint an opportunity in the frustration? And are there risks I can take to surmount the problem?

Today's Takeaway

Galvanize your self-esteem by holding yourself in high regard, treating yourself with respect, being your own person, and affirming and liking yourself on a daily basis.

DECEMBER 4
Open Your Arms to Hopelessness

Here is a truth, a truth by which to live: there is hope.
There is always hope. If we choose to abandon it,
our souls will turn to ash and blow away.
—John Connolly

There will be times when we feel as if all hope is gone for our writing dreams. I don't know of a writer who hasn't felt hopeless at one time or another, but that doesn't make it true. Hopelessness is fear based. The author Robert Ludlum said, "Hope is the only thing stronger than fear." When things get overblown and we feel hopelessness, it could mean we simply have lost perspective.

No matter how impossible the writing hurdles seem, there's always hope amidst adversity. But it's important to permit ourselves to feel hopelessness while knowing that our feelings are not facts. Feeling hopeless isn't the same as abandoning hope. Allowing ourselves to feel hopeless relieves the impulse to abandon our sense of hope and hope springs eternal.

Here's a counterintuitive challenge. Close your eyes and imagine opening your arms and accepting any feelings of hopelessness. Spend one minute in this exercise knowing that it can actually restore a deeper sense of hope.

Today's Takeaway

Give yourself permission to feel hopeless without abandoning hope or depriving yourself of your writing dreams, and hope will reappear along with inner peace.

DECEMBER 5
Let Passion Keep Your Soul Alive

*Passion, for better or worse. It can keep a soul alive even
if all that survives is a shimmering. I've even seen it.
I've been bathed in it. I've been changed by it.*

—M. J. Rose

For most of us, writing is a passion, a deep personal calling. It's an intense abiding love for the craft—an all-consuming flame that burns within us. It keeps us going, rekindles the fire in our writing, and propels us through insurmountable odds.

Successful writers carry this passion in their hearts and souls into everything they do. I've seen it. I've been inspired by it. The passion that resides within us is more powerful than the writing challenges on the outside of us. We owe it to ourselves to connect with that passion, bathe ourselves in it, and remember the taste of it in our hearts and souls.

When we seek patience and passion in equal amounts, everything we do makes an impact, if only a slight shimmering trace. We can write with passion just as easily as we can with doubt or dread, writing through storm clouds with the same passion with which we write on a sunny day.

Today's Takeaway

Get in touch with your writing passion, taste it, bathe yourself in it, let it shimmer in everything you do, everywhere you go, and passion's glow will be written all over you.

DECEMBER 6
Don't Be Afraid of Your Shadow

*The demand for the perfect is the
greatest enemy of true goodness.*
—Richard Rohr

All writers are flawed in one way or another. Our shadows—the hidden and denied parts of ourselves that we don't like—are part of our human condition. The challenge is not to be afraid to accept our shadows. If we don't recognize and name our shortcomings, it's inevitable that we will project and hate them onto other people. The key is to accept our human fallibilities and imperfections.

Author Richard Rohr said, "The 'last' really do have a head start in moving toward 'first,' and those who spend too much time trying to be 'first' will never get there." Successful writing has "getting there last" built into it. We grow as writers much more by "doing it wrong" than "by doing it right." Otherwise, we become scribes who think we're above and beyond imperfection, and our egos have a field day over-defending us.

Most of us have difficulty embracing the road not taken. There comes a time in our lives when we realize if we don't go where there is no path, we might never get another chance again. Practically speaking, if you took the unbeaten path and left a trail, describe what that would look like in your everyday writing life.

Today's Takeaway

Embrace, instead of fear, your shadow and allow yourself to get it wrong as often as necessary; that imperfection eventually will take you to the right turn in the road.

DECEMBER 7
Meditation Practice: WAIT with Kindness

The deepest truths are the ones we most often forget.
One of these is that if we don't regard our inner life with
kindness, it's difficult to open our hearts to others.

—Tara Brach

It's amazing how many seasoned authors speak about the importance of kindness to others. It's important to be kind to others because we never know what burden they might be carrying. And it's not a bad idea to put *us* somewhere in the mix. As we practice self-compassion, it spills over into goodwill toward others. I developed a quick and easy acronym WAIT as a tool for practicing self-compassion:

- Watch what's going on inside when you're triggered by writing stress.

- Accept the stressful experience and your internal reactions, just as they are.

- Invite the activated feelings to relax, and with curiosity and compassion soothe them.

- Tell your inner reactions in a mental whisper, "I'm here with you" or "We've got this."

When we get frustrated with our writing or things don't turn out the way we had hoped, most of us react instead of act. Once we start to WAIT, it inhibits our automatic reaction and gives us the space to bring calm and compassion to ourselves and then to others.

Today's Takeaway

Inwardly WAIT and treat yourself with compassion on a regular basis then watch how it quiets negative mental stories, softens your heart, and spreads kindness to others.

DECEMBER 8
Build a Backbone of Steel

Ever tried. Ever failed. No matter.
Try Again. Fail again. Fail better.
—Samuel Beckett

Our sense of how others see us and what they approve and disapprove of can be a negative influence on our writing. Some of us are so afraid of failing that we're willing to avoid any possibility of failure or adapt ourselves to the approval of others. And because acquiescing to the whims of others is a form of giving up, we fail in the truest sense of the word and the worst way.

Our strength doesn't come from arm wrestling or verbally sparring with someone. It comes from knowing and accepting ourselves and our steadfast belief in our abilities, no matter what. Strength develops from trying, failing, trying again, and failing again in a much stronger way.

We can't change the failures that have already happened. They will always be there. We can't change the fact that the future will contain more failure. We either let failures bring us down or build a backbone of steel. We can worry about past failure or let them go. We can avoid future failure and play it safe or take the risk, try, and fail again. Each time we fail better than the time before, we build a stronger backbone.

Today's Takeaway

Build a backbone of steel by making sure after each time you fail that you try again, and if you fail again, make sure you fail better than the time before.

DECEMBER 9
Replace Your Nail with a Spike

*The nail in my wall would no longer support the
weight of the rejection slips impaled upon it.
I replaced the nail with a spike and kept on writing.*
—Stephen King

After meteoric challenges, are you still in the writing game? Of course you are, so am I. It's easy to mistake rejection letters for "I'm not good enough," to have our feelings injured, and our egos bruised. We fret with, "Why can't I write?" or "Why do I keep failing?" But usually rejection isn't a reflection of our writing ability or creative mojo.

When we think this way, we're off track. It's time we hammer home a more resilient attitude. We're "spike writers." We reject the idea of rejection. We use rejections to fuel our fierce determination to persevere through literary storms—albeit bruised, bereft, and beleaguered.

Once we substitute a spike for a nail, we look at rejections differently. We consider it an honor to be in such an exclusive club. Every successful writer—from the Beatles to Stephen King to J. K. Rowling—has travelled this same path hundreds of times. I shudder when I recount the number of rejections I received. When rejection threatens to stop us, or gear us in the wrong direction, perseverance and resilience are the tickets that will take us to our destination.

Today's Takeaway

Substitute your rejection nail with a spike, face rejections with fierce determination, knowing you're still headed in the right direction, never give up, and keep on writing.

DECEMBER 10
Welcome Writing's Contradictions

Trust to the contradictions and see them all. Never annul one force to give supremacy to another. The contradiction itself is the reality in all its manifoldness.

—Alfred Kazin

Writing has many contradictions. To achieve, we must fail. We cannot have success without failure. Accomplishment is built on falling down. We fall down in order to stand up. Success and failure are flipsides of the same coin. The way up is the way down.

Ask this question, "Is water good or bad?" Neither and both. It's soft and powerful at the same time. When it refreshes and sustains us, we can't live without it. When its powerful force threatens to destroy us—carving through rock, flooding homes, even drowning us—we can't live with it. In this way, the potential for success is embedded in our shortcomings.

The goal is to hold the opposites together. We are turned down for a gig to read at a festival and we're upset. At the same time, we plan to submit our writing to another juried festival. We hold the uninvited situation in one hand with serene acceptance of the loss. We hold our plan to submit our work to another festival in the other along with a sense of hope. Holding our opposites imbues us with resilience and persistence.

Today's Takeaway

Embrace writing's contradictions, knowing that rejection, mistakes, and failures are not good or bad; they contain all the essential ingredients to become a successful writer.

DECEMBER 11
Take the Off-Ramp

*The first thing you want to do after being
shot is make sure you are not shot again.*

—Ace Atkins

Perhaps many of us keep reacting to disappointment in the same ways. We go back to the same people for the same rejections. We try to solve problems with the same strategies that we know don't work. We resist change and cling to sameness. We live in the past. We want most in our writing lives what we cannot have. The list goes on.

If we get shot, we make sure we don't get shot again. We take the off ramp and get the hell out of Dodge. In other situations, we avoid touching metal handles of hot cooking pots because we know *metal conducts heat*. We refrain from touching an exposed wire while standing in the bathtub because we know *water conducts electricity*.

Although similar principles govern our writing, they are less concrete, and so we don't always see the path on which we're walking. We must learn from mistakes and take a different action instead of doing the same thing, expecting different results, and ending up in the same unsatisfying place. Once we do something different in the heat of the moment, our lives change for the better.

Today's Takeaway

Take the off ramp from the self-defeating highway on which you're driving and find writing fulfillment on new routes you didn't know about.

DECEMBER 12
Think like a Writer

At all times, think like a writer, and keep those antennae
twitching—that way, you pick up new ideas.
—Ian Rankin

How does a writer think? If we write every day, we become accustomed to seeing our unfolding daily lives through writer's eyes. With antennae twitching, we watch what happens to those around us and ourselves— the bad things, the good things, funny stories—even the mundane.

Thinking like a writer means we write with honesty, meaning, and authenticity. We pen the beauty of early morning light streaming through a window the same as we would the horrifying scene of a vagrant gunned down in the street.

We let the story develop in a real way instead of trying to be nice, shaving off the terrifying edges or worrying about how readers will react to a word, situation, or character. In the words of writer Steven James, "Let the story kick and scream and bleed if it must. Don't remove its claws and fangs, or you won't be as honest with it as your art form demands."

When we think like a writer, we write equally about darkness and light, and our craft takes on an honesty that pulls readers into it. Contemplate ways you can think more like a writer—the bad, the good, and the ugly—and generate untamed work and hone your craft.

Today's Takeaway
Day by day think like a writer and use your honest observations and personal experiences as fodder to fertilize your imagination without holding back or seeking reader approval.

DECEMBER 13
Act in the Face of Fear

Courage is to feel the daily daggers of
relentless steel and keep on living.
—Douglas Malloch

The path to writing is paved with fear—real and imagined. The challenges and obstacles can be scary and intimidating at times. Even though running away from a scary situation might feel safer in the moment, we find it harder to live with ourselves later on. Being fearless isn't the goal. The way to cultivate courage, resilience, and steadfastness is to acknowledge the fear, feel it, and act in its face anyway.

We don't have to be braggadocios or martyrs to the literary challenges. We simply need to stand our ground, stay the course of our writing goals, and discover a connection to the power that dwells within us. With regular practice we learn that the power inside is greater than the challenges we face on the outside.

As we surmount hardships, we realize we're indeed heroes—reluctant ones perhaps—but the best in the world. Fist pump preferred but not required.

Today's Takeaway

Stand your ground when confronted with fearful writing challenges, as all writers are; each time you feel the fear and face it anyway, you're developing your craft of writing.

DECEMBER 14
Don't Sit on Your Hands

A life spent making mistakes is not only more honorable,
but more useful than a life spent doing nothing.
—George Bernard Shaw

It's amazing how many writers sit around waiting for a publisher or agent to knock on their door, willing to take on their manuscript. Some writers, usually novices, complete their submission, throw it out there, and wait for it to hit the bestseller list. Unfortunately it's not that simple.

Seasoned writers know that completion and submission of a manuscript is only the first part of getting published. For a submission to get the attention it deserves we must get up off our rumps and beat the bushes.

After waiting through the review period, if we haven't heard we need to check back to make sure the manuscript was received. Once an agent or publisher rejects it, we keep sending it out, no matter how hopeless it seems, no matter how many noes we receive. Even after double-digit rejections, we keep revising and casting the net as far and wide as possible. After we get an acceptance and sign a contract, we still don't sit on our hands. We begin the next project to keep the momentum going. That's what writers do.

Today's Takeaway

Don't sit on your hands when defeated or when you see other writers give up; get up and take steps that lead in the direction of your writing dreams, no matter how big or small.

DECEMBER 15
Posture Yourself with Fierceness

You, be the Master: Make yourself fierce; break in.
And then your great transforming will happen to
me. And my great grief cry will happen to you.
—Rainer Maria Rilke

When the odds are great, the road is long, and we face one difficulty after another, we must have the audacity to remain fierce. We must hold on to the dogged faith in our writing dreams. When the odds go low, we must go high.

Every time we face a roadblock we remind ourselves that we are not fragile writers. We are strong and resilient. No mountain is too high, no river too wide. We carry ourselves over, under, or around obstacles. When the road is long and bumpy, we are fierce in the face of uncertainty. We reject fear and cynicism, accepting what is best in ourselves. In the face of hardships, we soften our hearts and lengthen our strides.

Ask what it is that can make you fierce every time you're discouraged. Is it something stubborn inside? Or is it a loved one or friend who cheers you onward? Is it a one-liner from an agent who says you have a strong voice or you're a talented writer? Or is it something a wise person once said that you carry inside?

Today's Takeaway

Find the fierceness that dwells within, immerse yourself in it, and have the audacity to posture yourself with it as you encounter the hard writing battles that lay ahead.

DECEMBER 16
Take Time off the Grid

What I still ask for daily—for life as long as I
have work to do and work as long as I have life.
—Reynolds Price

After putting her family second to her writing and neglecting herself for a year to get published, debut author K. L. Hallam was running on empty. When her publisher went belly up, she had to step back and learn from the devastating experience. Although all she wanted to do was write, she realized there's more to writing than writing: "It's by living fully with love and trust, trust in your path and its outcome."

Most of us writers have long periods of agonizing self-doubt punctuated by brief moments of affirmation followed by more self-doubt. And we must accept that events rarely fall in place the way we expect or want them to. Sometimes there's more to writing than writing. It's not about sitting in front of our keypads. It's about living in all quadrants of our lives: relationships, play, self-care, and writing. And it's about faith in ourselves and trusting in our paths and their outcomes.

Today's Takeaway

Your effectiveness and growth as a writer is determined not by the number of hours you pound the keypad but by how fully you trust and live your life on and off the grid.

DECEMBER 17
Swim in Your Own Lane

What lies behind us and what lies ahead of us are
tiny matters compared to what lies within us.
—Henry Stanley Haskins

Most of us have our favorite writers that we emulate. But if we put them too far up on a pedestal and ourselves too far down, we create a form of self-sabotage. The ones we idolize have a long way to fall, we have a long way to climb, and both of us lose. Whether or not we realize it, when we compare ourselves to another writer, we set both of us up to fail.

What good are comparisons, anyway, other than to make us feel cheated? Since the outcome of comparisons is usually self-inadequacy, why would we compare at all unless we're insecure about our talents? Comparing our writing robs us of happiness.

We can never be like another writer. We can only be like ourselves. There will never be another Ernest Hemingway or J. K. Rowling, and there will never be another you and me. Another's talents don't diminish our own. So instead of comparing our literary work, let's value and affirm our unique writing talents and appreciate what we have.

Today's Takeaway

Swim in your own lane, admire and respect the talents of others while affirming your own, and see your would-be comparisons pale in relation to your own unique voice.

DECEMBER 18
Have the Audacity to Accept Criticism

*I suspect that most authors don't really want
criticism, not even constructive criticism.
They want straight-out, unabashed, unashamed,
fulsome, informed, naked praise ...*

—Neil Gaiman

One of the essential traits of a good writer is the ability to accept criticism. If we would rather be ruined by praise than saved by criticism and if our egos are too fragile to appreciate and receive constructive criticism about our writing, then we should be on a park bench feeding pigeons, not pounding out words on the keypad.

No writer can survive a career if they're allergic to constructive criticism. The audacity to accept criticism is the best vaccination against writing failure. Truth is hard to swallow and can be hurtful. That's why we call them growth pains. Words can harm *and* heal. When we flip our outlook, we realize that praise can destroy writing efforts and criticism can save them. Like good medicine, this attitude adjustment makes a bitter pill go down easier.

Do you have the audacity to handle constructive criticism without getting defensive or taking it personally? Can you listen to criticism with a dispassionate ear and see it as helpful? If not, what do you need to fix within to understand that there are problems with the manuscript, not problems with you?

Today's Takeaway

Trust yourself enough to have the audacity to put your defensive ego aside and really examine criticisms of your writing; it will save and strengthen you over the long haul.

DECEMBER 19
Honor Your Commitments

If we can't make and keep commitments to ourselves as well as to others, our commitments become meaningless.

—Stephen Covey

All of us look for meaning and purpose in our writing, and we find it by devoting ourselves to the craft in many different ways: volunteering behind the scenes at a conference, agreeing to speak on a panel at a bookstore, reviewing a manuscript, offering writing tips for an online magazine, serving as a judge on an awards panel, penning a blurb for someone's book, or speaking at a book club.

Our commitment starts with calculating if it's possible to agree to a request before committing to it. We think about the required timeline and all that is involved. We ask ourselves if our hearts are really in the commitment. Is it something meaningful that stirs or moves us enough to honestly devote ourselves to it? Or are we succumbing to pressure or appeasement?

When we make a writing commitment, our integrity is on the line. Let's ask how we truly want to devote ourselves to writing then put our hearts and souls into the promises we make. Or if after consideration we can't make a meaningful commitment, let's give ourselves permission to say no and feel good about the decision.

Today's Takeaway

Before you put your heart and soul into a writing commitment, make sure it has meaning and purpose and that you have the time to follow through with your commitment.

DECEMBER 20
Serve in the Trenches

Blessed the man and woman who is able to serve
cheerfully in the second rank—a big test.
—Mary Slessor

Authors looking for glory are unlikely to find it in the nitty-gritty world of writing. In many ways, the job of writing is a service industry that takes many years to build. Successful writers aren't too good to work in the trenches: reading at nursing homes, entertaining sick children in hospitals, or appearing gratis to support a fundraiser for a good cause.

Great writers are not puffed up with pride. They stand on the shoulders of giants who came before them. Willing to travel the back roads of small towns, they appear at festivals, firehouses, fish fries, and tiny bookstores off the beaten path—even if it's speaking to only two or three eager fans about their craft.

Successful writers have their share of insecurities too, but are able to withstand rejection of a manuscript, no-shows at advertised book signings, or searing self-doubt. They are able to embrace their flaws and keep going, willing to join the second ranks and forego the glory until the spotlight finds them despite, or in spite of, their hard work deep in the trenches.

Today's Takeaway

Be willing to build your reputation as a writer through selfless service working in the trenches for the welfare of others, giving your talents freely until the spotlight finds you.

DECEMBER 21
Welcome Old, Uninvited Friends

Negative emotions like loneliness, envy, and guilt have
an important role to play in a happy life; they're big
flashing signs that something needs to change.
—Gretchen Rubin

One of the most important skills we writers must learn, perhaps even more important than the craft itself, is to prepare for old, negative friends who show up uninvited to spoil the party.

We invite and hope to see Triumph, Joy, Success, Happiness, Approval, Hope, and Excitement. We overlook old negative friends—Loneliness, Self-Doubt, Rejection, Worry, Disappointment, Heartbreak, and Anxiety—but they crash the party anyway. Although we avoid them like the plague, they refuse to leave whether we like it or not.

As writers, our best bet is to accept ahead of time that our persistent, negative friends will show up on the doorstep along with invited guests. There's little we can do to stop them, so we might as well welcome them, give them party hats, and let them take part in the event. They have an important role to play on our writing journey. If we prepare early, send them invitations, and accept their presence, it's easier to cope when they appear out of nowhere like an embarrassing distant relative we try to keep under wraps.

Today's Takeaway

Perfect both your craft of writing *and* your ability to accept and deal with negative thoughts and feelings because craft alone won't carry you through the writing hurdles.

DECEMBER 22
Develop 20/20 Eyesight

We keep searching and searching,
when everything is already within us.
—Don Miguel Ruiz

Once there was a starfish that lived in the ocean. "Pardon me," he said to the whale, "could you tell me where I can find the sea?"

"You're already in the sea," said the whale. "It's all around you."

"This?" asked the starfish. "This is just the ocean. I'm looking for the sea." The frustrated starfish swam away to continue searching for the sea.

"Look around you," yelled the wise old whale. "*Seaing* is a matter of *seeing.*"

When we hit writing snags, we get frustrated and impatient, and sometimes disillusioned. The best resilience remedy is an inside job. Marcel Proust said, "The real voyage consists not in seeking new landscapes but in having new eyes." We see disappointments and letdowns with new insight and greater clarity. We don't wish for something to be different. We ask how we can look at the downturn in a way that benefits us.

There's an old adage that hindsight is 20/20. Think back on your last or most recent writing disappointment. How did you react? If you look back with a pair of new eyes, do you notice anything different? Can you carry this new perspective into future writing voyages?

Today's Takeaway

Resilience comes from the ability to shift your perspective when met with defeat—to change directions, not on the outside, but on the inside where the misery lingers.

DECEMBER 23
Bounce Higher Than You Fall

Life ain't about how fast you run or how high you climb.
It's all about how good you bounce. A man cannot
be comfortable without his own approval.

—Mark Twain

Sometimes it's hard to bounce back after a writing setback. The hole feels too deep, too dark. Perhaps we lose weight, can't stop crying, or obsess over the loss. Maybe we're bitter and mean-spirited. It's important to acknowledge and allow ourselves to feel all emotions and give ourselves time to bounce back. It's also important to recognize that every one of us has a "springback" inside that can bounce us forward after a big letdown.

In metalworking, the term "springback"—also known as elastic recovery—is when metal returns to its original shape after undergoing compression and tension (stretching). Like metals, we have an elastic limit to which we can stretch. We're like elastic bands that can bend and stretch to a certain point before we return to our original shape.

After a big setback, we writers need to access our inner springback and bounce back like singer/songwriter Prince: "I have a very thick skin. I take everything that comes and let it bounce right off me." Consider how well you bounce and if you can bounce higher than you fall after the next downturn in your writing aspirations.

Today's Takeaway

Think of yourself as an elastic band that can bend and stretch to a certain point before you spring back higher than you fall.

DECEMBER 24
Remove "Fatal" from Your Attraction

Some fatal attraction draws me down into the abysses
of thought, down into those innermost recesses,
which never cease to fascinate the strong.
—Gustave Flaubert

Sometimes writing can feel like a fatal attraction that refuses to give us the time of day, yet we can't resist the chase. Like moths to a flame, many writers attest to the irresistible chase for writing success, being seduced and pulled in with false promises of glory, fame, and fortune.

Some of us can become so infatuated we're willing to stop at nothing and do whatever it takes, putting ourselves under intolerable conditions, short of boiling rabbits, to achieve writing success. The desire to succeed can create a greater determination to stalk our prey and steamroll over anything or anyone who stands in our way.

In the extreme, the very attraction that draws us to writing ultimately can have fatal consequences. When we're caught in an obsessive-compulsive pattern for writing success, it can lead to the destruction of our reputation or even death, known as *karoshi*—a Japanese term for death from overwork.

There's a difference between healthy determination of writing goals and a fatal attraction that goes overboard. Let's ask ourselves where our perseverance needle falls: on an outer extreme of the spectrum? Or somewhere in the middle where balance resides?

Today's Takeaway

Instead of being a moth to a flame, regulate your attraction to writing so you can maintain a healthy "favorite attraction," not a destructive "fatal attraction."

DECEMBER 25
Duck the Holidaze

The Holidays are only holy if we make them so.

—Marianne Williamson

Holidays are supposed to be fun and holy. Right? But they often turn into hectic instead of meaningful times. Between shopping for gifts in the crush of crowds, popping in on endless streams of parties, and adhering to mandatory family traditions, there's little time left to relax and find meaning in the blur of the season.

One of the biggest myths about the holidays is that we have to do things as we've always done them: to excess. That requirement can throw us into a frenzied whirlwind of shopping, parties, and baking—on top of an already hectic writing schedule. Traditions are part of the season, but just because we've done things a certain way doesn't mean we can't power down the holi*dazing* and still celebrate select and meaningful traditions.

We don't have to let the holiday commercialization trump the true meaning and joy this time of year brings. We can celebrate the season by having the kind of holiday *we* want, not what merchandisers want for us. We can take the emphasis off grand gestures and gift ourselves with simple "literary" gifts such as extra time to write or time off from writing.

Today's Takeaway

Be an angel to yourself after loved ones have gone to bed, gifting yourself a moment alone in front of holiday decorations, contemplating what the season means to you.

DECEMBER 26
Tip the Scale in Your Favor

The weight of the world is love, under the burden of
solitude, under the burden of dissatisfaction.
—Allen Ginsberg

For many writers, confidence trails self-doubt. It's as if we're carrying the weight of the world on our shoulders. How can we lighten the load in pursuit of our goals when we get the constant message from others and ourselves that we don't measure up?

The choreographer and author Martha Graham said, "No artist is pleased. There is no satisfaction whatever at any time. There is only a strange, divine dissatisfaction, a blessed unrest that keeps us marching and makes us more alive than the others." Here are a few ways to keep our thumbs on the dissatisfaction scale and tilt the needle in our favor:

- We don't surround ourselves with people who *weigh* us down.

- After hours, we leave the *weight* of unfinished work on the paper or computer.

- We make sure we pull our *weight* to the best of our ability.

- We don't compare our abilities to other writing *heavyweights*.

- We *weigh* in with positive opinions of our writing worth on a regular basis.

- We are able to objectively *weigh* the merits of our writing.

- We don't throw our *weight* around.

Today's Takeaway

Tip the scale in your favor and give yourself credit as a writer, because the weight your writing carries in others' eyes is in direct proportion to the amount of weight you give it.

DECEMBER 27
Perform Carpool Karaoke

Claim your space. Draw a circle of light around it. Push back against the dark. Don't just survive. Celebrate.

—Charles Frazier

When pressures come at us from all angles, it's time to depart from our literary pursuits, push back against the dark, and find a healthy outlet to release daily writing stressors. What better way to claim our space and draw a circle around it than carpool karaoke? It's free and doesn't take extra time out of our busy schedules. We can perform it while running errands, picking up kids from activities, or when we just want to be alone and let off steam.

T. S. Eliot said, "There is no feeling, except the extremes of fear and grief, that does not find relief in music." So what are we waiting for? The car can be our theater where we get our freak on when nobody's watching. We can crank up the music and rock out with Beyoncé, Adele, or the Rolling Stones. We can belt to the top of our lungs, flaunt our hipness, and groove with effortless on-beat hand twists.

After the refuge of carpool karaoke, the only drawback is that we might not want to get out of the car. But when we drop the mike, we're more clearminded, calmer, and in a better position to face our writing woes.

Today's Takeaway

Push back against the dark and let off steam with carpool karaoke, feeling every cell of your body throb with music, every fiber of your being thrill like harp strings.

DECEMBER 28
Avoid Being a Desk Potato

I don't exercise. If God had wanted me to bend
over, He would have put diamonds on the floor.
—Joan Rivers

The typical American spends an average of ten hours a day sitting, whether it be in a car, at the computer, or in front of the TV. Okay, I admit it. I'm an average American and a writer to boot. I sit more than I move. Plus I agree with Joan Rivers that working out sucks. There, I said it. But listen up: our bodies are not designed to be deskbound for long periods. Writing at our desks for hours on end is an occupational hazard that puts our health at risk.

Parking it for more than four to six hours a day puts us at an 80 percent greater risk of dying from cardiovascular disease. Prolonged sitting is as bad for us as smoking cigarettes. It reduces blood and oxygen flow, causes weight gain, and leads to heart disease and diabetes.

Just fifteen minutes of daily exercise lessens stress, promotes better health, creates sharper clarity, and develops a longer writing trajectory. Take a second right now to identify one physical activity to do today. Take short five-minute strolls outside on a nice day or walk up and down a flight of stairs in bad weather. Exercise at your desk. Or stand, take deep breaths, twist, or stretch out the built-up tension and get your blood flowing.

Today's Takeaway

Offset hazards to your literary health by taking frequent work breaks, moving around, and writing while standing to keep your attention alert, health good, and writing optimal.

DECEMBER 29
Cultivate Good Literary Stewardship

Be a good steward of your gifts.

—Jane Kenyon

A steward is an Old English word for one who manages the property or affairs of another, as in an entrusted guardian or keeper of the house. Writers are privileged members of a literary community, entrusted to take care of what belongs to us all: the craft of writing. Words belong to the masses. We don't own them; we're merely entrusted caretakers of them.

Good stewards are committed to selfless service for the common good. We devote time for the betterment of literary organizations. We live the values and carry on traditions of previous wordsmiths. We preserve the history and culture of literature. We believe in the sustainability of fellow writers. We're team players, giving credit and supporting others' work. In the end, we're accountable for our stewardship.

Poet Jane Kenyon's passages contain the most ennobling tenets for writing stewards to live by: "Protect your time. Feed your inner life. Avoid too much noise. Read good books, have good sentences in your ears. Be by yourself as often as you can. Walk. Take the phone off the hook. Work regular hours." These wise words remind us of our privileges and responsibilities as writers. Contemplate ways you can be a good steward.

Today's Takeaway

As you weave words into sentences into paragraphs into pages, be a responsible caretaker of the communal property that all of us in the literary community are privileged to share.

DECEMBER 30
Restock Your Writing Reservoir

*Attempting to revise while still writing, like exercising
while eating, may shut down the body's production of
creative juices and lead to dry-well syndrome.*
—Chris Roerden

Once we fully immerse ourselves into the well of writing, dry-well syndrome is a possibility. At the beginning of this book, I told you I would reveal my writing strategies to deal with dry-well syndrome, so here they are in three steps.

First, the realization hit me that I had tried to accomplish two competing tasks at once: revising while creating—a prescription for dry-well syndrome.

Second, I put the manuscript aside to provide an incubation period for my creative juices. Stepping away from a manuscript after burying heart and soul into it might sound counterproductive, but the survival mind doesn't give us the best creative advice.

Although we're hardwired for survival, swimming toward shore in a riptide drowns us, just as pushing through writer's block can backfire, drying up any leftover creative juices. An old adage says whatever we resist persists and that applies equally in the writing arena.

Third, I pursued a different creative activity. Writing a proposal for the book you're holding refilled my creative reservoir and replenished my writing mojo; then I went back, finished my novel, and ended up with a second book to boot.

Today's Takeaway

Restock your artistic pond by swimming with the tide, putting the project aside for a month, and pursuing another endeavor until the creative juices flow again.

DECEMBER 31
Endure to the End

*There will come a time when you believe everything
is finished. Yet that will be the beginning.*

—Louis L'Amour

Sometimes it's difficult to see that, just as the Phoenix rises from the ashes, we writers are beginning *and* ending all at the same time. Saying goodbye to a critique group. Completing a writing class. Finishing a manuscript. When endings fill us with grief, we can search for the gains in the losses, and that perspective becomes stronger, ruling in every situation.

We discover that out of an ending something is born. The end of summer shepherds the beginning of fall. New Year's Eve ushers in an upcoming year. The end of this book delivers an opportunity for you to put the readings to good use.

After you've been a writer for as long as I have, you learn that just when you're ready to throw in the towel, there's a breakthrough. So remember when something discouraging happens with your writing, something good comes right behind it. Persevere to the end of your song, poem, novel, memoir, cookbook, or thesis then ask what's starting anew from the endings.

Today's Takeaway

Never give up or let big publishing honchos intimidate you; keep writing every day as if you're an athlete training for the Olympics—the amazing moment the world learns of your craft.

INDEX

This book is organized so you can read one writing meditation for each day of the year. In this index, you will find key words that allow you the flexibility to select a particular writing issue that you might want to contemplate. You can pick and choose from the topics listed here, selecting the ones that resonate and draw you on any particular day or explore certain topics of your choice in more depth.

Adversity: March 23, April 27, May 7, May 20, May 21

Affirmations: February 10, May 29, June 11, July 1, July 23, September 4

Age and Writing: February 28, November 10

Anger: March 8, March 22, September 6, September 28

Animosity: July 16

Anxiety: April 27, May 31, August 1, August 16, October 15

Appeasement: January 26, June 5, July 6, July 7, August 1, August 29

Approval: June 5, August 1, August 5, August 20, August 23, August 29, December 8

Assertiveness: June 8, July 6, July 7, July 18, July 25, August 29

Attachment: June 27, October 28

Attitude: April 20, May 24, June 23, August 7, August 16, November 6

Autocorrect: November 27

Avoidance: March 2, July 20, August 29, October 20

Balance: March 20, August 6, August 21, August 31, December 16

Beginnings: January 1, July 11, September 23

Believing in Ourselves: April 17, May 5, July 23, September 13, October 29, October 30

Black-and-White Thinking: March 20

Blame: July 7, November 13

Blank Page Syndrome: February 23, August 4, December 1, December 30

Blessings: January 26, July 13, August 3

Blind Spots: July 27, October 31

Body's Stress Response: January 20, January 27, February 24, March 3, May 12, May 27, May 31, July 15, August 27, September 21, September 28, November 2, December 28

Bookstores: October 5

Boundaries: June 8, November 5, November 19

Brain: March 21, March 24, April 6, May 1, May 12, May 19, June 18, June 28, July 2, August 11, September 6, September 18, September 28

Breathers: January 18, June 15, August 28

Breathing: March 22, May 23, May 27, August 18, October 1

Broaden Your Outlook: January 6, January 22, April 15, August 20, October 3, October 17

Burdens: December 26

Burnout: May 23, June 23

Calmness: March 30, April 22, May 21, May 31, June 25, August 8, August 22, August 28, September 5, September 21, October 1

Carpool Karaoke: December 27

Celebrate Writing Triumphs: March 17, June 11, July 1

Challenges: April 8, April 13, May 1, May 20, June 9, July 2, July 26, August 18, August 30, September 1, September 8, September 23, September 30, October 4, October 21, November 8, November 15

Change: November 23

Choices: February 19, April 20, July 4, July 13, July 25, September 5, September 22

Clarity: January 29, March 20, April 6, July 16, August 8, August 22, October 11, December 22

Clutter: April 5, June 17

Cluttered Thoughts: January 12

Commercialization: June 24

Commitment (to Writing): January 17, July 29, July 31, October 13, December 19

Comparisons: December 17

Compassion: January 25, February 11, March 1, March 2, August 8

Confidence: February 7, June 14, July 10, July 20, July 23, July 28, August 8, September 20, October 27, November 14, December 26

Conformity: August 29, November 30

Connections: April 9, May 17, August 8

Contentment: November 18

Contradictions: December 10

Control: March 8, March 9, April 24, May 20, July 25, October 2, October 28, November 25

Courage: March 11, April 14, May 5, May 7, June 14, June 20, July 20, August 8, August 16, August 19, December 13, December 15

Creative Juices: January 18, May 22, May 28, July 20, July 22

Creating a Vacuum: January 28, April 5

Creative Flow: May 3, May 22, October 7, December 30

Creativity: April 2, April 30, May 3, May 15, May 28, June 23, July 10, August 8, August 21, September 16, October 15, November 8, November 17, November 30, December 30

Critical Voice: January 25, February 23, March 28, May 7, June 25, June 26, July 26, August 14, August 25, August 26, October 10

Criticism: April 7, July 3, August 6, August 23, December 18

Critics: February 9, February 20, June 7, June 16, July 3, October 9

Curiosity: July 4, July 22, August 4, August 8, August 25, September 9

Dark Hours: January 8

Dark Shadows: May 15, July 12, October 8, October 20

Deadlines: July 8, September 6, October 16

Decision Fatigue: February 27

Decisions: January 21, February 27, March 26, April 1

De-Cluttering: April 5, June 17

Deep Play: February 8

Defeat: January 23, April 17, May 17, May 24, July 23, November 7

Defiance: April 14

Despair: June 9

Detachment: July 26

Determination: July 2, November 11

Detours: November 7, December 11

Disappointments: January 21, January 31, February 4, February 22, March 9, March 23, May 6, May 7, May 17, May 18, June 22, June 23, June 30, July 13, July 19, July 23, August 10, August 24, September 6, September 7, September 9, September 12, September 20, September 26, September 30, October 3, November 7

Discipline: July 31, August 17, September 10, September 29, October 13

Discouragement: July 24, July 26, September 30

Dispassionate Eye: February 9, August 10, October 10

Dissatisfaction: July 24, December 26

Distorted Thinking: March 20, April 23, April 26, April 27, June 22, October 19

Distractions: February 3, July 30, October 16

Doing Nothing: January 11, April 22, April 28, May 28, December 14

Doubt: January 31, February 18, March 15, April 3, April 10, April 20, May 29, July 1, August 16, September 23, October 26, November 14, December 16

Eating: February 29, May 12, June 21

Ego: March 31, May 7, September 12, October 6

Electronic Devices: January 29, February 12

Emotional Prison: July 25

Empathy: February 11, September 12, October 27

Empowerment: January 29, May 26, June 2, June 3, July 7, July 13, July 25, August 24, September 5, September 13, September 22, September 30, October 9, October 15, October 26

Endings: January 1, September 11, September 26, December 31

Endurance: October 11, December 31

Envy: February 7, April 7

Exercise: March 3, May 12, June 29, July 15, December 28

Expectations: March 7, April 21, May 24, May 29, November 24

Failure: January 13, April 11, May 4, May 5, May 16, June 30, July 2, August 14, August 19, September 1, September 4, October 23, November 22, December 23, December 8

Faith: April 11, April 20, April 21, June 16, August 17, November 14

Fast Food: February 29

Fatal Attraction: December 24

Fate: January 21, March 4, March 9, June 2, June 3, December 15

Faultfinding: February 10, May 7, September 12, October 18

Fear: January 19, January 24, April 20, June 6, June 13, July 20, August 9, August 16, August 19, October 8, October 19, December 6, December 13

Flexibility: May 3, June 27, October 7

Focus: November 12

Follow Your Dreams: February 28, April 12, May 6, May 19, July 31, July 31, September 1

Forecasting: March 18

Forgiveness: January 28, April 29, October 16, October 24, November 9

Fortitude: July 2, September 26, October 11, November 11

Fresh Starts: January 1, June 19

Friendship: May 8, May 9, June 30

Frustration: February 4, March 16, May 17, July 18, August 1, August 17, August 18, September 20, September 26, September 29, October 16, November 27, December 1

Gains and Losses: May 6, November 26

Giving Up: March 10, May 7, May 19, June 1, June 9, August 14, October 23, December 31

Gobble, Gulp, and Go: February 29

Good Will: June 12, December 7

Gratitude: February 1, September 20, October 6, October 21, November 18, November 20

Grief: May 6, May 10, June 29

Growth as a Writer: March 9, May 20, July 13, July 16, July 18, July 21, July 28, August 24, September 1, September 2, September 10, September 11, September 30, October 20, October 26, October 30, November 17, November 21, December 18

Grudges: January 28

Guilt: March 25

Habits: September 10

Happiness: April 7, June 3

Hard Knocks: February 9, July 18, July 23, July 25, August 10, August 24, September 7, December 13

Harness Negativity: February 22, June 30, July 18, August 24, October 23, October 26

Heart: March 26, March 30, April 2

Heartbreak: June 29, September 4, September 27

Helping Other Writers: March 31, June 12, August 12, September 18

Holding On: January 28

Holidays: July 4, November 20, December 25

Hope: April 11, July 13, July 19, July 25, December 4, December 31

Hopelessness: April 14, May 19, June 9, June 23, July 18, July 19, August 1, November 7

Humility: July 9, August 5, September 9

Humor: August 9, August 30

Hurry: February 29, March 12, March 22, April 2, July 27, October 14

If-Then Plan: February 13

Loosening Up: May 3, May 28, October 19

Loss: May 5, May 6, November 26

Love: February 14, November 9

Love for Writing: April 10, July 18, July 31, October 11

Magnification: July 13, July 23, August 13

Marketing: March 31, April 19

Meditation: April 2, May 2, May 31, June 28, August 13 September 1, October 14, November 16

Mind/Body Connection: January 27, February 27, March 16, April 30, May 23, June 29, July 15, August 27, September 21, October 1, October 3, November 2, December 28

Mindfulness: January 14, March 2, April 2, April 23, April 26, April 28, May 2, June 4, July 23, July 26, July 27, August 7, August 13, September 14, October 31

Mindreading: April 18

Mindset: August 4, September 1, September 22, October 10

Mind Traps: June 22, July 13, August 14, November 28

Miracles: April 21

Mistakes: March 25, June 30, July 12, September 1, September 8, October 16, October 24

Monitoring Your Writing: January 4, September 19

Multitasking: August 6

Murder Your Little Darlings: April 4

Murphy's Law: February 21

Muse: April 25, April 30, May 14

Music: December 27

Naps: April 6

Nature: February 17, May 22, May 31, August 28, December 2

Negative Reviews: February 9, February 20, June 16, October 9

Negativity: January 5, January 20, January 21, February 6, February 21, February 25, March 28, April 26, May 19, May 30, June 16, June 22, August 7, August 14, August 15, August 23, August 25, September 3, September 9, September 12, September 17, September 24, November 3, November 6

Nutrition: February 29, June 21

Obsessive-Compulsive: December 24

Obstacles: February 4, March 10, March 23, April 3, April 8, April 10 April 13, April 17, April 20, April 27, May 1, May 4, May 19, May 20, May 24, June 9, June 17, July 16, July 18, July 20, July 21, July 26, August 18, September 3, October 4, October 19, November 7

One Step at a Time: January 23, April 13, May 13, July 26, August 1, August 21, September 10, October 4

Openness: March 7, June 13, July 26, July 27, August 3, August 4, August 14, September 23, October 11, November 21

Opposition: February 19, April 15, July 13, September 8, October 25

Optimism: April 11, July 13, August 7, September 3, September 24, October 30

Organization: June 17

Outlook: April 20, April 27, May 24, May 29, June 3, June 22, July 13, August 15, September 24, September 30, October 3, October 17, November 28

Overworking: February 24, August 31

Pantsers: June 10

Passion for Writing: January 8, February 26, March 30, July 31, August 18, October 11, December 5

Patience: April 1, May 13, July 17, August 21, September 29, December 5

Peace: May 21, May 31, August 22, September 12, October 2, October 7

People Pleasing: January 26, June 5, July 6, August 2, August 29

Perfectionism: January 10, November 3

Perseverance: January 3, March 10, March 14, April 11, April 14, May 25, June 3, June 20, June 30, July 1, July 12, July 18, July 30, July 31, August 1, August 19, August 24, September 8, September 25, October 2, October 10, October 11, November 7, November 11, November 14, December 31

Persistence: March 10, April 11, April 14, April 15, May 25, May 26, June 20, July 12, July 17, July 18, July 30, July 31, August 19, September 8, October 11, October 25

Perspective: January 22, February 9, March 9, March 20, March 23, March 24, April 20, April 23, April 26, April 27, May 20, May 24, June 3, June 22, June 30, July 13, July 27, August 4, August 10, August 15, December 22, September 3, September 17, September 30, October 3, October 6, October 17, October 30, November 17, November 26, November 28

Perspiration: July 17, July 31, August 4, August 18, October 11

Pessimism: February 6, August 7, August 17, November 6

Pilates: June 29

Planning: February 13

Plotters: June 10

Positivity: January 6, March 23, April 12, April 13, April 20, April 23, May 20, May 24, May 29, May 30, June 3, June 11, July 14, August 15, August 23, August 24, September 3, September 4, September 12, September 20, September 24, September 30, October 3, October 21, October 30, October 31

Postponement: June 2, February 28, September 11

Post-Traumatic Growth: March 23, May 20

Power Down: February 13, February 24, June 15, August 31, October 14

Present Moment: January 14, March 2, April 13, April 27, April 28, May 1, May 2, May 13, June 4, June 28, October 31

Pride: December 20

Prioritizing: January 17, March 5, July 29, September 15, October 13, November 1

Privacy: November 19

Procrastination: January 15, April 13, June 6, August 19, September 15, November 7

Productivity: February 16, March 30, June 1, August 6, August 18, September 15

Promotion: March 31, April 19, May 11, May 26, October 12

Psychological Space: May 8, November 4

Publishing Pressures: March 4, March 12, March 24, April 10, April 14, April 25, May 10, May 26, May 27, May 29, July 25, August 11, November 22

Putdowns: April 7, June 25, June 26, July 14, August 26

Quiet Mind: May 31, June 25, July 22

Quitting: April 8, May 7, May 18, August 14, August 17, October 23

Reactivity: January 21, May 14, May 19, May 21, July 4, August 13, September 6, September 9, September 17, September 27, September 28

Recharging Your Batteries: January 18, March 19, March 27, May 28, June 15

Rejection: January 13, February 6, February 9, April 17, July 17, July 21, August 13, August 24, September 4, September 26, December 9

Relaxation: January 27, February 27, March 19, March 22, April 22, May 28, June 15, August 22, August 28, September 21, October 1

Release: January 28, February 8, December 27

Resentments: January 28, April 29, July 16, September 24, September 28

Resilience: January 5, January 25, January 31, February 2, March 14, April 11, April 14, April 15, May 4, May 18, June 4, June 9, June 14, June 20, June 30, July 20, July 21, August 16, August 31, September 1, September 18, September 23, September 24, September 25, September 30, October 2, October 20, October 27, November 16, December 23, December 8

Resistance: April 24, June 25, July 20, August 3, September 27, November 23

Resources: February 2, September 20

Responsibility: November 13, December 29

Rest and Relaxation: February 27, March 22, May 21, May 23, June 17, August 22, August 28

Rewriting: April 1, July 24, October 2, December 1

Rigidity: May 3

Risk Taking: January 24, May 15, July 20, August 19, September 2, October 8, October 19

Sacrifices: July 29, October 11

Sadness: February 9, May 17, June 1

Safety: January 30, December 27

Sameness: December 11

Saying No: June 8, November 5

Scars: May 4

Second Book Syndrome: April 10, July 3

Second Chances: August 14, September 4

Second Wind: November 29

See the Light: January 8, July 12, August 1

Self-Attunement: July 23, July 26

Self-Betrayal: April 17

Self-Care: February 5, March 1, April 6, May 23, July 6, July 7, July 8, July 9, July 10, July 23, July 28, August 22, August 31, September 7, September 14, October 10, October 22, October 29, December 25

Self-Centeredness: March 31, July 9, October 22

Self-Compassion: January 25, February 5, March 1, March 25, May 7, May 8, May 29, May 30, July 23, July 26, July 28, August 1, August 13, September 7, September 28, October 15, October 29

Self-Defeat: March 18, March 25, April 16, April 17, May 16, May 24, June 20, July 26, October 10

Self-Esteem: April 16, April 28, June 5, July 14, July 28, December 3

Self-Fulfilling Prophecy: May 24, November 24

Self-Sabotage: May 13, May 16, August 7, August 26, September 28

Self-Talk: January 20, February 19, March 28, April 17, May 7, May 19, June 25, June 26, July 26, August 1, August 14, August 25, August 26, October 10

Self-Worth: April 16, April 28, May 16, July 14, July 23, July 24, July 25

Selfless Service: June 12, December 20, December 29

Setbacks: January 23, April 10, April 11, May 16, July 2, August 1, August 10, August 17, August 24, September 7, September 30, November 28, December 23

Shame: July 11

Shoulds: February 19

Silence: July 22

Sincerity: June 24

Sitting: January 27, April 22, June 1, November 2, December 28

Sleep: February 15, June 18

Slow Writing: March 13, March 19, April 25

Slowing Down: January 18, February 29, March 12, March 13, March 19, March 22, March 30, April 1, April 22, October 14

Solitude: January 18, March 27, March 29, May 31, July 22

Sophomore Slump: April 10, June 5, June 9, July 3

Soul Writing: April 25, June 26, October 11, December 5

Spiritual Experience: April 25, May 31, September 13, October 11

Spontaneity: May 28

Stewardship: June 12, December 29

Strength as a Writer: January 31, February 2, April 14, May 4, May 18, July 2, July 18, July 21, August 8, September 2, September 23, September 26, December 15

Stress: January 14, February 24, March 4, March 6, April 20, May 9, May 12, May 27, May 29, June 21, July 4, July 15, August 13, August 20, August 27, September 5, September 19, September 21, October 1, October 14, October 15, December 2, December 30

Stretching Yourself: July 20, August 19, September 2, October 20

Struggles: April 3, May 4, June 9, July 2, August 10, August 18, September 1, September 9, December 13

Success: May 5, May 16, July 17, August 14, August 19, September 4, September 12, September 21, October 16, October 23, November 22

Suffering: September 27

Support: January 30, February 14, March 29, April 9, June 11, June 12, July 11, July 30, August 12, September 7, October 5, October 29

Surrender: April 24, June 27, September 30, October 2, October 28, November 23

Thankfulness: October 6, November 20

Thick Skin: April 15, May 26, July 18, August 24, December 23

Thoughts: January 12, March 26, March 28, June 26, September 22, November 28

Time to Write: January 17, July 31, September 15

Transformation: November 27

Troublesome Thoughts: March 2, May 1, June 3, June 4, June 22, August 25, September 7, November 28

Writing Jags: March 3

Writing Mojo: April 3, May 28

Writing Self: May 8, May 11, June 5, June 24, June 26, June 30, July 25, July 28, August 29, September 2, September 13, September 16, September 29, October 8, October 11

Writing Style: June 10

Writing Sustainability: January 5, April 3, June 21, June 23, July 31, September 14, October 16, November 17, December 1, December 6

Writing Tribe: January 30, March 29, April 9, August 12

Writing Voice: February 26, March 28, March 30, May 15, June 5, June 26, July 26

Writing Woes: April 20, August 15, October 16

Yoga: March 16, December 28

Zingers: June 30, July 4, November 24

BIBLIOGRAPHY

Brach, Tara. *Radical Acceptance: Embracing Your Life with the Heart of a Buddha*. New York: Bantam, 2003.

Brown, Brené. *Rising Strong*. New York: Spiegel & Grau, 2015.

Cameron, Julia. *The Artist's Way: A Spiritual Path to Higher Creativity*. New York: Tarcher, 2002.

Carmen, Allison. *The Gift of Maybe: Finding Hope and Possibility in Uncertain Times*. New York: Perigee, 2014.

Chödrön, Pema. *When Things Fall Apart: Advice for Difficult Times*. Boston, MA: Shambhala, 1997.

Davis-Bush, Ashley. *Self-Care for Therapists: Restorative Practices to Weave Through Your Workday*. New York: Norton, 2015.

De Salvo, Louise. *The Art of Slow Writing: Reflections on Time, Craft, and Creativity*. New York: St. Martins Press, 2014.

Dweck, Carol. *Mindset: The New Psychology of Success*. New York: Ballantine Books, 2016.

Foster, Jeff. *Finding the Courage to Hold Everything in Love.* Boulder, CO: Sounds True, 2016.

Fredrickson, Barbara. *Positivity.* New York: Three Rivers Press, 2009.

Gallwey, Timothy W. *The Inner Game of Work.* New York: Random House, 2000.

Hanson, Rick, and Richard Mendius. *Buddha's Brain: The Practical Neuroscience of Happiness, Love, and Wisdom.* Oakland, CA: New Harbinger, 2011.

Hawlena, Dror, and Oswald Schmitz. "Herbivore Physiological Response to Predation Risk and Implications for Ecosystem Nurtient Dynamics." *Proceedings of the National Academy of Sciences.* New Haven, CT: Yale University, January 4, 2010.

Lama, His Holiness The Dalai. *The Art of Happiness.* New York: Riverhead Books, 1998.

Milton, John. *Paradise Lost.* London: S. Simmons, 1674.

Neff, Kristin. *Self-Compassion: Stop Beating Yourself Up and Leave Insecurity Behind.* New York: William Morrow, 2011.

Nhat Hanh, Thich. *The Heart of the Buddha's Teaching.* Berkeley: Broadway Books, 1999.

Rein, Glen, Mike Atkinson, and Rollin McCraty. "The Physiological and Psychological Effects of Compassion and Anger," *Journal of Advancement in Medicine* 8 (1995): 87-105.

Robinson, Bryan E. *Chained to the Desk: A Guidebook for Workaholics, Their Partners and Children and the Clinicians Who Treat Them.* New York: New York University Press, 2014.

———. *The Smart Guide to Managing Stress.* Norman, OK: Smart Guide Publications, 2012.

Rohr, Richard. *Everything Belongs: The Gift of Contemplative Prayer.* Danvers, MA: The Crossroads Publishing Company, 2003.

Shapiro, Dani. *Still Writing: The Perils and Pleasures of a Creative Life.* New York: Grove Press, 2013.

Tolle, Eckhart. *A New Earth: Awakening to Your Life's Purpose.* New York: Penguin Group, 2005.

Trungpa, Chogyam. *The Myth of Freedom and the Way of Meditation.* Boston, MA: Shambhala Publications, 2002.

GET MORE AT LLEWELLYN.COM

Visit us online to browse hundreds of our books and decks, plus sign up to receive our e-newsletters and exclusive online offers.

- **Free tarot readings • Spell-a-Day • Moon phases**
- **Recipes, spells, and tips • Blogs • Encyclopedia**
- **Author interviews, articles, and upcoming events**

GET SOCIAL WITH LLEWELLYN

Find us on  @LlewellynBooks
www.Facebook.com/LlewellynBooks

GET BOOKS AT LLEWELLYN

LLEWELLYN ORDERING INFORMATION

99 Keys
to a
Creative
Life

Spiritual, Intuitive, *and* Awareness Practices
for Personal Fulfillment

MELISSA HARRIS